MY 26 STANLEY CUPS

MY 26 STANLEY CUPS

Memories of a HOCKEY LIFE

DICK IRVIN

M&S

National Library of Canada Cataloguing in Publication Data

Irvin, Dick, 1932-
My 26 Stanley Cups: memories of a hockey life

Includes index.
ISBN 0-7710-4370-8

1. Irvin, Dick, 1932- . Sportscasters – Canada – Biography.
3. Hockey – Canada – History. I. Title.
II. Title: My twenty-six Stanley Cups.

GV742.42.I78A3 2001   070.4'49796962'092   C2001-900720-5

We acknowledge the financial support of the Government of Canada through the Book Publishing Industry Development Program for our publishing activities. We further acknowledge the support of the Canada Council for the Arts and the Ontario Arts Council for our publishing program.

Typeset in Janson by M&S, Toronto
Printed and bound in Canada

McClelland & Stewart Ltd.
The Canadian Publishers
481 University Avenue
Toronto, Ontario
M5G 2E9
www.mcclelland.com

1   2   3   4   5   05   04   03   02   01

Contents

For Wilma

Preface

·······························

On December 27, 2000, Mario Lemieux began his much-publicized comeback with the Pittsburgh Penguins. During a pre-game interview with Scott Russell on *Hockey Night in Canada*, Mario said, "Hockey has been with me since I was three years old." I've got him on that one, because hockey has been with me since the day I was born.

My father was coaching the Toronto Maple Leafs when I arrived on the scene and I have been hanging around the National Hockey League ever since. I did it the easy way by becoming a hockey broadcaster, which meant I could keep at it until I was almost seventy years old, when I retired in 1999. I don't think Mario will still be coming back when he's that age. Then again, with hockey the way it is these days, you never know.

Mario also never saw Rocket Richard play. I did, many times. I not only saw the Rocket play, he once worked with me in a broadcast booth at the Montreal Forum as a guest analyst on *Hockey Night in Canada*. So did Gordie Howe and Bobby Hull, Scotty Bowman and Bobby Orr, Howie Meeker and Don Cherry. The list of hockey greats I have been lucky to meet and know over the years is a long one.

Hockey people love to tell stories, and that's what this book is about. There are stories from the old days, and the newer days, and most are happy ones because I like happy ones the best. You won't find gripes or complaints about people, places, or things here, because as I look back on my life around hockey, I don't have any. That might not be fashionable in today's media, but that's the way I am.

This book is also about being in the hockey arena twenty-six times when the Stanley Cup was won. The first was in 1940, the last in 1994. Do those dates ring a bell with New York Rangers fans? There are stories about all twenty-six, along with some background of what was happening on the ice in those years, especially during the best time of the hockey season, the playoffs.

First, number twenty-six.

The Last One

....

I was in Madison Square Garden the night of June 14, 1994, when the New York Rangers defeated the Vancouver Canucks to win the Stanley Cup, but I didn't see it happen. I heard it, but I didn't see it.

I was part of the *Hockey Night in Canada* crew that had broadcast a very emotional final series, one that had gone to the limit of seven games. With about ten minutes remaining in the third period, and the Rangers leading 3–2, I left the broadcast booth "high above centre ice" as we say (and at MSG it's very high), where I had been working alongside Harry Neale and Bob Cole, and made the trip from the ninth floor to the fifth floor, which is ice level. For the fourth straight year I was to handle post-game interviews with the Cup-winning team. The previous three – two wins for Pittsburgh and one for Montreal – it had been obvious well before the end of the third period of the deciding game who the winning team was going to be. But not this time. When I got downstairs, it was still 3–2 Rangers, the game was still on the line, and HNIC had some decisions to make.

The producer was Larry Isaac. Even though he came from Vancouver, Larry had a hunch the Rangers were going to hang on. As the third period wound down, he had a couple of cameras set up in the home team's dressing room, cameras that were mobile enough to make a quick move down the hall should the Canucks come back and win. But that didn't happen. Final score: 3–2 New York.

I was in the Rangers' room when the last few minutes of the game were being played and had no idea what was happening on the ice. They had moved the cameras in, but forgot to set up a TV monitor so we could watch the game. All we had to go on was the ebb and flow of the crowd noise. When the final buzzer sounded and eighteen thousand Ranger fans celebrated their team's first Stanley Cup in fifty-four years, the noise level made it obvious which team had won. That's why I've always said that in 1994 I didn't see it happen, I heard it happen.

When the traditional on-ice presentations and celebrations were over, the triumphant Rangers whooped and hollered their way into the room followed by the biggest mob of people I had ever seen in a Cup-winner's dressing room, and I had been in quite a few. It was wall-to-wall humanity, with champagne corks popping and a lot of the bubbly stuff being shot around the room. Nevertheless, our show had to go on, and the interviews began with a lot of people watching. The game drew an audience of 4.957 million, the largest in the history of *Hockey Night in Canada*.

One of the first players to join me was Adam Graves. During our chat a spray of champagne came close to us and I flinched. Adam put his arm around me and said, "Don't worry, Dick. I'll protect you."

After two or three more interviews, Glenn Anderson moved in beside me. Anderson was celebrating his sixth Cup victory, having previously won five with the Edmonton Oilers. That was the good news. The bad news was he had a bottle of champagne with him.

I can't recall ever speaking with Glenn Anderson before that night, and I know I haven't since then. I'm not sure he even knew my name. As I was asking my first question, he had a smarmy grin on his face and I knew he wasn't listening to a word I was saying. I also knew what was coming next and, sure enough, with millions of Canadians watching, Anderson poured champagne on my head. While it probably wasn't the whole bottle, it sure felt like it. Where was my protector, Adam, when I really needed him?

The problem all that champagne poses for an announcer isn't just a wet head. It's the champagne in your eyes. The stuff stings like crazy and it's tough to keep your eyes open. A lot of us have gone through it. I recall a current legend in American sports broadcasting, Bob Costas, getting soaked after either a World Series or a Super Bowl, and I felt for him as I watched him gamely struggle on with the broadcast.

That's what I tried to do with Anderson and a couple of Rangers who followed him. My performance wasn't exactly an award-winner. During the next commercial break they told me my part of the show was over.

Getting out of the room was a chore. Dozens of people jammed the doorway trying either to get in or get out. One trying to get in was Doug Messier, father of the Rangers' captain, Mark. I finally pushed my way through and headed down the hall to the *Hockey Night in Canada* studio to dry off and clean up.

As I walked through the door, Ron MacLean was starting an interview with the losing coach, Pat Quinn. I tiptoed behind the camera and into a washroom where, to my surprise, I found myself

face to face with the coach in "Coach's Corner" himself, Don
Cherry. Don was leaning against the wall, and the minute I got
there he started talking, which didn't surprise me. What he had
to say did.

"They want me to go on," was his opening line. "I'm not goin'
on. I never went on when I lost. You never want to go on when
you lose. No way."

A stranger would have sworn Grapes was an employee of
the Vancouver Canucks, the losing team whose coach, at that
moment, was on.

"Your dad wouldn't go on. I'm not goin' on."

Minutes after having the glamorous job interviewing the
Stanley Cup champs, there I was with my head stuck in a sink full
of water, an audience of one for a Don Cherry rant.

Ron's interview with Quinn had ended and he called through
the door, "Okay, Don, two minutes."

Don's answer wasn't loud enough to be heard through the
door, but for the benefit of his audience of one he said it anyway.
"I'm not goin' on."

By this time I had pretty well combed my hair back in place and
I wanted to see how it all played out from the other side of the
washroom door. So I left Grapes the way I had found him, by
himself, and went back into the studio. By this time our executive
producer, my boss, Ron Harrison, had arrived but remained silent.
Ron MacLean kept talking to the door: "Thirty seconds, Don. . . .
Hey, Don, fifteen seconds." The washroom door remained closed.

Then it was "Cue Ron," and our host was on the air, flying solo.

From the standpoint of the show, Don Cherry was right
again. Ron had about twenty seconds of air time. Heck, Ron and
Don aren't even warmed up in twenty seconds. Ron said exactly
the right thing in wrapping up the show in his usual professional
style, and another *Hockey Night in Canada* season was over.

For me, it had been a somewhat bizarre finish to a night marking the twenty-sixth time I had been in the arena where the Stanley Cup was won.

∎∎∎∎

When I retired from the *Hockey Night in Canada* broadcast booth in 1999 after thirty-three years of playoff hockey, I looked back on 1994 as perhaps the best year. There was great hockey, dramatic story lines, and a lot of fun. To top it off, Ron Harrison assigned me to twenty-seven playoff games that year, my career high. I was being paid by the game, so it was good news for my many creditors.

The 1993–94 NHL season had been one of the most interesting in years. Teams started play in Anaheim, Miami, and Dallas, not exactly places Canadians thought of as hockey hotbeds. Scotty Bowman recorded his one thousandth NHL coaching victory. Referees and linesmen went on strike for sixteen days, during which they were replaced by well-meaning but out-of-their-league officials, most from amateur hockey. And a couple of class acts had impressive stats in seasons shortened by injury and illness. Mario Lemieux played only twenty-two games for Pittsburgh, yet compiled thirty-seven points, and Cam Neely scored fifty goals in forty-nine games for Boston.

It was a strange season for Wayne Gretzky, then with the Los Angeles Kings. The Great One became the NHL's all-time goal scorer, breaking Gordie Howe's record of 801. He won his tenth, and last, scoring championship with 130 points, and he won the Lady Byng Trophy. For years the Stanley Cup playoffs seemed to belong to Number 99. But the Kings managed just sixty-six points in eighty-four games, which meant that, for the first time in his career, Gretzky wasn't there when the two-month trail to the Stanley Cup began.

The Montreal Canadiens, defending the Stanley Cup for the twenty-fifth time, played the Boston Bruins in the first round. As always, the Canadiens series was my assignment. The teams split the first two games in Boston. Back in Montreal the next day, the Canadiens' goaltender Patrick Roy complained of a pain in his right side. He was sent to hospital, where tests showed his appendix was in trouble. He stayed overnight. When the pain was still there the next morning doctors told him he couldn't play in the game that night at the Forum. Patrick's pain became the number-one story in Montreal.

The Canadiens' 1993 Stanley Cup victory is still remembered for their ten wins in overtime. Roy blanked four teams through seventy-seven minutes and five seconds of playoff pressure. Now, in game three against the Bruins, Ron Tugnutt was in goal and Patrick Roy was in hospital. Admitting afterwards he hadn't prepared himself properly, Tugnutt, a good guy and a good goalie, was beaten on two fairly routine shots early in the game, which the Bruins won 6–3.

Two days later Roy was still in the hospital, where he told the doctors he had awakened pain-free. He was sent for more tests, "to prove I wasn't lying," as he put it. He wasn't. An hour later he was practising with his team and was in goal that night as the Canadiens won 5–2.

Two nights later, in Boston, Patrick Roy played one of the best games of the hundreds I saw him play for the Canadiens. The Bruins fired sixty-one shots at him and he stopped sixty. The Canadiens won on Kirk Muller's goal at 17:18 of overtime. But that was the Canadiens' last gasp. Patrick and his pals were running on empty by then and the Bruins won the next two games and the series. A few days later, doctors took out Patrick Roy's appendix.

There was another aftermath to that series that only became apparent two years later. When Patrick Roy left the Boston Garden after the final game, April 29, 1994, nobody, not even Patrick, had the slightest idea he would never again be in goal for the Montreal Canadiens during the Stanley Cup playoffs.

There were some surprises elsewhere in first-round play. The San Jose Sharks finished the regular season eighteen points behind the Detroit Red Wings, yet defeated the Wings in seven games. The Vancouver Canucks fell behind to Calgary three games to one, then came back with three overtime wins to take the series. Vancouver won game seven in a double-overtime thriller when Pavel Bure, a sixty-goal man in the regular season, scored on a breakaway.

On April 27, in Buffalo, the Sabres and the New Jersey Devils fought a classic playoff battle which lasted into a seventh period of shutout goaltending by the Devils' Martin Brodeur and Buffalo's Dominik Hasek. It finally ended when Buffalo's Dave Hannan scored at 5:43 of the fourth overtime period. The teams had played what then was the sixth-longest game in playoff history.

Hannan's goal had tied the series 3–3. New Jersey eliminated the Sabres with a 2–1 victory on home ice two nights later. Martin Brodeur was an amazingly poised rookie throughout that playoff year. He later told me that, before the playoffs, veteran teammate Bernie Nicholls had said to him, "Just remember, kid, in the playoffs if you get a shutout, we win the game." Speaking of the seven-period marathon in Buffalo, Brodeur said, "I got two shutouts that night, and we still lost."

During the second round I worked the first and last games of New Jersey's six-game win over Boston, and the last four games of the Rangers' five-game win over Washington.

The 1993–94 season was perhaps the best enjoyed by the New York Rangers in the long history of the franchise. During the previous season they had fired coach Roger Neilson, who was in constant conflict with the team's captain and acknowledged leader,

Mark Messier. Shortly after he was let go, Roger told me, "A coach should never go to war with his best player because he'll never win." Ron Smith served as interim coach for the balance of the season. A few days after they finished out of the playoffs (a career first for Messier), the Rangers hired Mike Keenan as head coach. Eyebrows shot up all over the hockey world. Keenan and Messier with the same team? Let the fireworks begin.

Mike Keenan arrived to coach in New York with a history of guiding teams to success but then wearing out his welcome. He had led each of his two previous NHL teams, Philadelphia and Chicago, to the Stanley Cup finals, but he didn't win and eventually lost his job. There were always post-firing stories of Keenan's arrogance, his rough treatment of nice guys who played for him, and the ill will he left behind. I've heard some of his former players describe the experience as "brutal," and a "nightmare." I've heard others say that while he was tough, he was fair, and when at his best a great motivator.

In Chicago he briefly gave up coaching to be the general manager but that didn't last long. Mike Keenan wants to coach. But Keenan eventually wanted to do more: he wanted to run the whole operation as coach and general manager and was often referred to as a control freak. When he did have control later with the St. Louis Blues and the Vancouver Canucks, it didn't work, and he left those teams amid much bitterness.

Mike Keenan and I have had some interesting talks about coaching. He appreciates how the job has developed over the years and a respect for the good coaches of the past. He has asked about my father and how he operated. That's why, during the Rangers' series against Washington in 1994, I was surprised when we were chatting and, instead of asking questions about my father, he asked about my mother.

The Rangers had set team records during the regular season with 52 wins and a league-high 112 points, and they were on a roll in the playoffs with seven straight wins. They swept the Islanders in the first round and were up 3–0 on Washington. On the morning of their fourth game against the Capitals, I was at the Cap Center sitting with the Rangers' general manager, Neil Smith, while the players went through a light skating drill. Keenan was not on the ice. Despite their team's great season, Smith and Keenan weren't getting along and their mutual antipathy was common knowledge. Suddenly I saw Keenan, in shirt sleeves, standing behind the glass at the Zamboni entrance, motioning at me to join him. I said to Neil, "Well, guess I'll get to work now," and left to chat with the coach.

Our producer, Ed Milliken, was watching the practice, and I like to think that when he saw me going one on one with Keenan he thought, "Look at Dick, down there getting a lot of information from the coach about his team. That's what our guys are supposed to do. Way to go, Dick." Had he been listening, the boss wouldn't have heard one word about the Rangers, or the game that night. Instead, he would have heard a conversation about a hockey family, the Irvins. For a change, a coach was asking questions of a reporter.

Mike Keenan wanted to know how my mother reacted to being the wife of a coach. Was she interested in hockey? Did she go to the games? Did she talk hockey with her husband at the dinner table? Did my father bring the games home with him? Did his son and daughter get involved in the discussions? The answers were yes to all of the above. Mike hinted to me he was having marital problems. That coach-reporter interview was different, for sure.

That night I was having my free pre-game meal in the press room when Neil Smith came over to me and said, "I saw you with

Keenan this morning. What were you guys talking about?" I lamely answered we were chatting about the team and the series. Lamely lied, I should say, but I wasn't going to get involved in that scene.

The Rangers lost that night but eliminated the Caps two nights later. After New Jersey disposed of Boston I was assigned to the Eastern Conference final series between the Rangers and the Devils. That's when the fun really began.

■|■|■

The playoffs on HNIC are tough on the egos of those both on and off camera. Who does what, and who gets dropped as the playoffs continue? I was treated very fairly over my thirty-three play-off years, except once when my ego took its biggest hit; more on that later.

At the beginning of the 1994 playoff year I was part of a broad-cast team that was together for twenty games. Chris Cuthbert handled the play-by-play, former NHL goaltender John Garrett the colour, and this old man was in the booth to handle replays of penalty calls, do interviews, and keep the young guys on track when it came to hockey history. Scott Russell was the studio host and Rick Bowness, then coach of the eliminated Ottawa Senators, was the analyst. Our producer was Ed Milliken.

With so many series to cover these days, *Hockey Night in Canada* often shifts people around from one to the other, east to west, and so on. The fact that we were together for twenty games was unusual, but very enjoyable. We dubbed ourselves the "B Team," figuring that Harry Neale, Bob Cole, Ron MacLean, and Don Cherry were the "A Team." Or perhaps whoever was broadcasting the Toronto Maple Leafs was automatically on the A Team? Centre of the universe, and all that?

We heard the CBC brass in Toronto didn't like the term B Team, so we switched to "The Happy Gang." We really were happy. We spent thirteen straight days living in the Dumont Plaza Hotel in Manhattan, corner of 3rd Avenue and 34th Street, a road-trip record for all of us. We rode a van through the Lincoln Tunnel to and from the games in New Jersey. We walked to the games at Madison Square Garden, but took cabs back afterward. We might have been happy, but at that time of night in NYC, we weren't all that brave.

It's not often a Stanley Cup year contains a long-remembered semifinal game, but the Rangers against the Devils in 1994 was an exception thanks to Mark Messier. The first game lasted until 15:23 of the second overtime period when Stephane Richer's wrist shot glanced off goalie Mike Richter's stick and into the Rangers' net to give the Devils a 4–3 win. The Rangers then totally dominated the second game, outshooting New Jersey 41–16 on their way to a 4–0 victory.

The third game, at the Meadowlands, was another marathon. Again the Rangers had a wide margin in shots, 50–31, but they didn't win until Stephane Matteau backhanded the winner past Martin Brodeur at 6:13 of the second overtime period.

Changing goaltenders during play became one of Mike Keenan's trademarks, and he was at it again in the first period of the fourth game. After Bill Guerin's goal gave the Devils a 2–0 lead at 16:54 of the first period, Keenan yanked Richter and Glenn Healy took over. The change didn't work. Jacques Lemaire's team battened down the defensive hatches and the Devils were 3–1 winners to even the series. Two nights later they whipped the Rangers 4–1 at MSG and headed back to home ice one win away from the finals. That's when Mr. Messier took over.

Three years after he finally retires Mark Messier will get dressed
in a tuxedo and be inducted into the Hockey Hall of Fame, one
of the oldest modern-day players so honoured. The Messier
stories that will be recalled might include a game he played in
Chicago when the Edmonton Oilers were on their way to an
unexpected Stanley Cup in the year 1990 AG (After Gretzky).

The Oilers were behind the Blackhawks 3–1 in the Western
Conference final. The fourth game, at the Chicago Stadium,
turned into the Mark Messier show. Oilers coach John Muckler
and Chicago goaltender Greg Millen talked to me about that
game when I interviewed them for previous books.

Muckler said, "That's probably the best game I've ever seen
Mark Messier play. He took two penalties on his first two shifts
as if to let everybody know this was going to be his night so they
had better get out of his way. After that he was the most feared
player on the ice and he had all kinds of space. He did everything a player could do. He scored, he backchecked, he was
physical, he just dominated the game. That turned the series
around for us."

Millen feels Messier's domination started the morning of the
game. Greg told me, "I saw him sitting with John Muckler during
the morning skate. I glanced at him and I made sure I didn't look
at him again, because he had that look in his eye and I thought
right away, we'd better be ready for this guy tonight. I played that
game. Messier two-handed someone right off the bat. He was on
a mission. They beat us 4–2. I thought we had a good chance for
the Stanley Cup but Mark Messier took it away from us that
night." Ironically, the Chicago coach Messier took the Cup away
from in 1990 was Mike Keenan.

After tying the series, Edmonton went on to eliminate the
Blackhawks in six games and Boston in five to win their non-
Gretzky Stanley Cup.

Four years later, the day after the Devils won game five, Messier told the media he was personally guaranteeing a Rangers win the next night at the Meadowlands. The New York tabloids had a field day with the quote.

After the first period of the sixth game Messier might have wondered about the wisdom of his statement – the Devils were leading 2–0. It was still 2–0 when the Rangers' Alexei Kovalev scored at 18:19 of the second period. Messier set up the goal and I'm sure one of the three HNIC announcers in the booth said something like, "That could be a big goal before this one is over." It was, but not as big as the three scored in the third period which looked like this on the official scoresheet:

NYR Messier 8 (Kovalev, Leetch) 2:48
NYR Messier 9 (Kovalev, Leetch) 12:12
NYR Messier 10 (SHG) 18:15

The last goal was into an empty net from 175 feet with the Rangers shorthanded to complete Messier's remarkable hat trick. After the game Jay Wells, a veteran NHL defenceman then with New York, echoed Greg Millen. "I played against Mark for nine years," said Wells, "and nothing scared me more than when he got that real serious look of determination in his eye. In the third period, he had that look."

Rangers fans were celebrating, but the Happy Gang wasn't all that happy on the van ride through the Lincoln Tunnel back to the Dumont Plaza. Before we left the Meadowlands, word had come from Toronto that Ron MacLean and Don Cherry would be replacing Scott Russell and Rick Bowness on the telecast of game seven. Our displeasure had absolutely nothing to do with Ron and Don and everything to do with the spirit within our ranks. At that moment I'm not sure Ron and Don even knew.

By the time we returned to our home away from home we had decided to fight the decision. That was even before we hit the hotel bar. When we did get to the bar, Chris Cuthbert got on the pay phone and made some late-night phone calls to the top decision-makers both at the CBC and Molstar, the company producing the shows. Chris was persuasive. Scott and Rick stayed, and two nights later Chris would call the play-by-play of a heck of a hockey game.

The Devils were down 1–0 and storming Mike Richter's net in what truly were the dying seconds of the third period when Valeri Zelepukin scored at 19:52, setting up the third overtime thriller of the series. About an hour later the Rangers won when, for the second time in the series, Stephane Matteau scored in the second overtime period. Through 84:24 of winner-take-all hockey, the teams had combined for eighty shots on goal and referee Bill McCreary had called just two minor penalties. A great game had ended a great series.

■ ▮ ▮ ■

When the Stanley Cup finals began at Madison Square Garden four nights later, only one member of the Happy Gang was there. Me. It sounds corny but I really did feel a bit awkward saying goodbye to the others knowing I was the only one who would still be working. It would be the fourth straight year I worked the finals in the booth with Harry Neale and Bob Cole. Ron MacLean and Don Cherry were downstairs in the "Coach's Corner."

The Vancouver Canucks had reached the final series for only the second time in their history. After defeating Calgary, the Canucks eliminated Dallas and Toronto, both in five games. They were the fresher team, but the Rangers were the favourites and would have won the series four straight had it not been for an outstanding performance by Vancouver's goaltender Kirk McLean in the first game.

The opener was another overtime game for the Rangers, with the final shots on goal 54–31 in favour of New York. But the final score was 3–2 in favour of Vancouver. As had happened twice in their series against New Jersey, the Rangers let a one-goal lead get away late in the third period when Martin Gélinas beat Mike Richter at 19:00. In overtime New York outshot Vancouver 17–9. McLean was outstanding. He was the only reason the game was still tied when Vancouver's Greg Adams scored at 19:26 of the first overtime period.

I found myself thinking back to a playoff game at MSG in 1986 when Patrick Roy, then a rookie goalie for the Montreal Canadiens, stopped thirteen shots in the first nine minutes of overtime, allowing his team to defeat the favoured New Yorkers. Montreal won that series, and later the Stanley Cup. I can get superstitious about things like that. But a week later it looked as if it was all over but the shouting up and down old Broadway.

The Rangers won the next three games, 3–1 in New York and 5–1 and 4–2 in Vancouver. The turning point in the fourth game came when Richter stopped Pavel Bure on a penalty shot that if successful would have given the Canucks a 3–1 lead in the second period. The next day the *New York Post* trumpeted the play as the greatest save in hockey history. As they say, only in New York.

Back in the Big Apple for the fifth game the *Post* was at it again. "TONIGHT'S THE NIGHT" was the headline on the front page, anticipating the Rangers' first Cup win in fifty-four years. Not quite.

After a scoreless, penalty-filled first period, Vancouver scored once in the second period and twice early in the third. Then the

Rangers scored three quick goals before the period was half over
and the Canucks were reeling. That's when I got the word: "Dick,
go downstairs."

The elevator service at MSG may be the slowest in the world,
so I made the trip via a back stairway. It took my sixty-two-year-
old legs about four or five minutes to walk from the ninth floor
to the fifth floor and then halfway around the building to our
studio where everyone was watching the game on the monitor.
Ed Milliken, another fugitive from the Happy Gang, was there to
work as the dressing-room producer. When I walked in he said,
"You should have stayed upstairs. It's 5–3 Vancouver." As soon as
he said that the Canucks scored again. Their three goals had come
at 9:31, 12:20, and 13:04 and I hadn't seen one of them. Final
score, 6–3 Canucks.

The next day a now rather weary band of hockey travellers
took off on another transcontinental flight westward to beautiful
downtown Vancouver.

I was on dressing-room alert again for the sixth game but a trip
downstairs (much shorter at the Pacific Coliseum) wasn't necessary. Halfway through the third period Vancouver had a 3–1 lead,
which became 4–1 before the game ended, and the series was
extended to a dramatic seventh game in New York. The media
wanted Messier to come up with another fearless prediction,
perhaps another guarantee. This time his line was, "What this is,
is an opportunity to go home and win the Stanley Cup."

What is most remembered about the final game is the way it
ended. Messier's power-play goal at 13:29 of the second period put
New York ahead 3–1. Trevor Linden made it 3–2 on a Vancouver
power play early in the third period. It was still 3–2 when Pat
Quinn pulled McLean late in the game. In the wild last few
minutes the Canucks hit goalposts and the Rangers iced the puck
a few times. When they shot it down the ice with the clock ticking

down to the final seconds it seemed it was all over. There was bedlam in the Garden, Brian Leetch and Mike Richter threw off their gloves and starting hugging one another. Then they noticed none of their teammates had come off the bench. They hadn't heard the linesman's whistle to call icing with 1.6 seconds left on the clock. Yogi Berra was right. It's never over till it's over.

One faceoff remained, Craig MacTavish of the Rangers against Pavel Bure of the Canucks. MacTavish won the draw, Steve Larmer made sure the puck stayed along the boards and, finally, it was over. What followed was the predictable on-ice celebrations and presentations, the dressing-room interviews, Glenn Anderson with his bottle of champagne, and me in the bathroom with Don Cherry.

▌▐▌▌▌

I'm sure there were only two people in Madison Square Garden that night of June 14, 1994, who had been in Maple Leaf Gardens in Toronto on April 13, 1940, the last time the New York Rangers had won the Stanley Cup. One was Norm MacLean, a long-time hockey writer from New York. His father, a Ranger fan, had driven his ten-year-old son to Toronto to see the game. The other was me. In 1940 I was the eight-year-old son of the coach of the Toronto Maple Leafs.

In 1994, Norm was in the Rangers' room after the game and when we broke for a commercial I asked him to join me for an interview. But that's when HNIC decided to go back to the studio. So the two guys who were little kids at the Rangers' Stanley Cup–winning game in 1940 didn't get on television together when they weren't little kids any more, after the Rangers' next Stanley Cup–winning game fifty-four years later.

Before My Time

· ·

The twenty-six times I have been in a building when the Stanley Cup has been won isn't a record. Not even close. Veteran Montreal hockey writer Red Fisher began covering the NHL in general, and the Canadiens in particular, in 1955. Since then he has been at forty-four Stanley Cup finals. I don't think anyone is a close second. There could be others who have been at more than I, such as the late NHL president Clarence Campbell, but my twenty-six likely puts me in the top four or five. Maybe three or four.

The Rangers' win in 1940 was my first and their win in 1994 my last. I continued to work playoff games for *Hockey Night in Canada* until I retired in 1999 but I was never again assigned to a final series. I might see another, but I won't go out of my way just to say I made it twenty-seven. Red's record is safe, from me and everybody else.

However, I might have him on one score. I once made news in connection with a Stanley Cup victory. I was thirty-seven days old. The first time a team called the Toronto Maple Leafs won the Cup was on April 9, 1932, when they defeated the New York Rangers to sweep the best-of-five final series. The next day, along with details of the Leafs' triumph, Toronto newspapers carried the story that the coach's infant son was very ill in Calgary. One headline claimed the coach "MAY NOT SEE SON ALIVE." So instead of enjoying various functions arranged to fete the new champions, the coach, Dick Irvin, boarded a train and headed west. Obviously, Dick Sr. did get to see Dick Jr. alive.

My problem was something called erysipelas, which the dictionary describes as "an acute infectious bacterial disease." I don't know how prevalent it is today, but in 1932 it was pretty serious stuff, especially for a thirty-seven-day-old Toronto Maple Leaf fan. But he made it.

The second full season my dad coached in the NHL was 1931–32, and it was the second straight year he coached in the finals. He would coach for a record twenty-six consecutive years, a mark that should stand the test of time. So should the fact that he coached in the Stanley Cup finals sixteen times.

In recent years Scotty Bowman has broken almost every coaching record, most of them previously held by Dick Irvin. Every time he reaches another milestone my father's name is mentioned, which is why I kid Scotty to keep going. Because of Scotty, younger fans today see and hear recurring mentions of Dick Irvin Sr. I detailed my father's playing career in my first book, *Now Back to You Dick*. Here is a capsule version.

Born near Hamilton, Ontario, in 1892, his family moved to Winnipeg a few years later. Dick Irvin became a star amateur hockey player, helping the Winnipeg Monarchs win the Canadian

Senior Championship – the Allan Cup – in 1915. He scored twenty-seven goals in eight playoff games that year, including the Cup-winner against the Melville Millionaires. In appreciation of the win the City of Winnipeg gave each player a motorcycle. Some of them immediately sold their rather unusual gift but Irvin learned how to ride his. Later, while the First World War was still on, he went overseas with the Winnipeg-based Fort Garry Horse Regiment, serving as a motorcycle dispatch rider.

When the war ended, November 11, 1918, Dick Irvin was in a military hospital in France. He often told the strange story of his war injury. While driving his bike down a narrow road he met up with a cavalry unit. He weaved his way through almost the entire line when the last horse, perhaps frightened by the noise of the bike, reared up and kicked my father in the head, knocking him unconscious. The effects of that injury caused him periodic bouts of severe headaches for the rest of his life.

Back in Canada he resumed his hockey career in Winnipeg and Regina, turning pro with the Regina Caps of the Western Canada League in 1921. Two years later Regina became his permanent home. In 1925 the Regina team transferred to the Pacific Coast League as the Portland Rosebuds, where he scored thirty-one goals, tying Bill Cook for the league lead. After that 1925–26 season the league folded. The NHL absorbed many of its players and the Portland franchise was purchased by Major Frederic McLaughlin, a flamboyant Chicago millionaire who named the team after a restaurant he owned, the Blackhawk.

The 1926–27 season was the first time the Stanley Cup belonged solely to the National Hockey League, which had been formed in 1917. The NHL winner had previously played off against a team from the west to decide the Cup-winner. The NHL grew from seven teams to ten with the addition of Detroit, Chicago, and the New York Rangers and was divided into two sections, Canadian and American. Because there were only four teams in Canada, two in Montreal and one each in Ottawa and Toronto, the New York Americans joined the Canadian section. Along with the three new teams, Boston and Pittsburgh were in the American section.

In his first NHL season Dick Irvin was thirty-four years old. He finished second to Bill Cook of the Rangers in the scoring race. Cook had 33 goals and 4 assists for 37 points. Irvin had 18 goals and 18 assists for 36 points. Howie Morenz of the Canadiens was third with 32.

The following season ended early for my father when he suffered a fractured skull in his twelfth game. He was leading the early-season scoring with five goals and four assists. He played the 1928–29 season, in which the Chicago team won only seven times in forty-four games and scored just thirty-three goals, a record for team futility that will stand forever. Irvin had six goals. Owner McLaughlin spent most of that winter in Florida. When asked why, he replied, "So I don't have to watch my team play hockey."

Dick Irvin retired at the end of that season, scouted for the Blackhawks for a year, then became their coach. On October 4, 1930, just before leaving for his first training camp in his new capacity, he married Bertha Bain. During his summers in Regina, Dick had worked as a salesman for the P. Burns Meat Packing Company. One of his customers was the R.H. Williams Department Store, where Bertha was the clerk at the candy counter. When they first met she was engaged to a man named Whitehead. In later years Bertha sometimes wore her two engagement rings. Maybe that was because her husband sometimes wore a watch engraved "To Dick, love from Ethel." Ethel lived in Portland.

∎∎∎

In the 1920s, coverage of sporting events was solely via news-papers. When the Rangers started out in New York, a paper called the *Sun* was still in business. During the team's inaugural season, one of the *Sun*'s editorial writers attended his first hockey game and wrote these first impressions:

> Hockey, the outstanding game on the winter scene in New York, is a combination of football, golf, soccer, prize fighting, tong war, and the latest prison riot in Herron, Illinois.
>
> It is a crime wave on ice.
>
> If a man dashes into another on a slippery street, knocks him down, and bashes him between the eyes, it is unpremeditated assault. If a man dashes into another, knocks him down, and bashes him between the eyes with a crooked stick in a rink, it's first class hockey.
>
> Here, at last, is a game played while every contestant is in the act of falling through space.
>
> It makes baseball seem like casual exercise prescribed by the doctor for old gentlemen with stiff joints. Beside it football looks like something thrown into the nursery to keep the children out of mischief.
>
> Hockey comes from the great open spaces of Canada, where men are ice hounds and women are fancy skaters. It is played between teams of six men each, none of whom cares a thing about his physical future.
>
> It is played with a small black rubber heel, the aim of each team being to deliver it into a cage guarded by a youth whose parents evidently never gave him any good advice.
>
> When it is time for a hockey game to begin the referee skates to the center of the ice and blows a whistle. This is a signal to all physicians, nurses, and interns to get ready for business. He then drops the rubber heel, and flees for his life.

The rubber heel is immediately battled for by the opposing teams on the theory of an eye for an eye, a tooth for a tooth, and a fracture for every try at the goal cage.

After the end of the final period surgeons examine the goaltenders. The game is awarded to the team whose goaltender has the best chance of recovery.

Now there's a real hockey reporter for you.

■ ■ ■ ■

The 1930–31 season was a good one for the Chicago Blackhawks. Team records were set for wins and points, and after eliminating Toronto and the Rangers in the first two rounds, the Hawks met the defending-champion Montreal Canadiens in the best-of-five Stanley Cup final.

The first two games were played in the fairly new Chicago Stadium, where a crowd of over eighteen thousand for the second game was a record for the NHL. The series went the five-game limit, the Canadiens winning the Cup with a 2–0 victory. Although he would coach another twenty-five years with several bitter defeats along the way, Dick Irvin always said 1930's game five was his biggest disappointment. Shortly after it was over he learned that several of his players had spent the night before the last game touring Montreal's hot spots, getting roaring drunk in the process. They were not in game shape for the big one the next night.

Some things don't change. I've had two NHL coaches tell me their players behaved the same way on the road the night before the seventh game of a playoff series, once in the 1960s, once in the '80s. I've always tried to have a high regard for hockey players and their approach to the game that earns them such a good living, but sometimes my faith is severely tested.

Coaching the Blackhawks to within one win of the Stanley Cup wasn't good enough for the team's nutcase owner. The Major fired my father the following summer. A few years later he fired Tommy Gorman after he had coached the Hawks to their first Stanley Cup win in 1934, and Bill Stewart early in the season after he coached Chicago to its second Cup in 1938. In his first ten years as owner, Major McLaughlin hired and fired thirteen coaches.

So Dick and Bertha were at home in Regina when the 1931–32 NHL season began. Dick was waiting for the phone to ring. Bertha was waiting for me to arrive. The phone rang first, a couple of weeks into the season. The caller was hockey's other Major, Conn Smythe, builder of the newly opened Maple Leaf Gardens in Toronto and owner of the team that played there. Smythe had just fired his coach, Art Duncan. Would the expectant father be interested in taking over? The next day Dick Irvin was on the eastbound CPR Transcontinental to become coach of the Toronto Maple Leafs. Bertha, fearful of the uncertainties of the coaching profession, headed west to her sister's home in Calgary.

Dad arrived in Toronto on November 28, 1931. The Maple Leafs had a home game that night against the Boston Bruins. Smythe would coach the team while Irvin sat nearby to observe. Halfway through the second period the Bruins had a 5–1 lead. Smythe said to Irvin, "Okay, Dick, you take over now." Great way to start, down by four before even changing a line. Somehow the Leafs came back and won the game 6–5. It was a portent of what would happen in the months to come.

The Maple Leafs had in the line-up such future Hall of Famers as Hap Day, King Clancy, and Red Horner on defence, and Ace Bailey and the famed Kid Line (Joe Primeau, Charlie Conacher, and Busher Jackson) up front. They finished third overall in the eight-team NHL and, much to their coach's delight, eliminated Chicago in the first playoff round. Then they met and defeated the Montreal Maroons and finally the New York Rangers to win the Stanley Cup. The finals were called the "tennis series" because the scores were 6–4, 6–2, 6–4.

Another oddity about the 1932 final was that the three games were played in three different cities. The first two were Rangers home games, but because the circus was considered more important than hockey, Ringling Brothers moved into the old Madison Square Garden on 8th Avenue after the first game. The Rangers' home rink for the second game was the Boston Garden. The Maple Leafs clinched the Cup in Toronto.

The circus still shows up around playoff time at the new MSG on 7th Avenue, but now plays second fiddle. I've broadcast many games from there when the elephants, lions, and tigers were housed not far from centre ice. You can always tell. Just inhale deeply.

∎∥∎∥∎

I don't have many personal memories of hockey in the 1930s. Too bad. The '30s was one of the most colourful decades in NHL history. A lot of the colour was supplied by guys off the ice, the managers and coaches, who were quite a group. Reading about some of their shenanigans you find yourself saying, "That sort of stuff never happens these days." Some examples:

March 15, 1932. During a game in Boston, referee Bill Stewart penalizes Toronto goalie Lorne Chabot at a time when goalies have to serve their own penalties. Back-up goalies haven't been invented yet, so a skater has to go in the net with a goal stick but no goal pads. In this case three Leafs, Horner, Clancy, and Alex Levinsky, take turns and the Bruins score once on each. (Unlike today, penalized players served the full two minutes even if the other team scored on their power play.) An irate Conn Smythe, sitting at ice level, grabs Stewart as he skates by and starts punching him. (No

Plexiglas around the boards in those days.) Everybody gets into the act and peace is restored only when Bruins president Charles Adams arrives with a couple of tough Boston Irish cops in tow.

March 14, 1933. Again in Boston, the Bruins' Eddie Shore scores with two seconds remaining in the third period to tie Chicago 2–2. Chicago coach Tommy Gorman starts screaming that a penalty should have been assessed against the Bruins before the goal. He calls referee Bill Stewart (again) to the Chicago bench, pulls his sweater over his head and starts pummelling him. Stewart gets his head out of the sweater and lands a few punches on Gorman. The police (again) arrive and quiet things down. The Chicago players then refuse to play the last two seconds of the game, which Stewart forfeits to the Bruins, 3–2.

March 12, 1936. The Maple Leafs are playing the Canadiens at the Montreal Forum. Smythe (again) is there and constantly haranguing Montreal's playing-coach, Sylvio Mantha. Late in the game, with Toronto leading 6–3, Mantha is penalized. Smythe goes to the penalty box, sits down alongside Mantha, and continues his tirade. Referee Mike Rodden gets into the act and a tussle develops involving all three. Toronto coach Dick Irvin races around the rink and joins the fray, throwing a punch at Mantha. Montreal team president Ernest Savard and NHL president Frank Calder arrive and join the wild scene, which now involves the two team presidents, the two coaches, and the president of the NHL. Calder is the main peacemaker. Before the debacle ends Smythe grabs a hat from an usher and jams it onto Rodden's head.

Those were the days, my friends.

That last episode involving the league president was repeated, after a fashion, some thirty years later in that same penalty box at the Montreal Forum during a wild night involving the Canadiens and the Maple Leafs. There were players from both teams in the box when a brawl broke out on the ice involving several more players. When everybody had been penalized the timekeepers had a terrible time figuring out who should leave the box, and when, what with all the overlapping penalties being served.

The game had been held up several minutes when an exasperated NHL president Clarence Campbell left his seat at the south end of the building and purposefully strode to the penalty box where he sat down in the middle of the confused officials and sweaty hockey players, grabbed the penalty sheets, and quickly sorted out the mess. Mr. Campbell explained to everyone what should be done, and when, and that was that. Has Gary Bettman been seen in a penalty box near you lately?

■ ■ ■ ■

Is hockey more violent today than in the past? Most people feel it must be. But is it, or does television just make it seem that way? Some old-timers will tell you that, taking into consideration the shorter seasons they played, there was far more rough stuff in the old days than there is today.

I once saw a photograph taken in the 1930s during a game between Toronto and the New York Americans that showed every player in uniform, except the goaltenders, fighting. Know who else is on the ice? Some members of the New York Police Department. They had to call the cops to stop that one. Imagine if that happened today. The hue and cry would be deafening and everyone from coast to coast would see it. If you missed it live and in colour you could catch a few hundred TV replays over the next few days.

Another wild episode in the pre-television era was the infamous Eddie Shore–Ace Bailey incident. On December 12, 1933, the Toronto Maple Leafs played the Bruins in Boston. In the second period, Shore, the game's top defenceman, charged Bailey, who was knocked unconscious when his head hit the ice. Toronto's Red

Horner then attacked Shore with his fists and cut him badly. Shore received a major penalty, Horner a match penalty. Bailey was taken to hospital where his life hung in the balance for several days. He survived, but his playing career was over.

That incident was seen only by those in attendance at the Boston Garden. There were no television cameras to record the mayhem as there was, for example, in Vancouver February 21, 2000, when the Bruins' Marty McSorley hit the Canucks' Donald Brashear on the side of the head with his stick. Brashear struck his head when he fell to the ice and, like Ace Bailey, was knocked unconscious. Luckily his career was not ended.

How often has that incident been replayed on television? How many times did we see Scott Stevens's bodycheck on Eric Lindros in the 2000 playoffs that ended Lindros's season? The images of those frightening incidents were flashed into our living rooms dozens of times.

Red Storey, who refereed in the NHL in the 1940s and '50s, made the point in an interview. He said, "I'd do a game in Chicago on a Sunday night and there might be a bench-clearing brawl. Two nights later I'd be in Detroit and nobody there knew anything about the fight in Chicago."

▮▮▮▮

My first clear recollection of the NHL is from the 1939–40 season when I first went to games at Maple Leaf Gardens, but only on Saturday nights. The Maple Leafs began the 1940s by losing in the Cup finals. A few days after that I became a Montreal Canadiens fan.

The Maple Leafs were in the finals five times in the eight years following their 1932 Cup victory, and lost every time. In his first ten years as a coach in the NHL Dick Irvin reached the finals seven times, and lost six of them.

During the 1930s, the two longest games in NHL history played a key role in drawing attention to radio as a growing part of coverage of the sport. In 1933 the Maple Leafs lost to the Rangers in four games after a tough start. The Leafs had eliminated Boston 3–2 in the semifinals. The fifth game of that series still ranks as the second-longest ever played. The Leafs became 1–0 winners on Ken Doraty's goal at 4:46 of the sixth overtime period. NHL president Frank Calder was at the game. After the fourth overtime period he suggested the teams toss a coin to decide the winner. Calder was concerned because the winner was scheduled to open the final series the next night in New York. The Bruins agreed to the coin toss but the Leafs didn't. Calder then called Lester Patrick, who was running the Rangers, and asked if he would postpone the opening game by one night. Patrick, who had not one ounce of human kindness coursing through his veins, refused. So the game in Toronto continued until Doraty ended the marathon at 1:50 a.m.

Foster Hewitt's radio broadcasts from the gondola at Maple Leaf Gardens were becoming famous by then. Hewitt worked alone. No colour man. No analyst. But he did share the microphone during the intermissions with Gordon Castle, a radio announcer who read the commercials. Castle also did post-game interviews with the players. That night, as he always did, Castle went downstairs during the third period. He left the gondola just before 10:30. But the game wasn't over after three periods. Castle, standing between the players' benches, waited and waited while the overtime periods went on and on. That left Hewitt to handle everything by himself, the game and the intermissions.

An exhausted Hewitt was faltering badly near the end of the fifth overtime period. The show's producer, Pas Pasmore, saw that Hewitt was on the verge of falling off his chair. (Years later Foster told me he was becoming disoriented as that period drew to a close.) Pasmore yelled and motioned frantically to Castle at ice level to come back upstairs. Luckily he got the message. Castle made the long climb up to the gondola in record time, took the microphone from the sagging Hewitt, and ad libbed a monologue to fill the entire fifteen minutes of intermission air time. Fortunately for Hewitt the Doraty goal came early in the next overtime. Save for a few minutes along the way, Hewitt had been on the air by himself for five and a half hours.

The late-night Toronto–New York train had been held at Union Station so the winning team could make the trip. It turned out to be the Maple Leafs, and Foster Hewitt was with them. A mere eighteen hours after their marathon against Boston, the Toronto team was facing off against the Rangers to begin the Stanley Cup final series, and Hewitt was back on the air. Ken Doraty, used mainly as a utility player, scored the first goal of the game. But the Leafs were exhausted and the Rangers coasted to an easy 5–1 victory. New York avenged what happened in 1932 by winning the series in four games.

■ ■ ■ ■

Three years later, at the Montreal Forum, the Detroit Red Wings and the Montreal Maroons played what is still the longest game, one which lasted 11:44 longer than the Toronto-Boston game. Again it was a 1–0 final score, with Detroit's Mud Bruneteau scoring after 116:30 of overtime. The goal was scored at 2:25 a.m. There was a two-man broadcast team doing that one: Charlie Harwood handled the play-by-play with veteran newspaperman

Elmer Ferguson on colour. As the game dragged on, Ferguson remarked how nice it would be to have a beer. A man listening in his apartment across the street promptly knocked on the Forum's back door and delivered a couple of beers. Knowing Fergy, I'm sure the gift was well used.

On May 4, 2000, the Pittsburgh Penguins and the Philadelphia Flyers played the third-longest game, in Pittsburgh. It lasted through 92:01 of overtime before the Flyers' Keith Primeau scored. That one was on *Hockey Night in Canada*. Two of my favourite partners during my last few years in the booth, Chris Cuthbert and Greg Millen, were the broadcasters. Just as Foster Hewitt had a game less than twenty-four hours after his 1933 marathon, Chris and Greg broadcast one less than twenty-four hours later, in Denver. I was proud of my two protegés the way they came through.

The Coach's Kid

....

I'm often asked what it was like growing up as the son of a hockey coach.

The truth is, I don't know.

From the time I was five until I was nineteen, give or take a few weeks, Dick Jr. never lived with Dick Sr. during the hockey season. My dad was in Toronto and Montreal while I was growing up in Regina. I use that term loosely because when you're a sports broadcaster, you never grow up. Why should we? It's too much fun getting paid to watch grown men play the same games we played when we were little boys.

Before I started school, the Irvins would divide their time according to the hockey seasons, living on Millwood Road in Toronto in the winter and on Angus Street in Regina in the summer. Once I took the big step into kindergarten, Regina, with the odd exception, became the year-round home for Bertha, Dick Jr., and my recently arrived sister, Fay.

A life in hockey was so different then. In my kindergarten year, 1937, Conn Smythe let coach Irvin take the train to Regina to spend Christmas with his family. Smythe was behind the bench for the three games played while his coach was away, winning two and tying one.

At one point during that same era, the Montreal Canadiens were struggling under the coaching of Newsy Lalonde, who had become a nervous wreck. The team sent Lalonde to Florida for some R&R. These days teams save themselves the cost of a Florida trip for a struggling coach. They fire him instead.

During the 1938 playoffs, Bertha and Dick Jr. travelled to Toronto and that's when I saw my first NHL game. I have no recollection of the trip save one. After the game, the second in the Stanley Cup finals, the Leafs took a train to Chicago. With some time to kill before leaving, a few players plus the coach and his family dropped in for something to eat at Murray's restaurant across from Union Station. I always had the memory of Busher Jackson holding me on his knee that night and in later years, when I asked my mother, she confirmed it did happen.

The date of that game was April 5, 1938, the final score 5–1 Toronto, tying the best-of-five at one win apiece. The Blackhawks then won the next two games in Chicago and the Irvins drove back to Regina in a brand-new 1938 Buick, the coach a loser again in the Stanley Cup finals.

That Buick was one of the reasons that I always figured we were pretty rich. Not as rich as the people who lived in the fancy homes on Albert Street South in Regina, mind you, but we must have been doing all right. Dad never worked in the summer, spending his time in our backyard tending to his pigeons and chickens and doing a lot of carpentry work around the house, two interests his son didn't inherit.

A few years after my father died, the National Hockey League sent me copies of some of the contracts he had as a player and coach in the 1920s and '30s. He earned $2,700 for his final season as a player in Chicago. His coaching contracts in Toronto were in the $3,500 to $5,000 range. In 1954–55 his final, and best, contract with the Montreal Canadiens was for $15,000. The next season he earned $20,000 with the Chicago Blackhawks, which made him the highest-paid coach in hockey history up to that point. It doesn't seem like much today but back then it was. The Irvins lived comfortably in nice homes and drove nice cars and I got a college education.

In January 1940, Dick Sr. moved wife, son, and daughter to Toronto for the remainder of what would be his last season with the Maple Leafs. We arrived on a Sunday, the morning after the Leafs had lost a home game to the New York Rangers, so Dad likely wasn't in the best of humour. He was a very hard loser, and if he had to take it out a bit on his family, so be it.

The upper duplex on Millwood Road that was to be our home for the next three months was much smaller than our house in Regina, so I'm sure my sister and I hated it immediately. Early that afternoon there was a knock on the door and in walked Gordie Drillon, one of the Maple Leafs' biggest stars and one of my early hockey heroes. I don't think he just happened to be passing by. I'm sure his coach asked (ordered?) him to be there. Those things happened back then. Dad had bought me a magnetic board-hockey game. That afternoon I was down on the floor playing the game against Gordie Drillon, who had become a legend in Canada through Foster Hewitt's Saturday-night broadcasts from Maple Leaf Gardens. Sitting on Busher Jackson's knee when I was six years old and playing magnetic hockey against Gordie Drillon two years later should have tipped me off that being the son of an NHL coach was worth a lot of perks.

Gordie Drillon was quite a character. In 1937–38 he won the NHL scoring championship with twenty-six goals and twenty-six assists. A Toronto Maple Leaf hasn't won it since. In the 1942 Stanley Cup finals, when the Leafs came from three games down against Detroit to win four straight and the Stanley Cup, Drillon was one of a few regulars benched by coach Hap Day when the historic comeback began. The next season he was in Montreal, playing again for Dick Sr. and scoring a career-high twenty-eight goals.

At the end of that season the Canadiens played exhibition games in California and Vancouver. When they got to Vancouver, fans at the game chanted, "We want Drillon . . . We want Drillon . . ." So did the Canadiens. Drillon, a handsome guy who loved wine, women, and song, especially the first two, had disappeared in California. The Canadiens, and the NHL, never saw him again. When he finally made it back home he joined the RCAF, and after the war did some playing and coaching in the Maritimes. In his final season as a player, at the age of thirty-five, he scored forty-eight goals in forty-nine games for the Saint John Beavers of the New Brunswick Senior League.

■ ■ ■ ■

Syl Apps. Now there was a hockey hero. Apps died December 24, 1998. Two nights later the Montreal Canadiens played for the last time at Maple Leaf Gardens and it was a great night for memories. Maurice Richard was introduced before the game and received an emotional ovation from the crowd, as did Ted Kennedy, the man who succeeded Apps as captain of the Toronto Maple Leafs. I was on the *Hockey Night in Canada* crew and Ron MacLean interviewed me about Syl Apps. I said that once upon a time every kid in Canada wanted to be Syl Apps, he was that popular.

There more of a mystique about the NHL and its players in those pre-television days. Thanks to Foster Hewitt's broadcasts, photographs in newspapers, Beehive corn syrup hockey cards, and our own vivid imaginations, hockey heroes were very much part of our growing up. A lot of us had their pictures on our bedroom walls. Don Cherry had Montreal's tough defenceman Ken Reardon on his. I had a picture of the Canadiens' Punch Line of Elmer Lach, Toe Blake, and Maurice Richard. But I'll bet Syl Apps led that league. After all, he was captain of the Toronto Maple Leafs, and that alone made him something special.

When we arrived in Toronto in 1940 and I got to see my first Saturday-night game (the Maple Leafs beat the New York Americans 5–1), Syl Apps wasn't playing because of a broken collarbone. But I saw him in the crowd, his arm in a sling, and my heart skipped. For a modern-day comparison to presence, image, and respect, think Jean Béliveau.

I also saw Foster Hewitt that night. Foster walked along the aisle at ice level directly in front of where I sat with Mother (red seats, box 4) on his way upstairs to broadcast the hockey game. I didn't meet him that season, but I would see him pass in front of us every Saturday night. Sometimes his son Bill would be with him. My youthful hockey dreams didn't include walking upstairs to a broadcast booth, which I eventually did about three thousand times. And there were quite a few games early in my career when my broadcast partner was Bill Hewitt.

My parents made it very clear that I was allowed to see the hockey games only on Saturday nights. The Leafs had a home game the Thursday after we arrived in Toronto and they tell me I threw a tantrum because I wasn't allowed to go. As it turned out I missed a bit of hockey history, at least as far as Phil Stein was concerned. Stein was a goaltender in the American League with Providence. The Leafs' regular goalie, Turk Broda, was injured, so Stein was called up and played in a 2–2 tie with Detroit. It was the only game Phil Stein ever played in the NHL. Taking the overtime into consideration his career goals-against average in the NHL was 1.71. Not a bad stat to quote to his grandchildren, providing they didn't ask how many games he played.

I got over the crushing disappointment of not seeing Phil Stein play, and spent the next three months attending grade three at Davisville School and going to Maple Leaf Gardens every Saturday night. I became a fan of Bingo Kampman, a tough 185-pound defenceman, who was a crowd favourite in Toronto. One reason was his ability to backhand the puck in the air almost the length of the ice, which he did frequently to great applause when the Leafs were killing penalties. Kampman got into a fight one night with a Chicago player named Cully Dahlstrom. The fight ended when Kampman picked up Dahlstrom and threw him over the boards and into the laps of some paying customers seated at ice level. Watching that with my eight-year-old eyes I was sure my hero Bingo was the strongest person in the whole world.

There were two Saturday playoff games at MLG that year, the second and sixth games of the Leafs-Rangers final series. I don't remember a thing about either one except the last shot in the last game. Bryan Hextall put it past Turk Broda, in overtime, right in front of where my mother and I were sitting and New York won the Stanley Cup. For the next few minutes the Rangers were celebrating while I was crying. Through my tears I saw the Stanley Cup presented at centre ice for the first time. Only twenty-five to go.

Dick Sr.'s last season in Toronto was tough on his nerves. He usually had a nap before dinner, and as he lay sleeping on the couch he tossed, turned, jumped, and twitched. It scared me. The whole Toronto scene with its annual playoff near misses was getting to him, and it happened again. In the finals, three of the four New York victories came in overtime. A lucky bounce in favour of Apps or Broda instead of a Ranger and the result might have been different. However, before it was all over Dick Sr. knew he was finished in Toronto and heading to Montreal no matter who won the Stanley Cup.

Late in the season NHL owners held a meeting to discuss the precarious plight of the Montreal Canadiens. For many years there had been two teams in Montreal, the Canadiens and the Maroons. The Maroons folded in 1938 and now the Canadiens were in danger of succumbing to the same fate. In 1939–40 they won only ten of forty-eight games. Crowds at the Forum were sparse. Yet the league knew it couldn't afford to lose the Montreal franchise.

One of the Canadiens' problems was a lack of discipline within the ranks of the players. Conn Smythe told his fellow owners, "I know who could straighten that out. How about Irvin going there to coach?" There was general agreement, so Smythe talked it over with my father even while their Leafs were still playing. Today they'd call it tampering. In 1940 it was an honest effort to save a historic franchise. Three days after Bryan Hextall's goal won the Stanley Cup for the Rangers, Dick Irvin became coach of the Montreal Canadiens.

He inherited a ragtag bunch. Toe Blake and Ray Getliffe were the only bona fide NHLers on the roster, but over the next four years things improved. In 1940 rookies Elmer Lach and Ken Reardon arrived from the west. The next year Émile "Butch" Bouchard joined the team. Another unknown kid, Maurice Richard, became a Hab in 1942. The best goaltender in amateur hockey, Bill Durnan, signed an hour before the start of the 1943–44 season. Years later all of those new players, plus Blake, would be inducted into the Hockey Hall of Fame.

Starting in '43–44 Montreal finished in first place four years straight. They won the Stanley Cup in 1944, the first for the Canadiens since they beat a bunch of hungover Blackhawks in 1931. They won the Cup again in 1946. They were somewhat aided by the Second World War. Several top NHL players, including their own Ken Reardon, left to join the armed forces. But in post-war play the likes of Lach, Richard, Durnan, and Bouchard proved they were far from being "wartime players," as many had charged.

■|■|■

After those three months on Millwood Road in Toronto, eleven years would go by before the Irvins would live together full-time during the hockey season. In the early 1940s, as the Canadiens were gradually resurrecting a great hockey franchise, Bertha and the Irvin kids travelled from Regina to Montreal for their Christmas holidays.

I lost a lot of my childhood innocence during our yuletide trip in 1940. First there was Santa Claus. I had been willing to give the old guy the benefit of any doubt when it came to sliding down our chimney in Regina. But crawling through a seventh-storey window in the Mount Royal Hotel was a bit much to believe, even for an eight-year-old.

More innocence was lost the first time Senior took Junior into the Canadiens' dressing room before a morning practice and the little guy heard grown men swear. I mean really swear. The presence of the coach's kid didn't inhibit them one bit and the coach wasn't shushing them. Four-letter words, five letters, seven, ten. You name them, I heard them.

The worst – or the best – was the captain, Toe Blake. How bad was he? Well, Blake was once banned from a poolroom located in the Forum because of his language.

■ I ■ I ■

Murph Chamberlain played for the Canadiens for most of the 1940s. His nickname was "Hardrock," and he lived up to it on and off the ice. Chamberlain had played for Dick Sr. in Toronto and the two men had, strangely, become good friends. I say "strangely" because Dick was a strict teetotaller and Murph was a drinker. Big time. But he was the kind of competitor the Canadiens needed and they purchased Chamberlain from Toronto for $7,500 a few weeks after Dick Sr. became the coach.

Once in a while Murph would go on a bender and disappear. The team would explain to the few newspapermen who came around that Chamberlain had some kind of injury and that would be that. A few days later Chamberlain would return with no questions asked. There's no way teams or players could get away with that kind of thing in today's media-driven sports world.

Years later, when he had beaten off the demon rum (as Gordie Drillon did after his hockey career ended), Murph told me about a time he went AWOL. "I finally showed up at the Forum," he said, "and wouldn't you know it, Dick is the first person I see when I walk in. I expected the worst, but all he said was, 'Get away from me. I don't want to talk to you.' And for a while he didn't. But he worked the hell out of me the next few days in practice. I sweated that one off pretty quick."

That was a case of a coach putting up with a hard-to-handle player because he needed the guy on his team. During the late 1950s Toe Blake, by then the Canadiens' coach, couldn't stand his unpredictable and temperamental goaltender, Jacques Plante. But

Plante was the best in the business and Blake didn't let his feelings get in the way of what was good for the team. During a later Montreal dynasty, Scotty Bowman stuck with a few of his least favourites like Rick Chartraw, Pierre Bouchard, and Pete Mahovlich. A lot of coaches don't seem to have that kind of patience today.

▌▐▐▌

The first time I saw Maurice Richard play was at the Forum, December 27, 1942. He was playing left wing and wearing number 15. Early in that game against the Boston Bruins he scored two goals, the fourth and fifth of his career. Late in the game Richard was dealt a terrific bodycheck by Boston defenceman Johnny Crawford and crumpled to the ice with a broken leg. Just like the Hextall goal in Toronto, it happened directly in front of where my mother and I were sitting. Richard's season was over and his future as a hockey player was doubtful.

Two short years later Maurice Richard had become hockey's flaming "Rocket." He was wearing number 9 and playing right wing on the Punch Line alongside Toe Blake and Elmer Lach. On December 28, 1944, the coach's kid, now twelve years old, was watching the game while sitting at the end of the Canadiens' bench when the Rocket set a record by registering eight points – five goals and three assists – as the Canadiens whipped Detroit 9–1. Seen a twelve-year-old kid watching an NHL game from the players' bench lately?

That was our last Christmas trip east until 1950. The next time the family was together during the holiday season was in the 1946–47 season when Dick Sr. flew west and spent New Year's with us in Regina. Assistant coaches hadn't yet been invented and Frank Selke, who was in his first year as the team's general manager, didn't take over as coach as Conn Smythe had done in Toronto in 1937. Captain Toe Blake ran the practices and served as playing-coach for one game, New Year's night in Chicago. We could pick up Chicago games on the radio via station WGN, so the coach was listening. At one point the Canadiens got a penalty to make them two men short. Dad said, "I'll bet Blake puts himself on." He did. Chicago didn't score.

The Canadiens won the game 5–2, with the Rocket scoring twice. Dad was sure Blake would run a tight ship up to and including that game in Chicago. He was likely also sure the boys would have a pretty good New Year's party during the twenty-hour train ride back to Montreal. If they did, the hangovers were gone in time for their next game, a 4–1 win over Boston on January 4. Dick Sr. was back behind the bench and didn't miss another game through to the end of his career in 1956.

∎▐∎▐∎

The coach's kid got his share of perks. Like comic books. During the war the cream of the crop, including Batman, Superman, and Captain Marvel, were available in the United States but not in Canada. Dick Sr. would buy them for me on road trips and I was the most popular kid in Davin School when a package containing the world's greatest comic books would arrive. Naturally I got to read them first.

While scratching around Rink 3 in Regina's Parks League system I had hockey sticks "right from the Canadiens' dressing room," as I liked to boast. I recall one batch of new sticks that all snapped in two after about a half-hour's play in the cold prairie outdoors. No wonder Rocket and Elmer didn't want them. I used hockey gloves my father had worn when he played for the

Chicago Blackhawks. I gave my friend Davie Malcolm goalie gloves that had been worn by the legendary Turk Broda.

During those years I learned that some hockey guys aren't as tough as you might think. My father spent his entire adult life working in a business where injuries come with the territory. He saw dozens of broken arms and legs and bloody cuts that required hundreds of stitches. And he likely never batted an eye. It was different on the home front, where his son managed to break his left arm four times in six years. The third break happened in the summer of 1942 when I was playing in a friend's backyard. His parents called my parents. Dad quickly arrived in the 1938 Buick and drove me home, which took about three minutes. By the time we arrived he was white as the proverbial ghost. Mother was sure he passed out briefly in the front seat when we got there. So my father, famed for his career in the rough, tough world of hockey, flaked out at home while my mother drove me to the hospital.

❚❙❚❙❚

Our last Christmas trip to Montreal was in 1950, eight months before we moved there permanently. It provided me with the highlight of my playing career which, up to then, had very few, if any, to report.

I was eighteen years old, attending the University of Saskatchewan in Saskatoon, and playing for the Huskies as the fourth-line centre on a three-line team. (I am living proof that athletic ability is not hereditary.)

I always took my skates on our holiday trips. It would be the only time all winter I would be able to go skating with my father, pass a puck back and forth, and, perhaps, learn something in the process. Those were rare but special times for me.

A few days into our 1950 visit Dick Sr. decided I would practise with the Canadiens, which really wasn't fair, either to the
players or to me. Nevertheless the equipment man outfitted me
and there I was on the ice at the Montreal Forum with future Hall
of Famers named Harvey, Lach, Richard, and Olmstead. Practices
in those days were mainly scrimmages, games between the Reds
and the Whites, and they could get rough. I tried to be Joe Cool,
but in reality I was scared to death.

A couple of days earlier I had heard my dad and Ken Reardon,
by then an executive with the team, talking about one of their
players, Ken Mosdell. A good centreman, Mosdell was usually
given the tough job of checking opposing stars like Milt Schmidt
and Sid Abel. His nose was broken many times, usually by
Schmidt. Reardon was saying how Mosdell could shift an opposing checker out of his jockstrap if the opponent played the body.
He said the way to play Mosdell was to forget the body and play
the puck.

So there I was, on the ice during my famous scrimmage and
here comes Mosdell out of his own zone, and here comes the guy
forechecking for the opposition. Me. Mosdell gave me his big
shift action but I was wise to that trick, thanks to Ken Reardon.
My eyes never left the puck and, bingo, I checked it away from
him. That's the only thing I remember about that day, other than
how scared I was. But like Fred Astaire sang, "They Can't Take
That Away from Me." The memory, that is, of my one and only
practice with the Montreal Canadiens.

Ken Mosdell was Maurice Richard's best friend on the team.
Several years ago Ken suffered a debilitating stroke. But he
battled back and it was touching to see him serving as a pallbearer
at the Rocket's funeral.

A Great Rivalry

·····························

D ick Sr.'s commuting was getting a bit tough to handle. A fifty-game season became a sixty-game season, and then a seventy. Training camp started earlier and the playoffs finished later. So in the summer of 1951 the Irvins left Regina in a 1950 Chrysler, which had replaced the 1938 Buick, and headed east to live in the big city year-round. I'm still there. My sister, Fay, lives in Ottawa.

House-hunting didn't turn up anything suitable right away, so from August until April we lived in an apartment building at 2075 Lincoln Avenue. And guess what? The Montreal Forum was just two blocks away. And the son of the coach of the Canadiens could walk into the Forum any time, free. Believe me, I took advantage of that perk, and then some.

I transferred to McGill University, which was quite a culture shock after the University of Saskatchewan. From a cozy campus of some two thousand students in Saskatoon I had moved to a campus of some six thousand located in the heart of what was then the biggest city in Canada. I enjoyed McGill, but I preferred the atmosphere in Saskatoon.

I managed to make the Redmen hockey team, although my performance was no better than it had been with the Huskies out west. At least as a Husky I once scored two goals in a game, against an intermediate team in Melfort. That turned out to be my career high. I managed to score a few goals in two years as a Redman, very few. I'm convinced the only reason I made the team – and I was the last one picked – was because we practised and played at the Forum. I'm told the school got a great deal on ice rental, and I'm sure Old McGill didn't want to take a chance on spoiling a good thing.

That was quite a set-up, a university team using the home rink of an NHL team. The Canadiens practised at ten in the morning and our practices began at noon. Players named Richard, Harvey, Lach, and Geoffrion would skate off at the end of their practice, then players named Schutz, Lupovich, Irvin Jr., and Kent would skate on at the start of theirs.

That first bunch of guys would draw crowds of fifteen thousand to their home games. The second bunch played theirs before "crowds" of a dozen or so parents and a few girlfriends. I don't know what the Canadiens' per diem was then, but we all got a voucher for seventy-five cents on practice days, which bought lunch at the Forum coffee shop.

■ ■ ■ ■

In the early 1940s my dad was contacted by a man named Alan Roth, a full-time tie salesman in Montreal whose hobby was sports statistics, something rarely heard of or used back then. Roth claimed a coach could learn a lot about the performance of his players, and the opposition, if he knew who won the face-offs, how many bodychecks each player delivered, who was on the ice when the goals were scored, and so on. Roth was a good salesman and the Canadiens hired him, likely paying him with a free ticket to the games. The sort of detail Roth provided was groundbreaking in the NHL.

Three or four years later Roth submitted a similar idea for baseball to Branch Rickey, who ran the Brooklyn Dodgers. My dad, a big baseball fan, wrote an accompanying letter of recommendation. Rickey liked the idea and hired Roth in 1947, the same year Jackie Robinson made his Major League debut with that team. Alan Roth spent the rest of his life working for the Dodgers in both Brooklyn and Los Angeles, and set standards for baseball statistics and research that are being followed, and expanded, to this day.

For a few years after Roth joined the Dodgers, the Canadiens' statistics were somewhat haphazard. So in 1951 Dick Sr., likely looking for an excuse to get his son into the rink without having to buy him a ticket, hired me as a statistician, without pay. On game day he would tell me what he wanted kept track of that night. Sometimes it was faceoffs, sometimes hits, and always who was on the ice for both teams when the goals were scored. Once in a while it would be giveaways, showing how many times his players passed the puck to opposing players. Only recently has the NHL added giveaways as an official stat. I was an unofficial statistician at every home game during the last four years Dick Sr. was coach of the Canadiens. Years later, my mother would complain that I used too many statistics on some hockey broadcasts. I always replied that I came by it honestly.

■|■|■

We moved to Montreal August 15, 1951. Eleven days later
Toronto Maple Leafs defenceman Bill Barilko disappeared in a
small plane while on a fishing trip in northern Ontario. It would
be eleven years before the plane, and Barilko's body, were found.
The Barilko tragedy occurred just four months after he scored one
of the most famous goals in the history of Maple Leaf Gardens.
The Maple Leafs defeated the Canadiens in a final series in which
all five games were decided in overtime. Sid Smith, Ted Kennedy,
Harry Watson, and Barilko got the game-winners for Toronto.
Maurice Richard scored Montreal's winner, his third of that
playoff year. Barilko's goal was the Cup-winner. It was also the last
hurrah for the Maple Leafs for the 1950s. The balance of that
decade in the NHL belonged to the Detroit Red Wings and the
Montreal Canadiens.

In 1951 the Canadiens defeated the Red Wings in the semifinals,
a monstrous upset considering first-place Detroit had finished
thirty-six points ahead of third-place Montreal. In the final league
game, in Detroit, the Red Wings whipped Montreal 5–0. The
playoffs began two nights later and it looked like a piece of cake
for Detroit. But the Rocket stole the cake right off their plate.

Montreal won the opener 3–2, Richard scoring the winning
goal on Terry Sawchuk at 1:09 of the fourth overtime period. In
the second it was 1–0 Montreal, Gerry McNeil besting Sawchuk
in a goaltenders' battle and Richard scoring another winner, at
2:20 of the third overtime period. It was only the third time a
player had scored back-to-back overtime-winning goals in consecutive games in the playoffs. The first to do it was Mel Hill of
the Boston Bruins in 1939. The second was Don Raleigh of the
Rangers in 1950. After Richard in 1951 the next was Montreal's
John LeClair in 1993.

Detroit won the next two games in Montreal. It seemed the
Canadiens had shot their bolt in Detroit. But the Rocket came to

their rescue again in the fifth game, this time with his fists. Richard KO'd Ted Lindsay during a scrum along the boards and scored a goal later in the game in a 5–2 upset victory. Dick Sr., never one to shrink from needling the hated Red Wings, said the Lindsay KO was the difference, calling it a "one-punch win" for his team.

Two nights later at the Forum, the Canadiens completed the upset with a 3–2 win. All the goals were scored in the third period, with Richard getting his fourth of the series. Not one penalty was called by veteran referee Bill Chadwick, who still remembers the game as perhaps the best he ever saw.

That series was the start of the best rivalry I have ever seen. I know many people think of the Toronto-Montreal competition as the best, "Forever Rivals" as the CBC titled a special on it, and maybe over the long haul it was. But for a few years in the 1950s the Red Wings and the Canadiens had something going the likes of which I had never seen, or ever saw again. Beginning in 1952 either Detroit or Montreal won the Stanley Cup for nine straight years. It was Detroit first and Montreal second in the regular season five out of six years. In the sixth it was Montreal first and Detroit second. Also starting in 1952 they met in the Stanley Cup finals four times in five years. The two teams were in a class by themselves. Nobody else was even close.

A rivalry like that can't happen in today's thirty-team league. In 2000–01 the Montreal Canadiens and the Detroit Red Wings played each other once, in Montreal, and that was it. The Canadiens didn't play in Detroit. In the days I'm writing about, they played each other fourteen times. That's right, *fourteen.*

There were other intense rivalries. For a long time the Canadiens and the Boston Bruins had a good thing going, especially when they played in Montreal. Bruins fans would arrive by the busload (I always wondered how they got so many tickets to the "sold-out" Forum) and create havoc on the streets, in the hotels, and at the games. It was great fun. In 2000–01 those teams didn't meet until the season was more than half over. The Leafs and the Canadiens now play five times. Not bad by today's standards, but it's a far cry from fourteen.

What does it prove to have teams play just once in a six-month, eighty-two-game season? It would be better if they didn't play at all, so there could be more games between teams who could get some kind of a rivalry going. The fans are the losers, and their displeasure is reflected in sometimes poor box-office receipts. The NHL has to address this issue somehow.

∎▌▌∎

The Detroit-Montreal rivalry in the early 1950s had everything. First and foremost it had two all-time great right wingers, both of whom wore number 9: Gordie Howe and Maurice Richard. They were at the peak of their prowess and arguments raged as to which was the best player in the game. Vern DeGeer was a veteran sportswriter working for the Montreal *Gazette*. DeGeer was from Gordie's home territory, Saskatoon. Even though he wrote for a Montreal paper it was obvious he was a Howe supporter. That made him the most disliked journalist in Montreal. Richard had no such media support in Detroit. There was a lot of cheering from the press box in those days.

In 1950–51 Howe won the first of four straight scoring championships, all by a substantial margin, but Richard was ahead of almost everybody else. Richard was second in '50–51 and, after an injury-plagued season the next year, finished third and second behind Howe the following two years. In 1954–55, the season Richard was suspended for the last three games, he was second to teammate Bernie Geoffrion, while Howe slipped to fifth place.

The next year Jean Béliveau was first, Howe second, and the Rocket third. That's what I mean by Detroit and Montreal dominating the league, as teams and individuals.

Detroit's Red Kelly and Montreal's Doug Harvey were the two best defencemen in hockey. There were arguments about that too. Detroit's great checking line of Glen Skov, Tony Leswick, and Marty Pavelich was on the ice when Richard's line was on. The Canadiens threw dogged defenders like Floyd Curry, Ken Mosdell, and Calum MacKay at the Production Line of Howe, Lindsay, and Abel.

Led by Ted Lindsay, the Red Wings had swagger and arrogance. You could sense the hatred coming from the crowd at the Forum, and from the Canadiens, the minute the Wings skated onto the ice. The feeling was mutual. Years later when I asked Ted Lindsay if he really hated Maurice Richard in those days he tersely replied, "I hated 'em all."

Red Storey refereed many a big game between the two teams. He told me, "One year I did twelve of the fourteen games they played. Seemed like every time I turned around, there I was again with those guys and they'd be fighting for first place. You could feel the tension the minute you dropped the puck, even if it was the first game of the season. But I'll tell you, they were easy games for me to do. Once in a while somebody would go crazy, but for the most part they stuck to pure hockey, and what great games they were. It was a pleasure to be on the ice with them."

Red and Dick Sr. were bitter enemies, but even with that, as the Old Redhead looks back he seems to hold more of a grudge against the Red Wings. He really got going on them when I chatted with him for my book on officials, *Tough Calls*, as follows:

"That whole Detroit team was bad in the '50s. First you had the boss, Jack Adams, who couldn't see across the rink but was always screaming at you. The coach was Tommy Ivan and he hated anything that didn't have on a Detroit uniform, especially the officials. Also behind the bench was their trainer, Lefty Wilson, and he was screaming all the time. He got more bench penalties than any trainer in history. They thought they should have total power over everybody and they hated it when you went back at them and they couldn't intimidate you. I figured that the worst thing they could do was have me fired but I knew none of them had the guts to come after me face to face."

The animosity between Jack Adams and Irvin Sr. dated back to when they played against each other in western Canada in the 1920s. It was comical at times. During one game at the Detroit Olympia, Irvin went on the ice and chased after referee Hugh McLean at the end of a period. Adams called the cops to have him arrested. The players heard about it as they got to their dressing room and went charging out into the lobby, sparks flying from the clash of skate against pavement, and rescued their coach before he could be taken into custody.

A couple of years later, after a rough game between the teams in Montreal, with the Rocket in the middle as usual, Adams said that Richard wasn't a hockey player, he was "Irvin's hatchet man." The next time the Canadiens visited Detroit, Irvin had one of his trainers, Gaston Bettez, don skates and dress up like a Québécois woodsman with a fake beard on his chin and a papier-mâché axe attached to the blade of a hockey stick. When the team went out for the warm-up, Richard stayed in the dressing room and Bettez made a grand entrance in his place. For the next few minutes the "hatchet man" skated amongst the Detroit players swinging his axe. At one point

Terry Sawchuk swung back. Adams likely tried to call the cops again.

■|■|■

For several years after the National Hockey League's 1967 expansion from six to twelve teams there were many who pined for the good old days. Veteran journalists and commentators tried to make you believe every game played in the Original Six era was a classic. Not true. Definitely not true.

There were some terrible teams in those days and they played some terrible games. During the height of the Montreal-Detroit rivalry in the mid-1950s, the Chicago Blackhawks were abysmal. During the '53–54 and '54–55 seasons the hapless Hawks played a total of 140 games and won only 25. Top teams in the league had a field day playing them. On January 9, 1954, the Hawks played in Montreal and were beaten 12–1. The Canadiens' Bert Olmstead had four goals and four assists, tying Maurice Richard's record of eight points in one game. Nobody would get eight points in one game again until Darryl Sittler recorded ten, against Boston, February 7, 1976. The Blackhawks of '53–54 surrendered nine goals in one game twice and their total of 242 against was sixty more than the next most-scored-upon team.

The following season, when Chicago was winning just thirteen games, the New York Rangers won only seventeen. On February 19, 1955, the Canadiens thrashed New York 10–2. Boom Boom Geoffrion scored five goals and Doug Harvey had five assists. Gump Worsley was the New York goaltender and that may have been the season he came up with one of the best of his many good one-liners. When the Gumper was asked what team gave him the most trouble he quickly answered, "The Rangers."

When Red Storey talked to me about how he enjoyed referee-
ing a Montreal-Detroit game he emphasized the point by saying,
"I loved those games but I hated it when Chicago or New York
were playing. They were awful teams and they didn't care what
happened. Those games were a lot tougher for me."

■ ■ ■ ■

What I remember most about the playoff years of 1952, '53,
and '54 are three goals. I saw two of them and was glad I didn't
see the third. There was a goal that wasn't scored that was also
a big story.

Maurice Richard was still the dominant Montreal player but the
1951–52 season was not a happy one for him. The Rocket missed
twenty-two games because of a nagging stomach-muscle injury. He
was constantly in and out of the line-up. On January 12 he scored
three goals as the Canadiens defeated Chicago 8–3, but after the
game complained his injury was still a problem. He missed a few
more games, came back briefly, then was sidelined for six weeks.
He spent most of that time in Florida, and then returned for the
last couple of league games. In later years I would hear Richard
blame the problem on a new style of skate he was trying out as a
favour to a friend in the hockey-equipment business. He still
managed twenty-seven goals and forty-four points in the forty-
eight games he played, but the Rocket was not a happy camper.

■ ■ ■ ■

The two teams out of the playoffs, Chicago and the Rangers,
played in New York on the final night of the season. That was the
game in which Chicago's Bill Mosienko scored three goals in
twenty-one seconds, still a record. After retiring from the

Blackhawks in 1955, Mosienko returned to his native Winnipeg and played four seasons for the Winnipeg Warriors of the Western Hockey League.

Fred Shero, who later coached the Philadelphia Flyers to two Stanley Cups, was a teammate of Mosienko's in Winnipeg. One of Shero's favourite stories was about the game in which another Warrior, Cecil Hoekstra, scored two goals in twelve seconds. The coach, Alf Pike, started to make a line change after Hoekstra's second goal. Mosienko yelled at him, "Leave him on! He's got a chance to tie my record!" Shero said, "That told you what kind of a guy Bill Mosienko was." Hoekstra took another shot before the twenty-one seconds were up, and hit the goal post.

■ ■ ■ ■

In 1951–52, Detroit ran away with the league championship, finishing with one hundred points, twenty-two ahead of second-place Montreal. Gordie Howe and Ted Lindsay finished one-two in the scoring race. The Red Wings were huge favourites to win the Stanley Cup, and that's exactly what happened.

Two individual performances dominated the 1952 playoff year. One was the goaltending of Detroit's Terry Sawchuk. The Red Wings always had a slight edge over Montreal during the time of that great rivalry and Sawchuk was the difference. I've seen a lot of great goaltenders but somehow the image of Terry Sawchuk at his best burns the brightest in my memory.

The first time I saw him play was at the Montreal Forum early in the '51–52 season. The Canadiens outshot the Wings 48–12. Detroit won the game 3–1. I may have been young and impressionable, but I've never forgotten that one. The Montreal Canadiens played against Terry Sawchuk in the playoffs five times, four when he was with Detroit and again in 1967 when he was a Maple Leaf, and beat him just once. That was the semifinal upset in 1951, Sawchuk's rookie year.

For most of the early 1950s the Canadiens' goaltender was Gerry McNeil. He was very capable, and was brilliant in the two long overtime games in Detroit when his team upset the Red Wings in 1951. McNeil was also the unfortunate victim of the Bill Barilko goal that same year. He's the one sprawled out in his crease as Barilko's shot hits high in the twine in the famous picture.

Gerry McNeil succeeded Bill Durnan, the best of his era, who left the goal crease in a strange way. In 1950–51 Durnan won the Vezina Trophy, his sixth in seven years, and was the NHL's First All-Star Team goaltender. But during the semifinals against the New York Rangers his nerves gave out. After a 4 – 1 loss in New York in the third game of the series, Bill Durnan, hockey's best goaltender, quit. He never played another game. McNeil took over and was the Canadiens' regular goaltender for the next four years. He was good and would play a major role in the Canadiens' Stanley Cup win in 1953. But Gerry McNeil wasn't quite as good as Terry Sawchuk. Nobody was.

In the 1952 playoffs, Detroit won the Stanley Cup in the minimum number of eight games, the first time that had happened since a new playoff format involving just four teams came into effect in 1943. The Red Wings swept both Toronto and Montreal. Sawchuk allowed just five goals in total. He had a shutout in each of the four games played at the Detroit Olympia.

The other great individual performance of that playoff year was what a lot of us consider Maurice Richard's greatest goal. It came in the 1952 Montreal-Boston semifinal series. While the Red Wings were cruising against the defending-champion Maple Leafs the Canadiens were locked in a bitter struggle with the Bruins.

The Canadiens faced elimination in the sixth game, in Boston, but stayed alive thanks to an overtime goal by Paul Masnick. That was the game when Dick Sr. was hit by a puck for the only time in his coaching career. In those days there was no room for coaches to stand behind their players at the Boston Garden, so they sat at the end of the bench. A puck was shot into the bench area during that sixth game. The players ducked but the coach didn't and it hit him smack on the bridge of his nose. Unhappily, they took the team picture the next day in Montreal, and in it the coach is sporting two beautiful black eyes. It was also the only time I knew my father to be in a foul mood after his team had won a game.

The story of the Rocket's greatest goal began in the second period of the seventh game at the Forum, April 8, 1952, when he was knocked out cold in a collision with two Bruin players, Hal Laycoe and Leo Labine. The teams were tied 1–1 late in the third period. Richard had not returned after his injury and the Canadiens were struggling. Then, with just a few minutes remaining in the third period he suddenly walked out from the dressing-room area and sat down at the end of the players' bench. The Forum crowd, and Richard's coach, couldn't believe it.

"You okay?" Dick Sr. asked. Richard nodded his head. The coach didn't believe him, but this was a seventh game, right? So on the next whistle the Rocket left the bench and lined up for a faceoff in the Montreal zone.

I was at my usual post upstairs, keeping statistics, and must have had a worried look on my face. Toe Blake, then coaching Valleyfield in the Quebec Senior League, was standing behind me as his two former Punch Line mates, Richard and Elmer Lach, got set for the faceoff.

"Don't worry, Junior," Blake said. "The Rocket will score."

The puck was dropped. Richard took a pass from Butch Bouchard, skated down right wing, swept around Boston defence-men Bob Armstrong and Bill Quackenbush, cut sharply to his left to the front of the crease, and jammed the puck past goaltender Jim Henry.

We all went nuts, of course. I dutifully tried to do my job and write down the numbers of the players who were on the ice when the goal was scored but my hand was shaking so much it was impossible. During my many years in the broadcast booth I saw a lot of big goals and did a lot of note-taking but was never so excited that I couldn't write. Only the Rocket could make that happen.

The Canadiens won the game 3–1. In the dressing room afterwards Richard broke down and sobbed like a baby, especially when his father arrived to congratulate him. I thought Dick Sr. was a bit callous when he complained on the ride home that Rocket's tears had spoiled the victory celebration. In later years Richard would say he didn't recall anything about the goal and would add, "I'm just happy I didn't put the puck into our net."

There were no television or film cameras in the Forum that night, which is a shame. Thanks to TV replays, future generations will be able to enjoy great goals scored by the likes of Gretzky, Lemieux and Yzerman. Most of Maurice Richard's greatest moments are locked in the memory banks of those of us lucky enough to have seen them happen.

■■■■

The season leading up to the 1953 playoffs was another case of same old, same old. Detroit easily finished in first place, fifteen points ahead of Montreal. Gordie Howe easily won the scoring title, with Ted Lindsay second and Maurice Richard third. But there was a big story about a goal that wasn't scored.

Until then Richard had been the only player to score fifty goals in one season. With one game left to play in '52–53, Gordie

Howe, Richard's big rival, had forty-nine. Howe's last game was in Detroit against, would you believe, the Montreal Canadiens. The game meant nothing in the standings but it meant everything to Richard. It would have been devastating for him to watch Howe tie, and maybe even beat, his cherished record.

The mercurial Rocket was in a terrible state the day of the game. Dick Sr. purposely shared a cab with him to the Olympia to monitor his star's mood. He could see there might be trouble. Early in the game he put Rocket on the ice when Howe was on, a "big mistake" he would say later. The minute the puck was dropped Richard charged from one side of the rink to the other and nailed Howe with a cross-check, drawing a penalty for his trouble. After that the Canadiens' number 9 spent most of the game on the bench watching his teammates try to stop the other number 9 from scoring a goal. Two players, Bert Olmstead and Johnny McCormack, went steady with Howe all night.

"I asked Dick what he wanted me to do," Bert told me. "All he said was, 'Go where he goes.' So that's what I did. Howe would go back to talk to Sawchuk and I would go with him and just stand there. I knew I was getting his goat."

It worked. The checking of Olmstead and McCormack plus a couple of good stops by Gerry McNeil kept Howe at forty-nine. The Rocket's record, set during a fifty-game season, wouldn't be equalled until Bernie Geoffrion scored fifty, eight years later, in 1960–61. Bobby Hull finally broke it by scoring fifty-four goals in 1965–66. Both feats took place during a seventy-game season. And the answer to the trivia question, Who was the first Detroit Red Wing to score fifty goals in one season? Mickey Redmond, who scored fifty-two in 1972–73.

∎∣∎∣∎

A big goal that was scored in 1953 enabled me to see the Stanley Cup won for the second time. Thirteen years after crying when Bryan Hextall scored the Cup-winner in overtime for the New York Rangers, I was cheering when Elmer Lach did likewise for the Montreal Canadiens. It was a great moment for Elmer, and for my father, who had helped bring him to Montreal as a rookie in 1940. The only way it could have been better is if the goal had been scored on Detroit's Terry Sawchuk instead of Boston's Jim Henry. But the big rivalry didn't extend into the playoffs that year. The Red Wings were derailed by the Boston Bruins in a shocking first-round upset.

After winning the first game 7–0, which might have been a bad thing for them, the Red Wings lost four of the next five. Veteran forward Woody Dumart threw a checking blanket over Howe and the result was very similar to the Canadiens' upset of Detroit two years earlier. The Bruins won in six games. Two semifinal upset losses in three years had critics in Detroit wondering about the Red Wings.

The Canadiens needed seven games to eliminate Chicago in the other semifinal. With his team facing elimination going into the sixth game in Chicago, Dick Sr. made several line-up changes, including replacing McNeil with a rookie goalie who would be appearing in his first playoff game. The kid's name was Jacques Plante. Dad phoned home before the game and said, "If we lose tonight I'll be fired." They didn't lose and Plante got a shutout.

Plante was still in the net two nights later at the Forum for a 4–1 win to eliminate the Hawks and the rookie started the final series against Boston. After a split of the first two games in Montreal, McNeil was back in goal and shut out the Bruins twice as the Canadiens won the next three games to take the Cup.

Game five was tied 0–0 at the end of regulation time. In the second minute of overtime a big left winger from Winnipeg,

Eddie Mazur, led a Canadiens rush into the Bruins' zone. Milt Schmidt checked him and shot the puck around the boards, right onto Elmer Lach's stick. Lach, who always claimed his shot couldn't break a pane of glass, wristed one at the Boston net and it got past Henry. The Stanley Cup was back in Montreal for the first time since 1946.

Elmer Lach is likely the only player to be injured after scoring a Cup-winning goal. When the red light went on the Rocket joyfully leaped into the arms of his long-time centreman, breaking Elmer's nose in the process. Richard was given an assist on the goal, but the film of the play clearly shows he never touched the puck. But it was at the Forum, and the Stanley Cup had been won, so who cared?

The aftermath to a Cup win back then was different from what it is today. For starters, nobody rioted and looted in the streets. Montreal would be the site of ugly scenes after Cup wins in 1986 and 1993.

The day after the winning game the players gathered at the Forum for a team picture with the Stanley Cup. The coach's kid was hanging around the dressing room again. I remember Maurice Richard walking past me with his uniform on saying, "I feel light on my feet today."

There was no Stanley Cup parade and there were no Stanley Cup rings. Two nights after the final game there was a private dinner for the Canadiens' official family, and their families, at the Windsor Hotel, and that was it. Everybody went their separate ways and it was "See you in September."

One of the directors of the Canadiens and the Forum operation was D.C. Coleman, father of long-time sportswriter the late Jim Coleman, and a former president of the CPR. I had seen Mr. Coleman, from a distance, at hockey games, and to my cocky young eyes he seemed like a crotchety old guy in a blue suit. I couldn't believe it when I heard he was going to MC the championship dinner. I was sure wrong on that one. D.C. Coleman was terrific at the microphone, sharp as a tack. I was very impressed and very surprised and said so on the drive home. Dad replied, "My boy, you don't get to be president of the CPR if you're a dummy." Lesson learned.

∎∎∎∎

When the next season was over, guess what? Detroit finished first, Montreal second. Gordie Howe won the scoring title, only this time it was Maurice Richard who was second, and Ted Lindsay third. In the semifinals the Red Wings eliminated Toronto in five games and Montreal swept the Bruins in four. A true meeting at the summit was about to take place in the Stanley Cup finals.

After a 2–0 win in Montreal, the Red Wings had a 3–1 series lead and seemed primed to win the Cup on home ice the next night. But Gerry McNeil got in their way, besting Sawchuk in a 1–0 goaltenders' battle. Ken Mosdell scored the only goal, in overtime. Back at the Forum the Canadiens tied the series with a 4–1 win. It was down to a winner-take-all seventh game at the Detroit Olympia.

Floyd Curry gave the Canadiens the lead in the first period and Red Kelly tied it in the second. Goaltenders Sawchuk and McNeil took over and it was 1–1 at the end of the third period. The Stanley Cup would be won in overtime. It was the defining moment in hockey's greatest rivalry.

Just past the four-minute mark Detroit's Tony Leswick flipped a long shot towards the Montreal net. Doug Harvey would often knock a floating puck out of the air with his glove and at the same time start rushing out of his zone. That's what he tried with the Leswick shot, only he didn't make solid contact. The puck caromed off Harvey and deflected into the net behind a helpless Gerry McNeil. Game over. Cup won.

Tony Leswick described it to me this way: "There was a line change. I came over the boards, and the puck came right to me. Apparently, so they say, because at times like that you don't always realize what happened, the puck went off Harvey's shoulder, or arm, and went into the net. I just let it go towards the net. Harvey told me after he could read the label on the puck as it was coming at him."

Poor Gerry McNeil. Even today, especially at playoff time, he gets calls about the Barilko goal and the Leswick goal. I'm sure nobody ever asks him about his 1–0 shutout that won the Cup in '53. He often says, "You guys call it the Leswick goal. I call it the Harvey goal." Except for a fill-in stint of nine games with the Canadiens three years later, Gerry never played again in the NHL.

Elmer Lach retired after the 1954 playoffs. A few weeks after his final game an obviously bitter Elmer said to me, "We had them on the ropes but we couldn't score on Sawchuk. He beat us."

As for Dick Sr., he had experienced another loss in the finals, his third in four years and the eleventh of his career. It can't get much worse for a coach than overtime in a seventh game.

Danny Gallivan liked to tell me about the train trip back home to Montreal after that seventh-game loss. Danny and some newspapermen gravitated to the coach's compartment as the train left Detroit. The mood was gloomy and nobody was saying very much. The coach pulled a calendar out of his pocket, studied it for a few minutes, did some figuring on a piece of paper, then said, "Gentlemen, I want you all to note that training camp starts in one hundred and fifty days."

Dick Sr. was already thinking of next season. It would be his last as coach of the Montreal Canadiens.

Changing Allegiances

....

By the middle of the 1950s the Montreal Canadiens were
giving the Detroit Red Wings stiffer opposition. At the
end of the season capped by the Leswick goal the Wings
had finished seven points ahead of Montreal. The next year they
were first again, but only by two points, and it wasn't decided
until the final game of the season.

During the early '50s the Canadiens added good, young players
who would eventually become great players. These included
Bernie Geoffrion, Dickie Moore, Tom Johnson, and Jacques
Plante. Doug Harvey had become the game's best defenceman,
Bert Olmstead a premier left winger. And, after a bit of a delay,
Jean Béliveau arrived.

I first saw Jean Béliveau in the spring of 1951 when his Quebec
Citadelle were playing the Barrie Flyers in the Eastern Memorial
Cup finals at Maple Leaf Gardens. I had flown to Montreal after
my exams in Saskatoon (my first plane ride) to join my parents

and drive with them back to Regina. Mother had spent the last three months of that season in Montreal.

The first stop on the trip was Toronto to see the junior game, on a Saturday night, exactly one week after the Bill Barilko goal. Béliveau was the biggest name in junior hockey, but that night Barrie defeated Quebec rather handily to win the series. The crowd was pro-Barrie, and as the Flyers got nearer to winning the Eastern championship their supporters got louder and mouthier. One guy in particular, sitting right behind us, was really giving it to Béliveau. He knew the coach of the Montreal Canadiens was hearing everything he said so his remarks started to include cracks about the Canadiens too. Dick Sr. suffered in silence but, finally, after a particularly vicious crack about Béliveau, Bertha turned around and told Mr. Loudmouth to shut up. Then she hit him with her program.

The wimpy Irvin men wanted to crawl into the nearest manhole, but the guy did shut up. Finally, trying to make peace with Bertha, I guess, he said, "That Béliveau will never be another Rocket Richard." He might have been right. While the Rocket will forever be first in the hearts of Quebec hockey fans, Big Jean is definitely second.

Our next stop was Detroit to visit friends and take in some ball games. The Boston Red Sox were in town to play the Tigers, so I saw Ted Williams. We were walking in the downtown area when a car pulled over and the young driver called out, "Hey, Mr. Irvin. Guess you ran out of miracles." He was referring to the Canadiens upsetting the Red Wings, then losing to Toronto. Dad went over to the car and got a kick out of chatting for a few minutes. It may have been the only time those two ever had a chat. The young guy driving the car was Gordie Howe.

■|■|■

When the next hockey season began, Jean Béliveau was playing for the Quebec Aces senior team and we had moved to Montreal. He would attend the Canadiens' training camp, then go back to Quebec where he could make as much money as the NHL team was offering. As he told me, "They used to tell me, 'Go to the camp. But remember, whatever they are offering in Montreal, same here.'" For two years he opted for the "same here," and he led the Senior League in scoring both years.

The Forum would be packed every time Big Jean and the Aces were there to play the Montreal Royals, usually on a Sunday afternoon. I recall a couple of Sundays when hundreds were lined up outside the Forum hoping to get in while a box-office employee was yelling through a megaphone from a second-storey window, "Please go home! All the tickets are sold!"

After attending the 1953 training camp Jean Béliveau finally signed with the Canadiens. It was October 3. That night he played in the All-Star Game, at the Forum. Béliveau had led the good life – and got married – during the summer. When he reported to camp he was far from playing shape. But lest he upset the big kid during the contract negotiations being conducted by Frank Selke, Dick Sr. didn't work him too hard. Once the contract was signed, it was a different story. Béliveau was put through some extra-tough conditioning drills. The fact that he worked hard and never complained told Dick Sr. a lot about Jean Béliveau.

∎∎∎∎

Sometime during a training season in the mid-1950s, the Canadiens played an exhibition game against the Valleyfield Braves senior team, in Valleyfield, on a Sunday afternoon. Toe Blake was coaching the Braves. Maurice Richard was nursing a minor injury. After the second period, Dick Sr. told him to take the rest of the afternoon off. The Rocket changed into civvies and went into the stands to watch the third period.

Some of the fans didn't like to see the Canadiens' star player watching, not playing. So they started to heckle him. "Hey, Richard, you too much of a big shot to play in Valleyfield?" Stuff like that. One guy was particularly vocal and with his buddies urging him on he decided to get right into the Rocket's face, nose to nose. Big mistake.

The Rocket silently took the abuse for a couple of minutes, then ended the one-sided conversation his way. He drilled the guy with a straight right hand, sending him tumbling down the stairs, out cold. His teammates saw what was happening and charged into the stands with sticks and fists flying. Just your typical Sunday afternoon of hockey in Quebec in the good old days.

A few nights later I was with my father at a Montreal Royals baseball game and we ran into Toe Blake. Dad asked him, "Is the guy the Rocket hit going to sue us?"

"Sue?" Blake replied. "He's the happiest guy in Valleyfield. He's walking all over town, pointing to his big black eye and saying, 'Look what the Rocket gave me.'"

I often use that story in speeches and follow it up with the one about the Maurice Richard Arena. It was built by the City of Montreal in the early 1970s and the Rocket was there to cut the ribbon at the opening ceremonies.

A few years later an arena was built in the north end of the city and named in honour of Howie Morenz, the late, great Canadiens star of the '20s and '30s. It was located in a neighbourhood where a local hockey hero of the '50s and '60s, Dickie Moore, had grown up. One of Moore's buddies called the city and asked why it wasn't being named for Dickie instead of Morenz.

"We never name arenas after anyone who is still living."

The caller quickly replied, "When did Maurice Richard die?" The civil servant hung up in his ear.

One way or another, the Rocket was king in *la belle province*.

∎∎∎∎

Jean Béliveau (who has an arena named after him in the Montreal suburb of Longueuil) did not enjoy a good first season in the NHL. Most reports about the contract he signed pegged its total value at around $125,000 for five years. (In 2000–01 Jaromir Jagr and Paul Kariya made that much in three games.) Tough opponents drew a bead on the highly publicized, highly paid rookie. Early in the season he suffered a cracked ankle bone, later a broken cheekbone. He missed twenty-six games because of injuries and scored only thirteen goals.

George "Punch" Imlach had coached Béliveau in Quebec City. Imlach was at a Canadiens game in Toronto during Big Jean's rookie year and proclaimed to everyone within hearing distance that Irvin wasn't coaching Béliveau properly and could ruin Jean's career. Of course Punch knew exactly who was the best coach in the history of hockey. He saw him every time he looked in a mirror.

A couple of years later, when Dick Sr. was coaching the Chicago Blackhawks, Imlach showed up at their training camp looking for players for his American League team. He arrived to a chilly reception and left without any players. Irvin and Imlach both loved to hold court with newspaper reporters. They never coached against each other. Had they done so there would have been plenty of verbal fireworks.

It would appear coach Irvin didn't exactly ruin Jean Béliveau's career. In his second season, with Irvin still coaching, Jean played the full seventy-game schedule and had seventy-three points. The following season, under Toe Blake, he had eighty-eight points and led the league. The rest, as they say, is history.

■I■I■

On Thursday, March 17, 1955, the Canadiens played against the Red Wings at the Montreal Forum in a game that will forever be remembered for all the wrong reasons. This was the occasion of the Richard Riot.

The previous Sunday, in Boston, Maurice Richard became involved in a stick-swinging fight with the Bruins' Hal Laycoe. During the melee, Richard hit linesman Cliff Thompson. A hearing was held at NHL headquarters in Montreal, and on the morning of March 17 league president Clarence Campbell announced his decision. Because he struck an official, Richard would be suspended for the remaining three games of the regular season, plus all of the Stanley Cup playoffs. Sportswriter Andy O'Brien summed it up best when he wrote that, after the verdict was announced, the city of Montreal was "in a state of stun."

Those in the Richard camp claimed that because of pressure from owners of other teams, principally Detroit, Campbell had made his decision before the hearing was even held. I tend to agree, but of course in those days I was very much in the Richard camp. Still am.

The whole scenario was weird. Gordie Howe was having a rare off year and Richard, who had never won the scoring title, was leading the league. The Canadiens were locked in a first-place battle with the Red Wings and the teams were scheduled to play each other two of the last three games.

On the seventeenth, Clarence Campbell, who was never late for anything, arrived at the Forum several minutes after the game began and was greeted by fifteen thousand booing Montreal fans.

The Red Wings led the dispirited Canadiens 4−1 after one period. Campbell remained in his seat during the intermission. A fan pretended to want to shake his hand, and then hit him instead. A minute or so later a tear-gas bomb exploded. Police ordered the evacuation of the building, the game was forfeited to the Red Wings, and the Richard Riot took place in the streets of downtown Montreal. (Some, including Ken Reardon, still maintain the police planted the bomb.)

To paraphrase Don Cherry, "I want all you young people out there . . ." to consider something. Let's say the same punishment had been dealt to Wayne Gretzky at the peak of his career, or Bobby Hull, Bobby Orr, Gordie Howe. Would there have been a riot in the streets of Edmonton, Chicago, Boston, or Detroit? I don't think so.

Maurice Richard was a man of the people to Quebecers. He hadn't been scoring a hundred goals a year as a minor hockey player, so he didn't arrive in the NHL as a young phenom the way Gretzky, Béliveau, Mario Lemieux, Guy Lafleur, and others did. My dad always said Richard had to fight his way to the top. His was a success story the public could relate to.

Red Storey, who was the referee the night of the riot, often says, "Hockey is a religion in Quebec, and the Rocket was bigger than the Pope." I'll let deeper thinkers argue whether the riot was a major flashpoint in heightening French-English tensions in Quebec, leading to the Quiet Revolution and beyond.

The season ended with the Canadiens defeating the New York Rangers two nights after the riot, then losing the last game of the season in Detroit. Bernie Geoffrion picked up enough points in the final weekend to win the scoring title. He had seventy-five points, Richard seventy-four, Béliveau seventy-three. Boom Boom was booed at the Forum for finishing ahead of the Rocket.

He claims that to this day there are still old-time hard-liners who haven't forgiven him.

Detroit and Montreal met again in the Stanley Cup finals. Despite the Rocket's absence, the series went to a deciding seventh game, won by the Red Wings 3–1. The game marked the twelfth final series loss for Dick Sr. and, after fifteen years, the last time he would coach the Montreal Canadiens.

A couple of sidelights to all of the above. Perhaps the most important game in 1955 wasn't the one on March 17, but rather the fifth game of the Montreal-Boston semifinal series played at the Forum, March 31. Why? Because starting on defence for Boston, alongside future Hall of Famer Bill Quackenbush, was a player named Don Cherry. It was the only game Don Cherry played in the NHL. If you didn't know that already you haven't been paying attention during "Coach's Corner" on *Hockey Night in Canada*, lo these many years.

Another sidelight was when Montreal filmmaker Brian McKenna produced a docudrama on the Richard Riot that aired on Global TV on the forty-fifth anniversary of the event, March 17, 2000. A camera crew came to our house to record my memories of the fateful evening. As always when interviewed about the riot, I told of being hit in the face by the tear gas.

Two parts of the story were dramatized: the hearing in Clarence Campbell's office and the fight in Boston. Brian invited me to play the part of my father during the hearing sequence and I quickly accepted. Finally! My chance to make it big in show biz.

A boardroom in a bank building in Old Montreal was used as Clarence Campbell's office. A combination of professional and amateur actors assembled early on a Saturday morning. My dad's hair was snow-white, so they used powder to whiten mine, although they didn't need much. The wardrobe department dressed everyone in 1950s-style suits, which my wife, Wilma, thought wasn't really necessary in my case. She claimed my current wardrobe would have sufficed.

It was a long, drawn-out day. I had a non-speaking part but did a lot of reacting to the camera while the arguments raged between actors playing Campbell, Ken Reardon, Richard, Hal Laycoe, and the linesman Cliff Thompson.

You say you didn't see me? You must have blinked. After all day on the set, and after the editing was completed, the finished product contained one brief glimpse through a doorway of the "actor" playing Dick Sr. Very brief. It was an interesting experience for a guy who considers himself a movie buff, and the show was a good one.

■■■■

During the last few weeks of the 1954–55 season, Dad was feeling, and looking, poorly. We felt the pressures of the first-place race against the Red Wings and the Richard situation had combined to wear him down. We didn't know he had bone cancer.

When he got home from the last game in Detroit he talked to me about something that happened in the dressing room, which normally he didn't do. He said, "I said things they'd never heard me say before." He never told me what he had said, or what might have made him say it. But something had happened and it clearly bothered him. It was also pretty clear he knew his coaching days in Montreal were over.

The owner of the Chicago Blackhawks, Jim Norris, contacted Dad about coaching his team. Frank Selke didn't fire him and he could have stayed with the Canadiens in some kind of an advisory position. But coaches want to coach and there was a very nice offer from Mr. Norris on the table. Dad took it, and signed a two-year contract with the worst team in the NHL for $20,000 per year. It was the richest contract he, or any other coach, had ever signed.

Dick Irvin coached the Montreal Canadiens for fifteen years, yet hardly anyone from the organization called to say goodbye or wish him luck, but that's not unusual in hockey. Ask Scotty Bowman.

When Alain Vigneault was fired as coach by the Canadiens during the 2000–01 season he told a news conference about being at home watching his old team on television in its first game after the firing. The other team scored the first goal, and his children cheered. Alain admonished them, saying they should still support the Canadiens, their hometown team. I'd be surprised if, silently, Alain practised what he preached.

There was no such sentiment in the Irvin family. Dad never said anything one way or another, but we became instant fans of the Blackhawks. It would be a few years before I again saw the Montreal Canadiens in a positive light. Not that it mattered. All they did while I didn't particularly like them was win five straight Stanley Cups.

∎∎∎∎

A short while after signing with the Blackhawks, Dad became quite ill. The doctors diagnosed the cancer and told Mother, who decided not to tell her husband. Pills were prescribed, which got him back on a pretty decent track. We constantly worried during his season with the Hawks, but he didn't miss a game, or a practice.

Dick Sr. took over a last-place team in Chicago, and when the season was over it was still in last place. Tommy Ivan, once Dad's coaching rival in Detroit, was in his second year as general manager in Chicago. I doubt they ever spoke when they were involved in the bitter Detroit-Montreal rivalry. Now that they worked for the same team they managed to coexist, but I don't think they became good friends.

There aren't many good memories of the Blackhawks of 1955–56. The team won nineteen games, six more than the previous season, but they were eleven points out of the playoffs when it was over. Chicago would remain at or near the bottom of the league for two more years. Some good young players were being developed in the organization. Bobby Hull was one. Elmer "Moose" Vasko was another. So was Pierre Pilote. Pilote likes to remember the night he made his debut with the Blackhawks. It was in Toronto, February 4, 1956, when the Hawks and the Maple Leafs were in a battle for the final playoff spot.

"I was playing in Buffalo when they called me up. A lot of my relatives around Toronto wanted to come to the game but I told them not to bother. The *Globe and Mail* used to print the ice times for players. Whenever I checked I'd see that anyone called up from the minors usually played about one or two minutes, maybe only thirty seconds.

"Before the game, Dick announced our starting line-up. When he said, 'On defence, Martin and Pilote,' I just about fell off my chair. On the first shift Tod Sloan got the puck for the Leafs, went around Eddie Litzenberger, and then went around me with a shift that almost put me out on the street. He went in alone on our goalie, Hank Bassen, who made a terrific save and got me off the hook. I played almost thirty minutes, and none of my relatives were there because I told them not to bother. And if Bassen didn't make that save I probably wouldn't be here today."

By "here," Pierre meant the Hockey Hall of Fame, where we were when he told me the story. He was being modest. I was at that game. Later in the first period he hit the elusive Tod Sloan with one of the best open-ice bodychecks I have ever seen. He made the team with that one and never went back to Buffalo. Pilote played thirteen NHL seasons, won a Stanley Cup, and was voted to the All-Star Team eight times.

The Blackhawks beat the Maple Leafs that night in Toronto and also the next night in Chicago to move past them into fourth place. That would be the highlight of their season. They won only three of their final seventeen games.

■|■|■

The night of April 10, 1956, was a tough one for the Irvins because the Montreal Canadiens, coached by Toe Blake, won the Stanley Cup. Dad watched it on television. There must have been a lot going through his mind as the team he had coached in seventh-game losses to Detroit the previous two years defeated the Red Wings at the Forum.

I was surprised he watched the telecast until the post-game celebrations were over. I figured he'd take off when the game ended, if not before. But he watched it all, saying little, if anything, before going to bed. The next day he seemed to be his usual self, or at least he let on that he was, and sent a note of congratulations to Toe.

By the following September Dad was a very sick man. He went to the Blackhawks' training camp in St. Catharines, but it was obvious he was too sick to continue coaching. After a few days he told Tommy Ivan, and the players, he couldn't go on.

Forbes Kennedy, a rookie who was in the room when Dick Sr. announced he was leaving, told me Dad said, "Fellows, you know I've always told you that if you didn't give me 100 per cent you couldn't play on this team. Well, now I can't give you 100 per cent so I'm leaving. I can't coach any more. I have to go home. Good luck."

So Dad went home, and his health deteriorated rapidly. He spent most of March 1957 in the Royal Victoria Hospital. and at times was well enough to have visitors. One was Clarence Campbell, who was going through a tough time with his employers, the NHL owners. Campbell wanted somebody to tell his troubles to, and Dad was a good listener.

When the Toronto Maple Leafs were visiting Montreal another unhappy old friend, Hap Day, dropped in to see him. Day had been captain of Dad's 1932 Stanley Cup–winning Maple Leafs. In 1940 he succeeded him as coach in Toronto and compiled a great record, winning five Stanley Cups. Day retired as coach in 1950 to become Conn Smythe's assistant. By 1957 Smythe's son Stafford, and some of his friends, were moving into the management picture at Maple Leaf Gardens and Day told Dad he was being pushed out. At the end of that season Hap Day quit the Maple Leafs and never worked in hockey again.

Dad hadn't been in contact with any of the Canadiens players since the last game in Detroit in 1955, but Doug Harvey got a few of them together, including Maurice Richard, to visit him in the hospital. At that time Richard was getting close to his five-hundredth career goal. Dad told him to hurry up and score it because, he said, "I won't be around much longer."

Dad was home but completely bedridden and heavily sedated when the Canadiens won a second straight Stanley Cup the following April 16. He had been watching but was asleep when the game ended and the Cup was won. He passed away exactly one month later, May 16, 1957, at the age of sixty-four.

There wasn't time for Maurice Richard to score his five-hundredth goal that season, but when he did, on October 19,

1957, he dedicated it to Dad. A few weeks later Rocket presented mother with a trophy to mark his historic milestone.

∎∎∎∎

Toe Blake's Canadiens were a better team than Dick Irvin's Canadiens while the Red Wings weren't as good as they had been. Following the Wings' Cup win in 1955, Jack Adams, claiming his team needed new blood to avoid complacency, traded away several players. The biggest shock was when Terry Sawchuk was traded to Boston. Glenn Hall replaced him. Hall would become one of the greatest during an eighteen-year career, which included ten seasons with the Chicago Blackhawks, but in his rookie season in Detroit he wasn't quite Sawchuk. The Red Wings wouldn't win the Stanley Cup again until 1997.

Was Toe's team the greatest of them all? Many say it was. While I don't agree, I never argue the point too strenuously. My choice is Scotty Bowman's Canadiens of the late 1970s. Fans in Edmonton likely disagree with both calls. But hockey had never seen a team as dominant as the Montreal Canadiens, 1956 to 1960.

For starters, Toe's team won five straight Stanley Cups. You can close the book on that record. They finished first four times in those five years by margins of 24, 19, 18, and 13 points. Detroit finished first in 1956–57 but lost to Boston in their semifinal. Two years later the Red Wings ended up in last place.

During their five Cup-winning years the Canadiens played forty-nine playoff games, losing only nine. In ten series they were extended past five games only twice, and never to seven games. In 1960 they swept to their fifth straight Stanley Cup with eight straight wins.

The stars of that team are legends today. Plante. Harvey. Béliveau. Geoffrion. Moore. Maurice and Henri Richard. In my

book *The Habs*, some of those legends talked about that team.
First, Jean Béliveau:

"We had great players. And it was very important that we also
had the day-to-day kind of guys you could count on when we
played on the road. I remember a guy like Bob Turner, who was
a defenceman, but who would move up to play forward on many
occasions.

"Billy Hicke, Ab McDonald, Claude Provost, André Pronovost.
I think that as a whole we had all the elements you need to make
a championship team."

Bernie Geoffrion:

"I have to say that was the best team that ever played hockey.
With all my respect to Toe Blake, he didn't have too much to do.
I can tell you that right now.

"But I will say that Toe Blake was a man of discipline. He knew
how to handle the guys, what to tell the guys. . . . He would grab
a guy and talk to him. I remember him giving hell to Doug
Harvey. He didn't give a damn who you were. . . .

"The five in a row? Man, what a team that was! What a team!"

Defenceman Tom Johnson:

"Everyone talks about us winning five in a row. I often think
how close it was to eight in a row.

"We won in 1953. In 1954 we lost to Detroit in overtime in
the seventh game. The next year we lost again in the seventh
game. The score was 3–1.

"So while we won five straight, when you think about it we
were just two or three goals away from winning the Stanley Cup
eight straight years."

The only one of the five-in-a-row Cup-winning games I
attended was number four, in Montreal, in 1959. The Canadiens
played Toronto in the finals, and that leads me into a beef with
my long-time employer, *Hockey Night in Canada*.

Fast-forward to the 1994–95 season and the lockout, when the NHL didn't start up until late January. The CBC filled the Saturday-night void with a variety of programs and movies until just after Christmas when they returned to hockey. HNIC's executive producer John Shannon came up with the idea of showing tapes of "Classic Games" from the past. One example was the 1975 New Year's Eve thriller played at the Forum between the Canadiens and the Soviet Red Army. The idea, and the shows, received rave reviews.

Ron MacLean and I co-hosted the series at the CBC studios in Toronto. One week we showed a game from the 1959 Toronto-Montreal Stanley Cup final. Now, here's the beef.

Those teams met in the finals two straight years, '59 and '60, playing a total of nine games. Montreal won eight, Toronto won one. Guess which game was aired? It was the one played April 14, 1959, at Maple Leaf Gardens. Final score: Toronto 3, Montreal 2. Dick Duff scored the winning goal, in overtime.

Doing my Rodney Dangerfield impersonation, I complained loudly that the CBC in Toronto didn't give us guys in Montreal no respect, or something like that. To no avail, of course.

Had the NHL season been wiped out, and it was close, they were going to continue the "Classics" series. I'm sure they would have found a Canadiens win somewhere in the archives. (Only kidding, John.) But after the series had run three or four weeks the millionaire players made peace with the millionaire owners, and we got back to reality.

■ ▮ ▮ ■

As the Canadiens' five-in-a-row streak moved from year to year, Maurice Richard became less and less of a major factor. The Rocket had his moments, but they were becoming the exception rather than the rule. In the last three years of the Cup run, and of his career, Richard missed 121 games because of injury. He played just twenty-eight games in 1957–58 but still managed thirty-four points, fifteen of them goals.

The Rocket's real last hurrah was in the 1958 playoffs when he scored eleven goals in ten games. One of them provided the early years of *Hockey Night in Canada* with a well-remembered moment.

Montreal met Boston in the finals and the teams split the first four games. The pivotal fifth game at the Forum was tied 2–2 after three periods. During the intermission preceding overtime the host of HNIC, Tom Foley, interviewed the Canadiens' general manager, Frank Selke. Foley asked Mr. Selke what he thought was going to happen.

"Maurice Richard hasn't done much tonight," Mr. Selke said. "He usually comes through at a time like this. I think he'll score the winning goal."

And, being the Rocket, that's exactly what Maurice Richard did, at 5:45 of the first overtime period. Three nights later, in Boston, the Canadiens won their third straight Stanley Cup.

I remember only one thing about the game in 1959 that marked the third time I had seen the Stanley Cup won. When the final siren sounded at the Forum, the Canadiens had defeated Toronto 5–3. As usual, all the players not on the ice at the time leaped over the boards to start celebrating. All but one. Maurice Richard.

The Rocket, who was the team captain, lagged far behind. He lazily climbed over the boards and slowly skated to where the celebration was taking place. Once there, he stayed on the perimeter, watching rather than participating. He had gone through another injury-plagued season, missing twenty-eight games. He had dressed for only four of eleven games in the playoffs, with no goals and no assists.

A lot of us wondered if Richard would play another year, but he did. Again injuries took their toll and he missed nineteen games. The Rocket played in all eight games in the 1960 playoff sweep, scoring his final goal in the third game of the finals against Toronto.

Richard reported to training camp in September. During a morning scrimmage at the Forum he scored four times on the best goaltender in hockey, Jacques Plante. It was a great way for him to bow out, typically Richardian. That afternoon the Rocket retired.

The Canadiens wouldn't win the Stanley Cup again for five years. By then Harvey, Plante, Moore, Geoffrion, and others from the glorious five-straight era were no longer with the team. But initially the loss of Maurice Richard, and all he stood for, hurt the most.

Frank Selke, Jr., was the Canadiens' publicity director during that era and, like all of us, a great Rocket fan.

"When the Rocket retired in 1960," Frank said, "he not only took his talent and skills with him, he took his heart too. I think maybe that had more to do with the team not being able to win the next year, win a sixth straight, than anything else. It wasn't the same without his fire."

Maurice Richard est mort

....

On Saturday, May 27, 2000, Wilma and I were finishing an early supper and getting ready to watch *Hockey Night in Canada*'s show from Dallas where the Stars and the Colorado Avalanche were about to play the seventh game of their Western Conference final series.

Two or three minutes before showtime, (6:30 in Montreal), the phone rang. The caller was from a Regina radio station and said, "We have a report that Maurice Richard has died. Could I do an interview with you?"

Richard, Montreal's all-time greatest hockey hero, had been gravely ill for days and there had been several false alarms. I asked the caller if he could get back to me in about twenty minutes, hung up, and switched from the CBC to a local French-language station. A reporter was on camera in front of the hospital Richard had been in for several days. Written across the bottom of the screen were the words "MAURICE RICHARD EST MORT." The fabled Rocket had fought long and hard against a rare form of cancer but his battle was now over.

I switched back to the CBC just as HNIC's pre-game show began. Ron MacLean welcomed the viewers, set the scene in Dallas, and they went to a commercial. As the commercial was on air I was wondering how I could get word about Richard to HNIC when the phone rang again.

"Dick, it's Paul Graham." Paul was the *Hockey Night in Canada* producer in Dallas. Behind him I could hear his assistant counting down to Ron's return on camera. "Seven . . . six . . . five . . ."

Paul asked, "Did Rocket Richard die?"

"Yes."

"We're going with it!" he yelled to Ron over the intercom.

"Three . . . two . . . one . . ." Paul slammed down the phone, and before I had hung up Ron was on camera, coast to coast, with the news of the Rocket's death. It was the start of an amazing few days.

Maurice Richard's death immediately became the biggest news story in Canada, in both languages. While the CBC's English and French networks carried the hockey game, one of the local French-langauge stations in Montreal immediately cancelled all Saturday-night programming and devoted its entire broadcast schedule until midnight to the Rocket and his passing.

Don and Ron were in the "Coach's Corner" as usual when the first intermission began in Dallas and introduced a special tribute to Maurice Richard. There was film of him scoring spectacular goals, of the Richard Riot, and of the ten-minute ovation he received the night they closed the Forum. But what intrigued me most was the voice of the narrator. It was mine. I kept asking myself, "When did I do that?" I couldn't remember.

The game went into overtime, ending fairly quickly when Joe Nieuwendyk scored on Patrick Roy to send the defending-champion Stars into the Cup final against New Jersey. The conclusion was fitting, I thought, as the Rocket had scored more playoff overtime goals than anyone in hockey history.

Ten minutes after the telecast Paul Graham was on the phone again from Dallas, apologizing for cutting me off so quickly on his first call and thanking me for the information I had supplied earlier. I told him I was puzzled by the intermission feature. He replied, "Don't you remember? You and I put that together two years ago when there were all kinds of rumours he was going to die then." Obviously I hadn't remembered.

Paul then added a bit of an eerie twist. "When we heard Rocket was in hospital again we looked all over the CBC for that feature but couldn't find it. Today I got a call that someone found it just this morning. Imagine. He died a few hours later."

Beginning from the next day until I worked on the CBC network telecast of his funeral the following Wednesday, I did twenty-seven interviews about Maurice Richard. There were calls from all over Canada, from San Diego, Miami, Chicago, and New York. *Sports Illustrated* hired me to write a piece on his death. Red Storey, a much better raconteur that I am, did over forty interviews and worked on the CTV network telecast of the funeral.

What were my main memories of Maurice Richard? Naturally I talked about his breaking his leg the first time I saw him play, and of my sitting on the bench when he set the record of eight points in a single game. I told how he was the last player picked on a junior team and how people wondered if he would have quit hockey if he had been passed over. There were stories of his famous feuds with the tough guys of his era like Ted Lindsay, "Wild Bill" Ezinicki, and Bob "Killer" Dill. I mentioned how opponents would try to stop him with constant hooking, holding, and interference and how Richard never ran to the nearest reporter to complain, as too many of today's stars often do.

Instead, the Rocket got even by doing what he did better than anyone else, scoring goals, and if necessary applying his fist to an opponent's jaw. He could really fight. I still say he was hockey's best one-punch KO artist.

I talked about Rocket's passion for the game, but I wondered if I was really getting across to people who had never seen him play the intensity with which Richard played.

What I should have done, but didn't, was read what long-time hockey executive Emile "The Cat" Francis told me when I interviewed him in 1991 for my book *The Habs*. Francis had a brief career as a goaltender in the NHL and described playing against Maurice Richard this way:

"From the blueline in I have never seen a player as exciting as Rocket Richard. The thing I didn't like about him, although you had to admire him for it, was that when he scored he didn't just put it in the net, he tried to put it right through the net. That's where a lot of players today make a mistake. They think they've got the goalkeeper beat and they don't really bear down, and the goalkeeper recovers.

"But Richard, when he came in on you his eyes would just light up and I can still see him coming in off that right wing.

"The best play I think I've ever seen in hockey was made by him. Bill Gadsby was a big defenceman in those days, and Ralph Nattrass was another. They were a year out of junior and I had just been brought in to Chicago from Regina in the Western Senior League.

"Rocket came in from the blueline and he carried both those guys on his back and then he beat me. So he beat three of us on the play. The two guys were tugging on him and hanging on to him all the way from the blueline in. He was on his knees by the time he got to the net and so help me he got the shot away and put it past me in the top corner. Like I said, that was maybe the greatest play I ever saw, certainly as a goalie."

∎∎∎∎

The day before his funeral, the body of Maurice Richard lay in an open casket for public viewing at the Molson Centre. People began lining up before dawn. The doors opened early in the morning and remained open until past midnight, until the huge procession of mourners had ended. There was no exact count of how many viewed the body. The accepted estimate is 115,000.

My main memory of that day is of young fathers and mothers lifting up their very young children and quietly explaining to them who the man was they were looking at. It was a totally touching scene, from start to finish.

A few weeks earlier, when Richard was again hospitalized, I had received a call from Bob Babinski, a CBC sportscaster in Montreal. He explained how his station was planning to provide local coverage of Richard's funeral whenever that would be and I agreed to take part in the broadcast with him and news anchor Denis Trudeau. Between the time of Rocket's death and his funeral, those in the ivory towers of Canadian broadcasting decided the story was of national magnitude. That's why at 9:30 a.m. in Montreal on May 31, 2000, every TV network in Canada, English and French, came on the air from the Notre-Dame Cathedral, and why I was sitting in the CBC booth alongside Canada's top newscaster, Peter Mansbridge.

The day before, I received a call from one of the producers outlining plans for the show. Babinski and Trudeau would be roving reporters while I would provide background and anecdotes about the Rocket's career. I said, "Oh, just like Jack Granatstein." He laughed. Jack Granatstein is a Canadian historian who often

Team photos looked like this in 1913. Dick Irvin, Sr., my Dad, is the short guy in the middle, back row, with his brother Alex to his right.

Dick Irvin, Sr., when he was coaching the Toronto Maple Leafs in the 1930s. The glum expression may be due to all the Stanley Cups they almost won.

If I was dreaming of the NHL at the age of three, it was to be a player, not a broadcaster.

Bertha, Fay, and I spent long winters at home in Regina while Dad was in Montreal, coaching the Canadiens.

ordie Drillon, the last Maple Leaf to win the scoring title, and one of my early heroes.

osing with Dad and Maple Leaf star Busher Jackson after a duck-hunting trip in askatchewan. They did all the shooting.

Do general managers still send Christmas cards to their coaches? This one, from Frank Selke, Sr., to Dick Irvin, Sr., reads: "Another Rocket – another Cup. Happy Landings in 1947."

On February 14, 1952, the Canadiens surprised a battered Boom Boom Geoffrion with a cake on his twenty-first birthday after beating Toronto 3-1 at the Forum. We don't see photos like this any more.

As a starstruck eighteen-year-old I posed with the Rocket after he scored a hat trick against Detroit in 1950. This might be my all-time favourite photograph.

The definitive photo of the Rocket, eyes blazing even in a publicity shot.

Fay and I with our parents shortly after moving from Regina to Montreal in 1951.

Dick Sr. arrives in Chicago to coach the Blackhawks in 1955. On the right is team owner Jim Norris. The players, left to right, are Ed Litzenberger, Harry Watson, Hank Ciesla, and Red Sullivan.

Another type of team photo you don't see today. The Montreal Canadiens posed wearing their new team blazers after winning the Stanley Cup in 1953.

This picture taken at the Forum in the early 1950s shows the coach of the Montreal Canadiens trying to teach his son something about hockey. It wasn't easy.

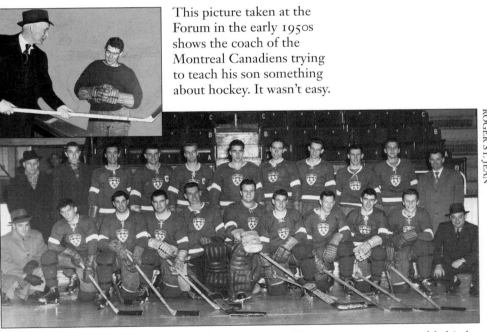

The McGill Redmen at the Montreal Forum, 1953. The twenty-one-year-old third from the right, front row, retired after the season. He eventually returned to the Forum as a broadcaster.

My first publicity picture, CFCF-TV, May 1961. I guess they put "Sports" over my head so viewers would know what I was supposed to be talking about.

appears on the CBC with Peter Mansbridge or Don Newman on shows with a political or military theme.

I had never met Peter Mansbridge until the morning of the funeral when he greeted me with a smile and said, "Hello, Jack." I replied, "You can call me Jack as long as I can call you Danny."

The telecast was tastefully done. The camera shot of two white-haired hockey legends entering the Notre-Dame together was a classic. Their names: Jean Béliveau and Gordie Howe.

I wondered if I might get somewhat emotional during the telecast, but I didn't. I did later when looking at pictures of the eight pallbearers at the funeral. Seven of them – Elmer Lach, Ken Reardon, Gerry McNeil, Ken Mosdell, Butch Bouchard, Dickie Moore, and Jean Béliveau – were the Rocket's teammates when my father was their coach. The eighth was his brother Henri, the Pocket Rocket, who played on eleven Stanley Cup–winning teams, a record that will be in the Richard family forever.

■|■|■

When Maurice Richard retired from playing hockey, September 15, 1960, he held or shared eighteen NHL regular-season scoring records and fourteen Stanley Cup playoff scoring records. When he died he still had the record of six goals in playoff overtime. He was proud of that record. Today a player could be in as many as twenty-eight playoff games in one year. Richard was in the playoffs seventeen years and never played more than twelve games in any one of them. And that happened only once.

When he retired, there were some who said he was pushed out by Canadiens' general manager Frank Selke and the team's owners. Ken Reardon took part in some of the meetings about the future of the Rocket and says nobody coaxed him into retirement. Whoever made the decision, it was the right one.

The Rocket was thirty-nine and his playing talents were slipping. Danny Gallivan liked to tell how he and some of his card-playing cronies were talking about Richard after his retirement and someone wondered out loud how much he weighed when his career ended. Danny phoned Toe Blake, Rocket's coach at the time. "I don't know," Blake said. "He wouldn't get on the scale." Blake was strict about having his players maintain correct weight levels. But he made an exception when it came to his old Punch Line right winger.

During an interview with me many years after he retired Rocket talked about his career after the riot:

"Some people said I played differently after that, had a different approach to the game. They said I mellowed quite a bit, but I don't think so. I played the same way except that I was overweight at the time, especially the last three or four years. I was too heavy and my reflexes weren't the same. I remember a few times I would get hit and I couldn't retaliate. By then it wasn't the same for me. Not the same at all."

Maurice Richard scored his last goal at Maple Leaf Gardens, April 12, 1960, beating Johnny Bower with a backhand. It came in the third game of the Canadiens' four-game Cup-final sweep of the Maple Leafs and an unprecedented fifth straight championship. It was the only playoff goal Richard scored in the final two years of his career.

Ken Reardon told me, "I think he wanted to retire after that last goal in Toronto. He saved the puck. I think he felt he might never score another one."

■|■|■

For the rest of his life, Maurice Richard's association with the Montreal Canadiens, and hockey, was a love-hate, on again–off again affair. The Canadiens gave him a job but he hated it. I met him at the Montreal airport a year or two after his retirement. He was on his way to a sports dinner in the Maritimes. "That's all they want me to do," he snorted. "Just go to dinners." He soon quit. Over the years that scenario would be repeated several times.

"What kind of a mood is he in?" was often the question when the Rocket would appear at golf tournaments or charity functions. Sometimes it would be great, sometimes sour. He kept you guessing.

In the 1980s a fundraising Skate-A-Thon was held on a Sunday afternoon at the Forum. The headliners were Gordie Howe, Bobby Hull, Ted Lindsay, and Maurice Richard. Quite a line-up. I covered it for my TV station and attended the post-skate lunch where the four hockey superstars sat at the same table. Lindsay, whom the Rocket despised when they played, said to me, "Isn't this wonderful? Who would have thought after the way we hated each other for so long that Rocket and I would be together at something like this, raising money for charity and sitting at the same table?" As Ted was saying all that I glanced at Rocket, who looked very much like a man wishing he were somewhere else.

But he wasn't always sour, not at all. In the early 1960s I organized and broadcast a TV series, *Montreal Minor Hockey*, featuring bantam-age players. We would often have celebrity referees and the Rocket took that role a few times. He was great with the kids. One coach told me he couldn't get his players to concentrate on the game. They were too excited because the legendary Rocket Richard was the referee.

When I was doing research for *The Habs*, I called Richard and asked about the incident in Boston, March 13, 1955, when he hit a linesman, resulting in his suspension and the riot. I knew he was touchy about the subject and I thought he might hang up on me, but he was fine. With the noisy exuberance of some of his grandchildren in the background the Rocket, as always, didn't deny drilling linesman Cliff Thompson, whom he blamed for the incident. (Thompson never worked another game in the NHL.) He thought both his main adversary in the fight, Bruins defence-man Hal Laycoe, and referee Frank Udvari didn't say "the right things," as he put it, at the hearing. Remember, there were no TV cameras in the Boston Garden that night. It was strictly their word against his. And of course he didn't agree with Clarence Campbell's decision and he had plenty of company there. Like about two million people in the province of Quebec.

For years Rocket travelled across the country with teams of Old-Timers, or Legends, as they prefer to be called, first as a player and then as a referee. He told me he loved making those trips and being with the boys, just as long as he didn't have to do too many interviews.

A newspaper interview, done in Winnipeg during a Legends trip, created an unnecessary stir across the country. The reporter wrote how sad it was that Maurice Richard was losing it, that he couldn't remember names or games from his career. It was picked up by the national wire services and received a lot of play. But the reporter had done a terrible job of researching his or her subject.

The Rocket had a poor memory for names and games from his playing days. I once did a nostalgia-type show for *Hockey Night in Canada* with him and several other former players. I knew the Rocket would have trouble recalling moments from the good old days, and he did. I had to prompt him to remember Johnny Bower's name.

But that was the Rocket. When he played, his concentration was all-consuming. Focus, passion, call it what you will. Mark Messier may have been close at times, but in my opinion there has never been a player who played the game with the same inten-sity. He couldn't have cared less what was going on around him.

Most players seem to have total recall. Richard didn't. My dad said Rocket couldn't tell you how he scored a goal after he scored it. The only thing he cared about was scoring a goal. When he did, he started right away thinking about scoring the next one.

Over the years there were numerous occasions when the Rocket would take part in a pre-game ceremony at the Forum. Even when other greats from the past were present, he always got the biggest cheer. But as the years went by the cheers abated somewhat. Time marches on, audiences get younger, and memories fade. So I didn't quite expect what happened March 11, 1996, the night they closed the Montreal Forum.

It was a marvellous ceremony, building to the introduction of nineteen Hall of Famers who had played for the Canadiens and the passing of a torch from former captains to then captain Pierre Turgeon, who carried the torch off the ice signalling its leaving the Forum for the team's new home, the Molson Centre.

The great players introduced included Béliveau, Savard, Worsley, Lach, Bouchard, Mahovlich, Lafleur, Dryden, Shutt, Henri Richard. They all received great ovations. Then came the final introduction: "NUMBER 9 . . . MAURICE RICHARD." There is really no way I can describe the ovation the Rocket received. It lasted almost ten minutes. On and on it went, and it wasn't staged. Nobody was prompting the fans to continue.

I was on the ice as one of the MCs along with Richard Garneau. As the ovation continued I walked over to one of the Hall of Famers, Tom Johnson, and reminded him of the story he once told me about the numbers 9 and 10. In the 1950s the Canadiens played a lot of exhibition games. Rocket wore 9, Tom wore 10. Johnson said, "When we were introduced before the game the cheer for the Rocket would last so long they'd be at number 15 by the time it stopped. Nobody ever found out who I was."

As I looked at the cheering crowd that night I was struck by how many people, men and women, were in tears. By my estimate, at least 75 per cent of the fans giving this hockey icon the greatest cheer any player ever received had never seen him play, not even on television. It had been thirty-six years since Maurice Richard had played his last game and scored his last goal. Yet there they were, eighteen thousand strong, totally wrapped up in the moment, and the man.

The ovation, seen coast to coast on television, produced a new generation of Maurice Richard fans. He was in demand again, especially for that fairly new phenomenon, sports-card shows. Other former players who also attended the shows told me he was much more relaxed than in the past. A year or so later, when it was revealed he had contracted a rare form of cancer, a nation prayed.

The National Hockey League introduced the Maurice Richard Trophy for most goals in a season, starting in 1998–99. The last conversation I had with the Rocket was at the NHL awards ceremony in Toronto where he presented the trophy to its first winner, Teemu Selanne. We chatted for several moments backstage at the Air Canada Centre. He talked about my father and said he didn't think coaches like him and Toe Blake would enjoy working with today's highly paid players.

The conversation ended on a poignant note when Maurice asked me, "How old was your father when he died?" When I answered, "Sixty-four," Rocket said, "That's all?" and shook his head rather sadly.

When Maurice Richard became the first player to score five hundred goals he dedicated number five hundred to my father, who had passed away a few months before. In an interview filmed a couple of years later he said that as he was being cheered at the Forum for scoring his historic goal he was thinking about "Dick Irvin, the man who taught me all I know about hockey." Now,

Dick Sr.'s son knows one of the Rocket's last thoughts before he
made the first presentation of the Maurice Richard Trophy was
of Dick Irvin.

That was the only time the Rocket would present the trophy
named in his honour. A year later I was back on stage at the NHL
awards ceremony, introducing a video tribute to the late Maurice
Richard.

■│■│■

A friend of mine, Lenny Lanteigne, manages a music-supply store
a couple of blocks from Notre-Dame Cathedral. A few days
before Christmas 2000 one of his employees said to him, "I feel
kind of sad. This will be my first Christmas without the Rocket."
The employee was twenty-three years old.

On the Air in the 1960s

....

My mother had always wanted to visit Williamsburg, Virginia, so in September 1958 we motored there and back. The day after we returned I received a call from Mr. Selke, who said he would like me to take on the job as official scorer at Canadiens home games. Before I had a chance to tell him I would think it over he said, "You weren't home when I called the other day so I have told the NHL you're the new scorer. You'll be starting when we play the Royals in an exhibition game tomorrow night."

Off-ice officials such as goal judges, penalty timekeepers, and official scorers represent the league but are appointed by the home team. In those days the Canadiens compensated you with two complimentary season's tickets and a trip to New York with the team. In my case the seats were the pair we'd had when Dad was coaching. They were great seats, ten rows up at centre ice. In 1958 the cost was eight dollars per ticket. (Today that same class of seat costs eighty dollars at the Molson Centre.) I was the scorer at the Forum, full-time and part-time, for eight years until I began broadcasting games.

The official scorer has the final say in determining who scored the goal and more importantly, as I would learn, who gets the assists. At the Forum there was a phone hook-up between where I was, upstairs in the press box, and the public-address announcer, who sat in the penalty box. When a goal was scored I would pick up the phone and say, "Number 4 from number 5 and number 12," I didn't enjoy it all that much, but at times it could get interesting.

Back then most players had bonus clauses in their contracts rewarding them for goals, assists, and points. The bonuses usually amounted to no more than a few hundred dollars, a sum more important to a player then than it is now. A scorer would feel the pressure near the end of the season when the boys were trying to reach their bonus targets. Either they claimed they got an assist they didn't get credit for, and usually didn't deserve, or someone else on their team would ask on their behalf. Doug Harvey was the worst offender. Often, after a Canadiens goal was announced, Harvey would grab the phone in the penalty box and curse me up and down for being stingy with assists. He'd scream, "They give them out everywhere else but you won't, you cheap bastard." In other words, other scorers in the league are dishonest and you should be too.

Replays weren't available in those days, so it was my word against theirs. I'm not a confrontational type, but I never changed anything after one of Doug's cheery little phone calls.

One night the Canadiens scored an early goal. I gave one assist. I saw Tom Johnson speak to the PA announcer, who then called me with the message. "Plante wants an assist on the goal." I didn't give him one. As it turned out, Jacques Plante, then the best goalie in hockey, had a rare bad game and the Canadiens lost

7–4. I delivered copies of the official scoresheet to the coaches after the game. That night Toe Blake was so mad at his team, and especially at Plante, you could almost see steam coming out his ears. I was tempted to say, "Here's the scoresheet, coach. And by the way your goalie, who just let in seven goals, wants an assist." But I didn't have the courage. It would have been like putting a lit match to a gas tank.

The Boston Bruins had a bad team in the 1960s. They lost a late-season game in Montreal something like 8–3. Afterwards two of the Bruins' top players chased after me down a corridor at the Forum looking for assists. No wonder they were last.

My favourite official-scorer story happened during a Canadiens–Maple Leafs game. Near the end of the second period Toronto's Bob Pulford picked off a pass by a Montreal player clean as a whistle, took off on a breakaway, and scored. No problem with that one. "Number 20, unassisted."

During the intermission Frank Selke, Jr., came by and we had a chat. We were still talking as the Leafs came out for the third period. Pulford skated straight to the penalty box and spoke to the PA announcer. My phone light flashed and I was told, "Pulford says Shack should get an assist on his goal." When I told Frank he said, "If I hadn't seen it, I wouldn't have believed it."

■ I ■ I ■

Eddie Shack broke into the NHL with the New York Rangers the same year I broke in as an official scorer. During a quiet period in a game at the Forum that season, with the Canadiens organizing a rush out of their zone, Andy Bathgate signalled to Shack to cover Boom Boom Geoffrion.

"I got him! I got him!" Shack yelled, and you could hear him all over the rink. At that instant the Boomer received a pass and took off, with Shack trying to catch up. It was no contest. Geoffrion took a couple of strides after he hit the New York blue-line and blasted the puck into the top corner of the net. The fans loved it and you could see them laughing. For the rest of the game, when Shack was on the ice, they would yell, "I got him! I got him!"

Early in the next season, during a game in New York, an Andy Bathgate shot hit Jacques Plante in the face, and history was made. After getting stitched up, Plante returned to the ice wearing his goaltender's mask, and the art of playing that precarious position was changed forever.

Over the years I have read and heard that Bathgate hit Plante with a wicked slapshot. Not so. A few years ago the good people who have published this book, McClelland & Stewart, produced a comic book about Jacques Plante aimed at children. They asked me to help with the research. I called Andy about the incident and he told me:

"Earlier in the game Plante went behind his net and gave me a pretty good hip check. The next time I got the puck I thought I'd get even, so I flipped it at his face. I didn't think I'd even hit him, but I did. It wasn't a hard shot. I just flipped it."

There was a dramatic photo taken that night of Plante, blood streaming down his face, putting on his mask. We all felt sorry for him, but we needn't have.

Plante had been lobbying for a mask, but Toe Blake was against it. One of Plante's teammates, Bob Turner, told me, "Jacques was hoping he'd get a puck in the face because Toe said he could wear a mask only if he got injured. Don't feel sorry for him. He was the happiest guy in the rink when he got hit."

■|■|■

I try not to be one of those who claims the old days were better. But I can tell you that the atmosphere surrounding the NHL was a lot different then and, in my opinion, more positive and more fun.

When the teams played each other fourteen times a season, the players became familiar to fans in the cities they were visiting. In the 1950s and '60s, when television coverage was increasing, players walking the downtown streets were instantly recognized, especially in Toronto and Montreal. Very few players wore helmets in those days, which made recognition that much easier. When the Detroit Red Wings were in town, everybody knew Gordie Howe, Ted Lindsay, Red Kelly, and Alex Delvecchio. The Chicago Blackhawks became a high profile team with young stars like Bobby Hull, Glenn Hall, and Stan Mikita. There were some great Toronto teams featuring Dave Keon, Frank Mahovlich, and Johnny Bower. When the Canadiens hit town there was Béliveau, Geoffrion, Moore, and Henri Richard. Today the entire Nashville Predators team could walk the same streets and only the most rabid hockey-card collectors and autograph groupies would have the slightest idea who some of them were.

The officials were in the same boat. Matt Pavelich, a Hall of Fame linesman, tells how he'd be out and about on the day of a game and people would yell, "Hey, Pavelich! Where's your seeing-eye dog?" Matt would work in each city twelve or fifteen times a season. With today's officials, it could be two or three times.

Once during the '50s Red Storey went for a walk in New York with one of his linesmen, Curly Davies, and a bunch of kids playing roller hockey recognized Red and started booing him. Perhaps some of them were at the game Red refereed at the old Madison Square Garden when Chicago was visiting the Rangers, a game that provided the Old Redhead with one of his favourite stories.

"I called a delayed penalty on Chicago. I put my arm up and the play kept going, and going, and going. Every time the Rangers got to the Chicago blueline they'd be turned away, so they'd circle and come back again. It happened three or four times. My arm was getting so tired I could hardly hold it up.

"Now, Chicago finally gets the puck, but I've forgotten who I was calling the penalty on. They had a tough guy, Larry Zeidel, and he happened to be close to me when I blew the whistle. I gave it the big action and yelled, 'Zeidel, you're gone!'

"Billy Mosienko rushed over to me saying, 'Red, you've got the wrong guy.' I said, 'I don't care. I'm just happy I didn't get the wrong team.'"

∎∎∎∎

From 1942 to 1999 only three broadcasters, Doug Smith, Danny Gallivan, and Dick Irvin, were known as "The Voice of the Canadiens" on the English side of the two-language broadcast scene in Montreal. But if Doug Smith hadn't written a letter to Dick Irvin, Sr., when Dick Jr. was only ten years old, the coach's kid wouldn't be on the list.

Doug Smith was working in radio in his hometown, Calgary, in the summer of '42 when he heard about an opening on the English broadcasts of Montreal Canadiens games. Smith, always a resourceful type, decided that instead of being one of many applying for the job to the radio station in Montreal, he would contact a fellow westerner from Regina who was coaching the team. He wrote Dad a letter. Then they talked a couple of times on the phone. Although he had never met Smith, the Canadiens' coach put in a good word for him and Doug Smith got the job.

Smith broadcast Canadiens games on radio for ten years. Molson was one of the major sponsors. In 1952 he signed with a competing brewery, Dow, to do sportscasts and Montreal Alouettes football games. So Doug Smith left hockey and a Maritimer,

Danny Gallivan, was brought in. Danny worked thirty-two years, with me as his sidekick during the last seventeen. After Danny retired in 1984, I hung around the broadcast booth until 1999.

In 1961 I was a restless twenty-nine-year-old bachelor who had worked in sales and accounting in the eight years since graduating from McGill. I had coached bantam hockey teams for a few years and enjoyed working with the kids. The two most nervous moments in my life were when I interviewed Bob Hope on *Hockey Night in Canada* and when I coached my bantam team in the 1961 Quebec Provincial final game. I was a basket case but the kids were cool. They won the game, and the championship, 6–0.

My minor-hockey coaching experience had me thinking of becoming a high-school history teacher. There was a shortage of teachers and I had been accepted by the Montreal Protestant School Board to start in the fall. My life was heading in a new direction, but I'd end up in front of a camera, not a blackboard.

On January 21, 1961, CFCF-TV signed on in Montreal. Brian McFarlane was the sports director. Brian was looking for offbeat stories and he liked the idea of the legendary Dick Irvin's son coaching a bantam team. He interviewed me on a show called *Sportsman's Club* the second week the station was on the air.

Brian was a one-man sports department and was desperately seeking an assistant. There was interest, but when the applicants learned the pay was seventy-five dollars per week, the interest immediately cooled. Brian talked to me about the job but finally said he needed someone with experience. I had none, so it was thanks, but no thanks.

Brian had whetted my appetite for the broadcasting business, big time. I called Doug Smith and he agreed to meet with me. In 1942, Dick Sr. played a big role in his career. Now, in 1961, Doug was about to play a big role in mine. I can't remember, but I hope

I didn't feel he owed me for what Dad had done for him twenty years before. He was a friend, and I knew he was plugged in to the industry.

I asked Doug if I was too old to start out in the business by working for a small-town radio station, playing records, reading news, and sweeping floors. He said I was. When I told him about the CFCF situation he said, "You're just the guy McFarlane needs. Can you write?" I let on I could, although I hadn't written anything since I was sports editor of the Regina Central Collegiate student newspaper. Doug was (and I now am) a firm believer that sportscasters should write their own material.

"Leave it with me," he said. "McFarlane owes me a favour."

Things happened quickly. That evening Brian called and, saying he had heard about me from someone whose opinion he respected, asked me to audition, which I did two days later. Three days after that, May 8, 1961, I started working as a sportscaster.

I've often thought of the money my parents spent so I could get a commerce degree at McGill only to have me spend most of my working life being paid to say, "Pittsburgh 3, Philadelphia 2" and "He shoots, he scores!"

I was on probation for the first three months. On August 8 I was sure I'd be told, "Thanks very much. Good luck as a history teacher." Nobody said a word. When my next paycheque arrived I had been given a raise, to $82.50 a week. As far as I am concerned, from then until I retired from the station in 1991, I spent thirty years at CFCF-TV working on probation.

And I'll always be thankful Doug Smith wrote a letter to my father, back in the summer of '42.

∎∎∎∎

In 1961 the Canadiens held their training camp in Victoria, B.C., instead of at the Forum, so I had to wait a bit before doing my first nervous interviews with the local hockey heroes.

The first time Brian assigned me to the Forum was the day before the season opened, when the team was going to name a new captain. Doug Harvey, who succeeded Maurice Richard as captain, had been traded to the New York Rangers in the off-season. As the players voted, the media waited outside the dressing-room door for the result.

When the door finally opened, the first person to come out was Bernie Geoffrion. The Boomer boomed out, took a sharp right turn, charged out the door onto Atwater Avenue and disappeared. It was obvious he wasn't the new captain of the Montreal Canadiens, and it was obvious he thought he should be.

Jean Béliveau was the winner. There were some solid veterans on the team like Geoffrion, Dickie Moore, and Tom Johnson. Geoffrion, coming off a career season in which he became only the second player to score fifty goals and won the Hart Trophy as league MVP, was the favourite of the ever-active Montreal rumour mill. But looking back, how could they have selected anyone but Big Jean? Has there ever been a better captain of any team, any time, anywhere? I don't think so.

Béliveau had returned from the west with his leg in a cast. He had suffered torn knee ligaments in an exhibition game against the Trail Smoke Eaters, an injury that would hamper him all season. As I chatted with the new captain his injured leg was propped over the back of a Forum box seat. So my first NHL interview was with Jean Béliveau. Nothing like starting at the top.

■|■|■

I almost made my first appearance on *Hockey Night in Canada* during the 1962 Stanley Cup playoffs. I had some holiday time owing that I had to take before the end of April. I had become good friends with Bob Turner, another Regina product, who had been Doug Harvey's defence partner. Bob had been traded to Chicago and the Canadiens were playing the Blackhawks in the semifinals. The Canadiens won the first two games at the Forum and I went to Chicago, on holiday, stayed with Bob and his wife, Betty, and saw the next two games at the Chicago Stadium.

Frank Selke, Jr., was the Montreal host of *Hockey Night in Canada*. He was also the Canadiens' PR director. (I can just imagine the hue and cry from some self-styled TV critics in the print press if that sort of thing were to happen today.) Frank spotted me before the second game in Chicago and asked me to stand by to be interviewed if there was overtime. I was on pins and needles that night, but my big debut was scrubbed by a 5–3 Chicago win. Bill Hay scored the winning goal in the third period. Bill, another Reginan, who played outdoors on Rink 3 when I did, is now chairman of the Hockey Hall of Fame, and I serve on the Hall's selection committee. Small world.

Hockey Night in Canada did something different during Chicago-Montreal playoffs in the early '60s. While the games were on in Chicago, Frank watched from a seat near ice level. There was a fan nearby who was loud, opinionated, and funny. He was Don Pincus, a Chicago accountant who did some work for the Blackhawks.

Frank got such a kick out of listening to him he asked him if he would come on TV and give HNIC's viewers his take on the games. Pincus did, and was just as opinionated and funny as he was in his seat at the Stadium. He was a big hit. Even though he was pro-Blackhawks, fans in Montreal loved watching the colourful

Pincus. HNIC even brought him to Montreal a couple of times.

Today's national HNIC host, Ron MacLean, could have a lot of fun with somebody like that. It wouldn't be "Coach's Corner," but it might be "Pincus's Podium."

■ ■ ■ ■

The best decision I ever made was when I decided I wanted to marry Wilma Dobson. The surprising thing to me then, and now, was that she agreed. We began a long-distance courtship when Wilma was working for radio station CKRC, in Winnipeg. Both of us were from Regina and that's where the wedding took place, at the Westminster United Church, which is in the same neighbourhood we both grew up in. Who says you can't go home again?

Wilma got an inkling on our wedding day, May 4, 1963, that there might be a touch of hockey in her future. I had breakfast that morning with Marlene and Bernie Geoffrion, who were staying at the same hotel while on a cross-Canada holiday. The best man was Chicago Blackhawks defenceman Bob Turner, and the happy newlyweds were driven from the church, in his flashy white Chrysler, by Montreal Canadiens forward Billy Hicke.

■ ■ ■ ■

I made my first appearance on *Hockey Night in Canada*, without much warning, at the end of a Montreal-Detroit game at the Forum, November 27, 1965. For the previous couple of years my official-scorer location had been in the catwalk, about ten feet away from the broadcast location of Danny Gallivan and his colour man, Keith Dancy. Perhaps that's one reason why I felt more comfortable than a rookie should have when I moved in beside the legendary Danny a couple of years later. I knew the territory.

Near the end of the third period of the game, Keith leaned over and asked if I would go on with him when it was over and pick the three stars. I gulped a bit, and agreed. It was a good thing he didn't give me much warning. No time to get nervous.

The siren went, and there I was, on camera with Keith playing the part of an expert after a 3–2 Canadiens win. Gordie Howe had played a very ordinary game but did score his six hundredth goal, a feat which normally would have earned him a star. Late in the third period Howe had drawn a stupid major penalty for high-sticking J.C. Tremblay, killing Detroit's chance to score the tying goal. So, despite his milestone goal, I didn't give Gordie a star, which made me some instant enemies in Saskatoon, Gordie's home territory.

The reason I know some people out west were upset with my non-pick of Howe was because I got mail. For the first several years after I joined *Hockey Night in Canada* Danny and I received lots of mail, from all over the country. It would be sent either to the CBC, or to the Montreal Forum. In those days emotions ran high, with half the country cheering for the Maple Leafs, the other half for the Canadiens. Most of the people who wrote were mad at us for something we said, but at least we knew they were out there.

Then, in my last several years on the show, hardly any mail arrived. The league had expanded and Canadians had the Canucks, Flames, Oilers, Jets, and Nordiques to cheer for. It wasn't a two-team country any more and, from coast to coast, some of the Toronto-Montreal emotion was gone. I missed the letters, even the ones that weren't exactly a boost to my ego.

■I■I■

By this point I had seen the Stanley Cup won only three times, but I made up ground quickly. Beginning in 1964, I was in the building when the Cup was won fifteen times in seventeen years. Starting in 1968, I was there thirteen times in a row.

The Montreal Canadiens went through a Stanley Cup slump in the early 1960s. After their fifth straight in 1960 the Habs didn't even get to the finals again until 1965. The Stanley Cup was won by Chicago in '61, and Toronto the three years after that. As I write this the Blackhawks' 1961 win is their only Stanley Cup in the last sixty-three years.

The Toronto-Montreal rivalry was at a peak when the teams met in the 1964 semifinals. The coaches, Toe Blake and Punch Imlach, were always going at each other in the press and often put on a better show than their players. The series went to a seventh game at the Forum. The Maple Leafs won 3–1, with Dave Keon scoring all three goals.

I interviewed Dave years later about the game and he said, "When the three stars were announced I was the third behind the goalies, Johnny Bower and Charlie Hodge. I had just scored three goals in a seventh game in the other team's building. I wondered what a guy had to do to be number one." Those controversial three stars, again.

The Maple Leafs went on to play the Red Wings in the finals. Terry Sawchuk was back in Detroit and the Wings led three games to two and had the sixth game on home ice. That's a well-remembered game, the one in which Toronto's Bobby Baun was carried from the ice with a broken ankle, then came back and scored the winning goal at 1:42 of the first overtime. Baun played in ninety-six playoff games and scored only three goals. But he became a legend with that one.

Brian McFarlane had moved back to Toronto and I called him the next day. I mentioned that Wilma and I would be driving to

Toronto on the weekend to visit some of her relatives. Brian kindly got me a pass to game seven, and I had a standing-room spot in the press box to see the Maple Leafs win 4–0. Andy Bathgate scored the Cup-winner on Terry Sawchuk on a break-away at the same end of Maple Leaf Gardens where Bryan Hextall scored the Cup-winner on Turk Broda, the night of my first Cup, in 1940.

■ ❚ ■ ❚

Bob Wolff is a veteran American broadcaster I first met in the early 1960s when he was in Montreal promoting a book he had written with Andy Bathgate. When the 1965 Stanley Cup final between the Canadiens and Chicago went to a seventh game, in Montreal, Bob was there broadcasting the game for American television. He asked me to be his statistician, so when that Cup was won I watched from a broadcast booth for the first time.

The Canadiens won the game 4–0. They scored all their goals in the first period, starting with one by Jean Béliveau just four-teen seconds into the game. Yvan Cournoyer was a flashy Canadiens rookie lacking in defensive skills so, even though the Roadrunner had a goal and an assist in the Habs' early outburst, Toe Blake didn't put him on the ice in the last two periods.

The home team won every game in that series. Glenn Hall was Chicago's goalie, while Gump Worsley and Charlie Hodge shared the Canadiens' crease. Gump hurt his knee in the sixth game and, although he said it felt all right, the doctors told him he couldn't play in the big one. He was in the Forum coffee shop with his wife before the game when the Canadiens' trainer, Red Aubut, came in.

As Gump relates it, "He said I had to go to the dressing room because I was going to play. I said, 'Yeah, sure I am.' He said,

'No joke. Toe told me to find you and tell you that you're playing.'" So Gump played, and got a shutout in the biggest win of his long career.

Bob Wolff invited Wilma and me to join him for a visit after the game at the Mount Royal Hotel, where the Blackhawks were staying. Unlike today, teams then didn't go straight home on a charter flight after the game. I had a chat in the lobby with their GM Tommy Ivan and coach Rudy Pilous, who were beside themselves complaining about the way one of their players had performed that night. He was a rookie, not a Hull or Mikita, and they were so down on him I was surprised they didn't trade him before the next season. In fact he played two more years in Chicago, then they traded him. Their whipping boy's name was Phil Esposito.

■I■I■

I began working alongside Danny Gallivan during the 1966–67 season when the CTV network started carrying games on Wednesday nights. Dan Kelly, who did colour for Danny on HNIC, was a CBC employee based in Ottawa, and they wouldn't let him appear on the rival network. When the NHL expanded the following season, Frank Selke, Jr., left to become general manager of the Oakland Seals, Kelly took his place as HNIC's host in Montreal, and I became the full-time colour man. The Danny and Dick show would run on the CBC for the next seventeen years.

The Canadiens, in a stretch of playing in the Stanley Cup finals five straight years, won again in 1966. Henri Richard scored the winning goal, in overtime, in Detroit. I wasn't there. Then, in 1967, fans in Canada got something that hasn't happened since, a Stanley Cup final between the Toronto Maple Leafs and the

Montreal Canadiens. With the NHL structured as it is today, it may never happen again.

In 1967 *Hockey Night in Canada* was produced out of Toronto and Montreal. With very rare exceptions, the Toronto announcers never worked in Montreal, and vice versa. In the finals, Bill Hewitt and Brian McFarlane were in the gondola in Maple Leaf Gardens, with Ward Cornell in the studio. In Montreal it was Danny and Dick upstairs, Frank Jr. downstairs. I had also done the odd interview and feature for the Saturday show that season. The CBC assigned Dan Kelly to handle play-by-play on radio during the playoffs and I moved into his spot on television. If you're getting the idea that Dick Jr. lucked out by being at the right place at the right time in those days, you got it.

The 1967 final is well remembered by those of us who were around then, and pretty well known to those who have come along since. I don't think a year has gone by since without a HNIC replay of the most famous goal of the series, the one the Leafs' captain George Armstrong scored into an empty net to clinch the Cup in the sixth game at Maple Leaf Gardens.

Foster Hewitt was the rare exception I mentioned when it came to HNIC people appearing in the other team's building. Foster would sometimes be on from the Forum, usually picking the three stars. Naturally those of us in Montreal would mutter about Foster being on our show while Danny seemed to be barred from MLG. To my knowledge Hewitt never did play-by-play on television in Montreal until the 1972 Canada-Russia series. Danny Gallivan never worked in the gondola in Toronto until late in his career when he was hired to broadcast mid-week Maple Leaf games for CHCH, a Hamilton station, in the early 1980s.

While I, like millions of Canadians, grew up listening to Foster Hewitt and admiring his work, once he and I had some personal contact via HNIC I wasn't too thrilled. Foster always acted as though we were meeting for the first time. Despite his long association with Dick Sr. in Toronto, he never mentioned him to me. When we met I'd always reintroduce myself and lean on the name *Irvin*, but it didn't work and he never once called me by name. I was always "Kid." Obviously my first broadcasting hero wasn't interested, or more to the point, I guess, wasn't impressed. Maybe he'd had a falling out with Dick Sr. Whatever, it was disappointing.

I have a totally different memory of Foster Hewitt's son, Bill, whom I first saw in 1940, then a little guy walking with his father up to the gondola at Maple Leaf Gardens. Bill was a great person and I enjoyed working with him. We did a few playoff games together, plus a couple of All-Star Games. We were the HNIC broadcasters at the Philadelphia Spectrum on a wild Sunday afternoon in 1974 when the Flyers defeated the Boston Bruins 1–0 to win the Stanley Cup. In fact, we were the only HNIC broadcasters there. Dave Hodge handled the opening, closing, and intermissions back in Toronto. It was a far cry from the entourage that covers the finals today.

Bill had one quirk that took some getting used to. A few minutes into the game, usually when you were saying something deep and profound like, "Let's look at that again on the replay," Bill would haul off and slap you on the back, then reach over and shake hands. It was his way of saying that everything was fine and we were off and running. The first couple of times he did it to me, it was quite a jolt. I learned to brace myself from then on.

Bill Hewitt received a lot of criticism for his work, especially in Montreal. In those days the Toronto crew wasn't too popular there, with Toronto feeling the same about the Montreal guys, but I always thought he was a fine broadcaster. Bill passed away a few years ago. I'm sorry he hasn't been elected to the media

section of the Hockey Hall of Fame so his name could be listed
among the winners the Foster Hewitt Memorial Award.

■ ■ ■ ■

The face of the NHL changed forever when the league expanded
from six to twelve teams for the 1967–68 season. Twelve teams
seems small compared to thirty today, but at the time it was quite
a departure. The old six comprised the East Division, the new six
the West. There was interlocking play during the season, but
divisional play in the playoffs, until the finals. That guaranteed
one of the new teams would be in the final, a condition of expansion that was to be in effect for three years.

The St. Louis Blues, coached by a young man named Scotty
Bowman, were the Western winners in each of the first three
years. The Blues played Montreal the first two years, and Boston
in the third. Their record in the three finals was twelve games,
twelve losses. Expansion didn't mean parity, not yet anyway.

A couple of hockey wives got into the act the first two years I
broadcast the Stanley Cup finals. In 1967 the Canadiens defeated
the Maple Leafs 6–2 in game one at the Forum. Before the second
game, Punch Imlach suckered me into a meeting in the hallway
outside the Leafs' dressing room. I thought he was going to favour
me with a scoop about his team. Instead, with his ever-present
worshipful group of Toronto newspaper reporters looking on,
Imlach lit into me about how biased Danny and I had been towards
the Canadiens during the 6–2 broadcast. He hadn't heard us of
course, but his wife had. Imlach claimed we were so bad the Missus
had called the Forum during the broadcast to complain. Obviously
I didn't think it was a very nice way for a tough old pro to treat a
rookie broadcaster, but it was vintage Imlach.

The next year, the wife of someone I'll refer to as a high-ranking executive of the Montreal Canadiens did her thing. The final series began in St. Louis. Scotty had a couple of long-time Montreal stars, Doug Harvey and Dickie Moore, in the Blues' line-up for a last hurrah. For them to be in the Stanley Cup finals against their old team was quite a story. Mrs. Executive watched the telecast of the first game in Montreal. When it was over she called her husband and demanded he have Gallivan and Irvin fired immediately because they had talked much too much about Harvey and Moore, and not nearly enough about her husband's team.

Mr. Executive was in a position to have us fired, but he never said a word. Danny got the story from a friend of his, who happened to be Mrs. Executive's brother. I am still friends with Mr., hence the bit of secrecy. But after the first game of the 1968 finals, Mrs. never spoke to Danny or Dick again.

■■■■

The Canadiens won four straight but the series was much more competitive than had been expected. The scores were 3–2, 1–0, 4–3, and 3–2. The Canadiens needed overtime to win the first and third games. As he had been throughout the playoffs, Glenn Hall, the Blues' goaltender, was magnificent. Nobody disagreed when Hall, a member of the losing team, was named the MVP of the playoffs.

I have some vivid memories of the 1968 Cup-winning game, which was played on a Saturday afternoon, at the Forum. When Clarence Campbell presented Jean Béliveau with the Stanley Cup, the Canadiens' captain was in civvies and on crutches because of an injury suffered early in the series.

I wasn't on HNIC's Cup-winner's dressing-room patrol yet, so my post-game wrap was with Danny, upstairs in the booth. The Forum was scheduled for a major renovation that summer and preliminary work had been going on for several weeks. Now that hockey was over they could start on the interior of the building. By the time we got downstairs after the game, dozens of workers were scattering to all parts of the building and had begun tearing out seats and demolishing the rink boards.

The first thing I saw in the Canadiens' dressing room was Toe Blake being interviewed live on CFCF Radio, via telephone, by sportscaster Russ Taylor. Russ had a major scoop: Blake was announcing that he had just coached his last game. He had won the Stanley Cup three times as a player, and eight times as a coach. When I shook his hand a few minutes later and congratulated him on his great career, Toe made me feel pretty good by saying, "Your father had a lot to do with it."

■|■|■

Claude Ruel, who had been coaching and scouting in the Canadiens' organization, succeeded Toe Blake. Ruel had been a good junior player whose career was cut short when he suffered an injury that cost him the sight in one eye. He had become a faithful employee of the organization, and still is, but his choice as Blake's successor was a surprise.

Anyone not knowing what was going on who walked into the middle of that news conference might have thought someone had died. There were nothing but long faces at the table. When the announcement was made all the brass, including Toe Blake, who had been hired as a consultant, bolted from the room. Ruel was left on his own to face the Montreal media onslaught.

It's not easy for a coach to take over a Stanley Cup champion, but Ruel was up to the task. In his rookie year the Canadiens finished first with a league-record 103 points, and won a second straight Stanley Cup.

The Boston Bruins were on the rise in the late 1960s. As I recall, it had something to do with a young defenceman named Orr and a former Chicago Blackhawk whipping boy named Esposito. The Canadiens swept the Bruins four straight in the first playoff round in 1968. They needed six games to beat them in the semifinals in '69, eliminating them on an overtime goal by Jean Béliveau, the only one of his career. That year Boston was second in the East with 100 points, three behind Montreal. Two years earlier the Bruins had finished dead last.

The second straight Montreal–St. Louis Cup final was another sweep for the Canadiens and their fourth Stanley Cup in five years. The Canadiens won the final game 2–1, in St. Louis. John Ferguson proved tough guys can also score goals by getting the winner in the third period.

The Cup was won on May 4, Wilma and Dick's sixth wedding anniversary. A daughter, Nancy Anne, had arrived in 1966 and a son, Doug, would join us in a few weeks. Wilma was in St. Louis and after the game we had dinner at Stan Musial's Restaurant, which was a couple of blocks away from the St. Louis Arena. Wilma and Dick are still in business. Musial's is long gone.

The Seals and Other Strangers

....

S peaking on behalf of my fellow media types in the east, the best thing about the 1967 NHL expansion was two teams in California. It was quite a change for the veterans on the beat, after years of seeing the same old cities in a six-team league, to find themselves travelling to sunny California and somebody else picking up the tab.

I joined the Montreal Canadiens' bilingual media entourage during the second season of expansion, 1968–69. Broadcast coverage of the team was sparse in those days. Television was limited to Saturday nights in both languages, and a Wednesday CTV English broadcast once or twice a month. The only radio coverage was via the CBC and Radio-Canada on Sunday nights.

In mid-January of that season the Canadiens played a Wednesday-night game in New York. Apparently it was an entertaining game with a final score something like 7–5, yet nobody in Montreal heard a thing about it until the 11:00 news.

That same night CFCF-TV showed a 1–0 game from Toronto that was a crashing bore. The next day I complained to Ralph Mellanby, the Montreal producer of *Hockey Night in Canada*, whose company held both the TV and radio rights to Canadiens games. Ralph's reply was, "Why don't you do something about it?" For a change, I did.

I spoke to my bosses at CFCF, which was a combined TV and radio operation, and they did some negotiating with the rights-holders and the Canadiens. An agreement was reached for the airing of a select number of games the rest of that season for a rights payment of a thousand dollars. A couple of weeks after my complaint I was airborne, headed to Oakland, California. My career as a radio play-by-play man, and my love affair with the Oakland Seals, had begun.

■■■■

The six expansion franchises were located in Philadelphia, Pittsburgh, St. Louis, Los Angeles, Minneapolis, and Oakland. The first four are still in business where they started. The Minnesota North Stars are now the Dallas Stars. Philadelphia, Pittsburgh, and Dallas have won the Stanley Cup. St. Louis and Los Angeles have reached the finals. Of the original new six, only the Oakland Seals disappeared. Well, almost.

The team lasted in Oakland until 1976. During that time it was called the Oakland Seals, the California Seals, the California Golden Seals, and, again, the California Seals. That, and the fact that the players once wore white skates, gives you an indication of what the franchise was all about.

It wasn't the players that did the team in, it was the ownership, particularly that of the flamboyant and unpredictable Charles O.

Finley. The first principal owner was Barend (Barry) Van Gerbig, a jet-setting playboy who had Bing Crosby as a godfather and the daughter of actor Douglas Fairbanks, Jr., as a wife. After one year he faded out of the picture and a group that included Crosby took over. Crowds were small, and the bank account smaller. The owners of the Harlem Globetrotters ran things, briefly. In 1970–71 Finley arrived.

Through all of the ownership mess some good people were trying to run the team day to day. Frank Selke, Jr., was first president, then general manager. Bill Torrey, who would build the New York Islanders dynasty of the 1980s, was there. They helped put together a team that, after winning just fifteen games in a dismal first season, made the playoffs the next two. Then Finley, and the World Hockey Association, combined to wreck the franchise.

Charlie Finley owned the Oakland A's baseball team. He made his baseball players wear white shoes, but he had some great players to put them on, and the A's won the World Series in 1972, '73, and '74. When he became the owner of the hockey team in Oakland, Finley changed its name to the California Golden Seals, and put white skates on the players. But they didn't win the Stanley Cup.

Finley once attended a game in Montreal and sat with long-time Canadiens player and executive Ken Reardon. Finley told Reardon, "I'm a good baseball man, but I know fuck-all about hockey." He had that right.

Finley set himself up as a one-man executive branch of the Seals. The league didn't approve and told him he had to have others in place, like a vice-president, or a board of directors. Finley got his shoes shined by a little kid who had set up shop on the street in downtown Oakland. When the league got after him about his lack of executive help, Finley hired the shoe-shine kid and listed him as the Seals' vice-president.

The kid went on to fame and fortune as rap singer M.C. Hammer.

When the World Hockey Association arrived in 1972 to upset some hockey applecarts, quite a few players on the Seals were courted by the new league. They included good NHLers like Gerry Pinder and Paul Shmyr. It wouldn't have cost the wealthy Finley all that much to keep the players in Oakland. But Finley was stubborn and, like most of his fellow NHL owners, arrogantly thought the WHA would never play a game. It did, and Pinder and Shmyr were among those who jumped to the new league. In all, the Seals lost nine players because Finley wouldn't pay a total of about $45,000, which he could well afford, to keep them. The team never recovered.

Games at the Oakland Alameda County Coliseum were fun and I'll always have a soft spot for the place because it was where I started my play-by-play career. When I flew to Oakland for my first radio game the Canadiens were already there and riding a ten-game unbeaten streak. I nervously began calling the play-by-play with Red Fisher as my colour man. Bobby Rousseau's goal gave them an early 1–0 lead, and I said "He shoots, he scores!" for the first time in an NHL game. It looked like a piece of cake for the good guys. But with someone named Joe Szura outplaying Jean Béliveau, and someone named Howie "Minny" Menard skating rings around Yvan Cournoyer, the Seals came back to whip the mighty Habs 5–1.

It got worse, for me. After the game I took a seat on the bus for the ride to the airport with the team. Jean Béliveau got on, walked down the aisle, and told me, "You're sitting in my seat." Not exactly a great start for the new guy on the road. But somehow I survived, and was a regular passenger on the Montreal Canadiens' bus for the next twenty-nine years.

One night at the Oakland Alameda County Coliseum the Canadiens were bombarding Seals goaltender Gilles Meloche, who must have faced fifty shots, but didn't score on him until the third period when Yvan Cournoyer got a breakaway. The fans saluted Meloche with a long, emotional standing ovation. It was the only time I saw a home-team goalie cheered after he had just been scored on. The game ended 2–2. I was sorry Meloche didn't win.

I had a memorable, for me, intermission interview in Oakland with "Peanuts" creator Charles Schulz, who I discovered was a great hockey fan, and a very nice man. Mr. Schulz apologized for not bringing along my all-time favourite cartoon character, who is also the World's Greatest Hockey Player, but Snoopy had a game that night.

It was sometimes hard for the Seals' players to take things seriously. After scoring an early goal against the Rangers, in New York, they lost the game 11–1. The captain, Joey Johnston, called a players-only meeting after the game. His teammates thought Johnston was going to rip into them but, after a brief pause for effect, he said, "I called this meeting because I'm confused. Who was the asshole who scored that first goal to make them so mad at us?"

Charley Finley's reign of terror, and error, cost the Seals talent on the ice and in the front office. Bill Torrey and Frank Selke, Jr., left, and so did the team's director of public relations, Bob Bestor. He had joined the Seals after working for the controversial owner of the Oakland Raiders football team, Al Davis.

Bestor himself wrote the following release announcing he had quit the team and distributed it in the press box during a game:

Bob Bestor, Director of Public Relations for the Oakland Seals of the National Hockey League, has resigned his post to accept

a position with ADvan Inc., an outdoor advertising firm head-
quartered in Berkeley.

Bestor commented on his resignation: "I was so happy when
ADvan offered me the job I damn near cried. As soon as I met
that tyrant Finley I knew there was no way I could work for the
son of a bitch. I thought Al Davis was a bastard, but Charlie
Finley makes him look like Father Flanagan."

He continued, "If hockey in Oakland can possibly be any
more fucked up than it already is, Charley Finley is the guy to
do it."

Bestor ended his remarks with a well known quote from
Martin Luther King, one of Mr. Finley's American folk heroes:
"Free at last, free at last; thank God Almighty, free at last!!!"

Finley gave up on the Seals in February 1974, and the league
ran the operation for the rest of the season. A West Coast hotel
man, Mel Swig, bought the team hoping a new arena would be
built in San Francisco. When that didn't happen, Swig moved the
team to Ohio and the Seals became the Cleveland Barons.

They played their games in the Coliseum, a beautiful new
building located in the middle of nowhere, in the town of Richfield,
halfway between Cleveland and Akron. They thought they would
draw fans from both cities. But not only did nobody from
Cleveland and Akron show up, nobody from Richfield did either.

The Barons had a major cash-flow problem and there were times
when the players threatened not to play unless they were paid.
One such threat came before a Canadiens game there and I
remember calling the radio station in Montreal to alert them that
the game might not take place. But it did.

The closest call was when the Barons were scheduled to play
at home, against Buffalo, and the team was a month behind with
the paycheques. Gilles Meloche told me, "We had a meeting that

afternoon in a restaurant and, as far as we were concerned, we weren't going to play the game that night. So we sat around eating and having a few beers. All of a sudden the president of the NHL, John Ziegler, walked in, and Alan Eagleson was with him. They told us the league was taking over the team and would be paying the players. So we played that night, but the Sabres were obviously in better shape than we were. They beat us 9–0, right in our own building."

A Barons defenceman from Charlottetown, Bob Stewart, was the team's spokesman when the media wanted news of the situation, and he was great. Front-office types were usually in hiding. Stewart was always available and he was patient, knowledgeable, and always made a lot of sense even though the situation was both chaotic and troubling. His answers were a lot better than our questions. I don't know where Bob Stewart is now, but back then he earned a lot of respect.

After two years of finishing dead last, the Barons were merged with the Minnesota North Stars in 1978. The Seals and the Barons had played a total of eleven NHL seasons and had missed the playoffs nine times, the last eight in a row. No matter. With former Seals, like Meloche, moving to Cleveland, and then Minnesota, in the minds of their loyal fans the team with the white skates was still, somehow, a part of the NHL.

How loyal are those fans? Well, the Seals Booster Club still lives. When the team was in Oakland it had a thousand members. Today, a quarter of a century after the team's last game, sixty-five Seals Boosters still meet regularly to reminisce about their long-lost hockey heroes. If Tony Bennett left his heart in San Francisco, the Seals left theirs with a lot of fans across the bay, in Oakland.

■▮▮■

The Kansas City Scouts were another team that, like the Cleveland Barons, had a brief two-year run on the NHL stage. However, unlike the Barons, who are a mainly forgotten blip in the league's history, the Scouts still get some exposure. Every once in a while someone will mention, or write, that the New Jersey Devils began life as the Kansas City Scouts.

The Scouts won the grand total of twenty-seven games (out of 160) in their two years in Kansas City. In 1976 the franchise was transferred to Denver, and renamed the Colorado Rockies. They made the playoffs just once in six years in Denver.

The best remembered season for the Rockies was 1979–80 because Don Cherry was the coach. He still talks about it, although not as much as he talks about his previous team, the Boston Bruins. The Rockies are the team Grapes is talking about when he says you can't expect to soar like an eagle when you're stuck with a bunch of turkeys.

According to Don, the biggest turkeys he found in Denver were the general manager, Ray Miron, and a goaltender, Hardy Astrom. I don't know if either was as bad as Don claims, but I do know Astrom allowed one of the strangest goals I ever saw.

Montreal defenceman Brian Engblom shot the puck from the Rockies' blueline. Brian's shot, which didn't remind anyone of Bobby Hull's, hit a couple of legs and trickled along the ice towards the net. Astrom was down on all fours. When the puck got to his crease he slammed his big mitt on top of it and the play was over. At least that's what he thought, and how I called it on the radio. Suddenly the puck reappeared, sneaking out from between Astrom's legs like a little black mouse, and rolled slowly over the goal line. When the red light went on Astrom was still on all fours, glove firmly on the ice, waiting for the referee to blow his whistle. It was hilarious, although Donald S. Cherry didn't think so.

Today's NHL arenas have million-dollar scoreboards and ear-shattering sound systems that constantly pound noise into the heads of the paying customers to help them stay awake. The Colorado Rockies had a different, and cheaper, idea. They hired a guy they called Crazy George, who ran around the rink pounding a drum and screaming like someone who was, well, crazy. They claimed he was a schoolteacher, so I thought his act was just that, an act, and he must be a serious scholar who liked to have some fun at hockey games. I interviewed him between periods and discovered that he really was Crazy George. The guy made no sense at all.

During the 1981–82 season there were persistent reports that the Rockies were being sold and would move to New Jersey. Peter Gilbert, a television entrepreneur from Buffalo, was the principal owner and the villain of the piece in the eyes of whatever fans the team had in Denver.

Late in the season the Canadiens played there on a Saturday night designated "Save the Rockies Night." There was a rare sellout, and the crowd, worked up by a media blitz in the week leading up to the game, let loose on Mr. Gilbert. All night they chanted, "Gilbert Sucks! Gilbert Sucks!" I tried to have some fun on my broadcast with their vocal display of bad manners. I said Mr. Gilbert must be a smart dresser because the fans were chanting something about his socks. (It's okay. My listeners didn't laugh either.)

"Save the Rockies Night" didn't. The team became the New Jersey Devils the following year. Another five years went by before the Devils made the playoffs. Since then they've won the Stanley Cup twice. The NHL returned to Denver in 1995, when the Quebec Nordiques were moved there. The team won the Cup in its first year as the Colorado Avalanche. It won again in 2001 when the Avs met the Devils in the Stanley Cup finals.

The Dallas Stars, who were once the Minnesota North Stars, won the Stanley Cup in 1999. When they did, a few of us remembered when the North Stars merged with the Cleveland Barons, a team that once was the Oakland Seals. The Seals Booster Club knew all along it would happen, somehow.

My Favourite Decade

· ·

People frequently ask me about my personal bests. Who's the best player I ever saw? What's the best team I ever saw? Or the best game, playoff, goalie, coach, and so on. But nobody has asked me what was my favourite decade? The answer is easy. It was the 1970s.

In the '70s I helped broadcast every Stanley Cup–winning game, saw Bobby Orr fly through the air after scoring his most famous goal, watched Jean Béliveau carry the Cup off the ice after his last game, and witnessed hockey take a turbulent turn when a team from Broad Street in Philadelphia bullied its way to a couple of championships. Best of all, in the last four years of the decade I saw almost every game played by the team that is my pick as the best. And it all began with something that hadn't happened in twenty-four years: the Montreal Canadiens missed the playoffs.

In 1946–47 the defending-champion Canadiens had a bad season. The fans in Montreal were outraged. My father was the

coach, and you might say he was getting a lot of heat. One
furious fan called the newspapers and said he would burn down
the Forum if Irvin was behind the bench at the next home game.
The Canadiens were in Toronto when the story broke. When
they skated onto the ice at Maple Leaf Gardens the players all
were wearing bright red hats like firefighters wear. (It was the
idea of goaltender Bill Durnan.)

The defending champions from Montreal didn't exactly have
a bad year in 1969–70, but it wasn't good enough. Only seven
points separated first and fifth in the Eastern Division. With a
week to go there was still a chance the Canadiens could finish
first. But they wound up fifth with 92 points, the most ever by a
team that didn't make the playoffs.

The Canadiens' season ended on a bizarre note. When the
Detroit Red Wings defeated the New York Rangers 6–2
in Detroit on the Saturday of the final weekend, they clinched a
playoff spot. The same teams played the next afternoon in New
York. The Rangers were in fifth place, two points behind the
Canadiens, who were to play that night in Chicago The game in
New York was televised nationally in the U.S., so the Montreal
players were able to watch it, and cheer for Detroit. But instead
of a hockey game, they saw a horror show.

The Canadiens sensed they were in trouble when they learned
that the Red Wings had left some regulars at home, to rest for
the playoffs. Then, in an intermission interview, Garry Unger
of the Wings laughingly talked about the big party he and his
teammates had the night before to celebrate making the playoffs.
By this time the Red Wings were down by three or four goals
and the Canadiens watching their TV sets were in shock. The
Wings obviously couldn't have cared less about the final score,
which was 9–5 for the Rangers. The Rangers racked up the

highest shots-on-goal total in the history of their franchise while the Red Wings barely broke a sweat.

The result left New York tied with Montreal for fourth place. The Canadiens would make the playoffs ahead of the Rangers by beating or tying the Blackhawks, or by scoring five goals. Total goals scored was used as the tie-breaker and the Rangers' nine against Detroit, which equalled the high for one game in the league that season, put them in the driver's seat.

The Canadiens were in a tough spot. Chicago needed a win to clinch first place, and had the best defensive record in the league. That was the season Tony Esposito, then a rookie, chalked up fifteen shutouts.

The Blackhawks scored two quick goals in the third period to take a 5–2 lead. Their fifth goal came with nine minutes and sixteen seconds left in the game. The Canadiens knew they wouldn't win or tie the game, But three goals would put them in the playoffs. Claude Ruel pulled goalie Rogie Vachon and the farce began. The Montreal net remained empty for the rest of the game, and the Blackhawks put the puck into it five times. The Canadiens couldn't score even one on Tony O. The 10–2 final meant the Hawks were first and the Habs were out.

I was at home listening to Danny Gallivan describe the game on CBC Radio, and he made no effort to hide his disgust, both at the fiasco in New York and the empty net in Chicago. Danny signed off the broadcast by saying, "This has been a bad day for hockey, and a black day for Canada." I wasn't sure about the last part, so I asked him about it. He said it because, with the Canadiens fifth and the Maple Leafs last, the Stanley Cup playoffs would begin without a team from Canada. That had never happened before and it hasn't happened since. A staunch Canadian, Danny took it personally.

Despite the absence of a Canadian team, *Hockey Night in Canada* still had playoffs to cover. Danny and I did most of the games in Boston. One left us with a sad memory.

The Bruins played the Rangers in the first round. Ed Giacomin was the Rangers' goalie and his back-up was Terry Sawchuk, then in the twilight of his great career. The series was tied after four games. The Rangers were ahead 2–1 in the third period of the fifth game when Boston scored two quick goals. Time-outs were not allowed then, so coaches would stall by changing goaltenders, and that's what New York coach Emile Francis did after the Boston outburst. Giacomin came out and Sawchuk went in.

The broadcast location in the Boston Garden was the closest to the ice of any rink in the league. We were seated directly above the New York bench and I can still see Sawchuk heading out the gate and taking his position in the crease. He entered the game at 7:59 of the third period. Giacomin went back after the next whistle, seventeen seconds later, at 8:16. Terry Sawchuk had played more games than any goaltender in NHL history. That would be his last.

Boston won the game 3–2. Two nights later in New York, with Giacomin playing the whole game, the Bruins eliminated the Rangers. A month later, Sawchuk and teammate Ron Stewart had a fight as a result of which Sawchuk sustained serious internal injuries. Three weeks later, on May 31, 1970, the man who was perhaps hockey's greatest goaltender died in a New York hospital.

Sawchuk was estranged from his family and in effect died alone. Emile Francis, who had been his only visitor in the hospital, was called to identify the body in a New York morgue.

Emile Francis:

"When I got there a man took me down a couple of flights of stairs and he opened the door and there were about thirty bodies lying there. The thing that hit me was that they were in bags just like the bags we use to carry hockey sticks in. And there he was, his head out of one end of a bag with a tag around his neck. They had "Terry Sawchuk" written on the tag. I thought to myself standing there in the morgue about what an awful way it was for him to finish up. He was only forty years old."

∎∎∎∎

The 1970 playoffs ended on an overtime goal by Bobby Orr. It wasn't the greatest goal ever scored and it didn't end the greatest series ever played. But it resulted in what surely was the most famous photo taken of a Stanley Cup–winner.

For the third straight year Scotty Bowman's St. Louis Blues represented the West against the East. In the previous two years against Montreal the games had been relatively close. But against Boston in 1970, the Blues lost the first three 6–1, 6–2, and 4–1. Only the fourth game was competitive, going into overtime on a Sunday afternoon at the Boston Garden.

Bobby Orr's domination of the game in 1969–70 was incredible. He won the Hart, Norris, and Smythe trophies, and it gets better than that. Orr became the first defenceman to win the Art Ross Trophy as the NHL's scoring champion. He amassed a total of 120 points, twenty-one more than runner-up Phil Esposito. The word "impossible" springs to mind, but it happened.

The Bruins' two losses to the Rangers were their only defeats in the playoffs. They swept Chicago in four, and did likewise to the Blues. Orr's Cup-winner was a basic bang-bang play at the goal crease on a pass from Derek Sanderson. Orr no doubt leaped, but he was given a further boost by St. Louis defenceman Noel Picard's stick. Bobby was about two feet off the ice and completely horizontal when the camera clicked. It was a magic moment, forever frozen in time by a photo, copies of which Bobby has autographed thousands of times.

Danny and Dick broadcast Orr's magic moment on *Hockey Night in Canada*. For the next several years, whenever HNIC replayed the goal, the play-by-play voice was Dan Kelly's, who called the game on CBS. I finally asked somebody from the CBC why we were using Kelly's call, not Gallivan's. He told me the tape of the game had been erased, along with several others because – are you ready for this? – the CBC was short of shelf space, so a bunch of old tapes were cleared out.

Glenn Hall, the Blues' goalie that day, is asked about it often. No doubt he's as tired of hearing about the Orr goal as Gerry McNeil is of hearing about the goal Bill Barilko scored on him in 1951. Whenever Glenn meets up with Bobby he asks him, "Is that the only goal you ever scored?"

███

Back to questions about my personal bests. When it comes to best player, I hedge and say Maurice Richard was the most exciting player I ever saw, and Guy Lafleur was the most exciting I ever described as a broadcaster. I don't have a favourite game because I've seen so many great ones, but I do have a favourite year. It's 1971, or at least that part of it ending with the Stanley Cup being won by the Montreal Canadiens.

The Habs got off to a shaky start in 1970–71 and in December replaced Claude Ruel with Al MacNeil, who had been a co-coach with the Montreal Voyageurs, the Canadiens' farm team in the

American League. MacNeil would be the last unilingual anglophone to coach the team.

So much happened in the last half of that season that a brief chronological summary may best convey how 1971 became my favourite year.

January 13: The Canadiens trade Mickey Redmond, Guy Charron, and Bill Collins to the Detroit Red Wings for Frank Mahovlich. It is the best deal ever made by general manager "Trader Sam" Pollock. Mahovlich plays the next night in Minnesota and scores a goal. Because the team did not have a number 27 sweater on the road trip, the Big M wears number 10. He will be the last player to wear that number before Guy Lafleur.

February 11: Jean Béliveau scores a hat trick against the Minnesota North Stars. The third goal is the five hundredth of his career. The non-televised game was broadcast on CFCF Radio and Dick Irvin called the play. As Béliveau neared the Minnesota net, Irvin yelled, "Here it is, five hundred!" For a change, his prediction is right. It is one of the biggest thrills in Irvin's long career in the broadcast booth.

March 14: Unknown goaltender Ken Dryden, who has been playing for the Voyageurs while studying law at McGill University, is called up and plays his first NHL game, in Pittsburgh. Montreal wins 5–1. Dryden plays five more games in the regular season, and twenty in the playoffs.

April 4: The regular season ends when Boston defeats Montreal 7–2. Phil Esposito scores three goals to reach the unbelievable total of seventy-six. Boston finishes first with a record 121 points, eleven more than second-place New York and twenty-four more than Montreal, whom they will meet in the first playoff round. Esposito wins the scoring championship with 152 points. Teammates Bobby Orr, Johnny Bucyk, and Ken Hodge follow with 139, 116, and 105 points. Cars in Boston have bumper stickers reading, "Jesus saves, but Esposito scores on the rebound." Jean Béliveau tops the Canadiens with 76 points.

April 7: The Bruins open their defence of the Stanley Cup against Montreal in Boston. The Canadiens make it close, but lose 3–1. After the game the Dick half of the Danny and Dick show is in the Boston dressing room doing radio interviews and overhears Bruins president Weston Adams, Jr., say, "The frogs gave it a shot, but that's as close as they'll get." Afraid of provoking an uproar in the Montreal French-langauge media, Dick is too chicken to report what Adams said, until now.

April 8: Boston leads the second game 5–1 late in the second period. Henri Richard scores for Montreal before the period ends. Then, led by Jean Béliveau, the Canadiens score five unanswered goals in the third period to win 7–5. It becomes one of the best remembered games in the history of the Montreal franchise.

April 15: Montreal wins the sixth game 8–3 to even the series. When it is announced that Ken Dryden, who by now is much better known, gets an assist on a late goal, the crowd at the Forum gives him a prolonged standing ovation.

April 18: Dryden continues his spectacular play in the seventh game and Montreal stuns Boston with a 4–2 victory. Several years later Bobby Orr admits to me that the Bruins took the Canadiens too lightly. Johnny Bucyk says, "Dryden beat us."

April 22: Minnesota North Stars defeat the Canadiens 6–3 at the Montreal Forum to even the playoff series at one win apiece. Canadiens firebrand John Ferguson, upset at Al MacNeil for not playing him in the third period, storms off the players' bench in the final seconds of the game and smashes his stick, and his fist, against a wall.

April 29: The Canadiens eliminate the North Stars in six games with 3–2 win, in Minnesota. The game ends strangely when Minnesota scores what would have been the tying goal just as the third period ends. The referee rules that time has expired. Half the Minnesota team is arguing with the referee and the goal judge, while the other half is at centre ice shaking hands with the Canadiens.

May 4: The Stanley Cup finals begin, in Chicago. The Blackhawks defeat the Canadiens 2–1 when Jim Pappin scores in the second overtime period.

May 13: The Blackhawks take a 3–2 series lead as Tony Esposito shuts out the Canadiens 3–0. After the game another Montreal veteran upset about lack of ice time, Henri Richard, says Al MacNeil is the worst coach he has ever played for. Richard's comments are immediately turned into an all-out language war in the French media. The Canadiens' coach receives death threats.

May 16: Bodyguards stand beside Al MacNeil during the sixth game of series, at the Forum. The Canadiens win 4–3. The home team has won every game, and the series goes back to Chicago for the seventh game.

May 18: On the day of the seventh game John Robertson writes in the *Montreal Star* that Jean Béliveau will be playing his last game that night. Montreal wins the Stanley Cup by defeating the Blackhawks 3–2. Chicago led 2–1 when Henri Richard scored the tying goal in the second period. Richard then scored the winning goal in the third period. When it was over, Frank Mahovlich had set a playoff record with fourteen goals, Ken Dryden was named winner of the Smythe Trophy as playoff MVP, and Jean Béliveau carried the Stanley Cup off the ice in his last act as captain of the Montreal Canadiens.

When the game ended I was sent downstairs to interview the Stanley Cup champions, the first time I was given that assignment by HNIC. There were many more to come.

On June 9, Jean Béliveau confirmed that he had played his last game, and retired. The next day the Canadiens, holding the first pick in the NHL draft, selected Guy Lafleur. Montreal had the first pick because of a deal Sam Pollock had made with a team he was sure was going to finish in last place in 1970–71, and it did. The team? The Oakland Seals.

The Flyers, the Flower, and Scotty

·····························

T he Montreal Canadiens were the Stanley Cup champions in 1971, but the Boston Bruins still had to be considered the number-one team. It's not easy for me to admit that. Red Fisher and I have argued about it for years. Red says Montreal's defeat of Boston was a massive upset, while I say it wasn't so big. More Montreal players than Boston players from that series are in the Hockey Hall of Fame. Despite finishing twenty-four points behind Boston in the regular season the Canadiens weren't exactly chopped liver. Nevertheless, Boston was the team to beat, and not too many teams beat them the following season.

The Bruins were the weak sisters of the NHL through most of the 1960s. Starting in '59–60 they missed the playoffs eight straight years, finishing in last place six times. In the two seasons starting in 1961 Boston won only twenty-nine of their 140 games.

Phil Watson coached the Bruins during their darkest days in the early '60s. Watson was a fiery guy who played for the Rangers and the Canadiens, coached in New York, and wasn't a stranger to the high life.

Watson's Bruins played a game in Montreal on a Thursday, and lost 10–1. They were scheduled for a day off on Friday before taking an afternoon train to Toronto for a game Saturday night. After the 10–1 shellacking, Watson ordered his players to show up at the Forum for a practice at 8:00 the next morning, which they did. The only person missing was Watson. The Bruins didn't see him again until Saturday when he walked into their dressing room, five minutes before game time.

As the '60s progressed they began talking about a saviour for the Boston Bruins, a kid from Parry Sound, Ontario: Bobby Orr. The Bruins first scouted him when he played peewee hockey. When he was fourteen, they signed him to a standard junior amateur contract and he began playing for the Oshawa Generals. The Montreal Junior Canadiens were in the same league and I watched Bobby play against them at the Forum. He would be on the ice for almost the entire game. When he felt extra-tired he'd trip somebody, get a penalty, and a two-minute rest. He was eighteen when he signed his first contract with Boston, reported to be worth $60,000, plus bonuses, over two years. What would he get today? The mind boggles.

In his first season in Boston, Orr won the Calder Trophy as the top rookie. The Rangers' Harry Howell won the Norris Trophy as the best defenceman. When he accepted the trophy, Howell said, "I'm glad I won it this year, because from now on that kid in Boston is going win it for a long time to come." Harry was right. Orr won it in each of the next eight years.

In '71–72 Boston finished first again. Esposito and Orr were one-two in the scoring again, and this time Boston won the

Stanley Cup, defeating the Rangers in a six-game final. The last game was played in New York and I did the broadcast along with Bill Hewitt. Orr scored the winning goal.

Players often talk about players, not teams, when assessing why they lost in the playoffs. Ask Jean Béliveau about Toronto's win over Montreal in 1967 and he'll answer, "Sawchuk beat us." Gump Worsley says the same thing.

In 1971, Boston captain Johnny Bucyk blamed Ken Dryden. When I asked him about the 1972 finals, New York goalie Ed Giacomin said, "The Bruins didn't beat us. Bobby Orr did."

It has always bugged me that Orr was so good in the 1972 playoffs yet, because of his bad knee, the best player in the world couldn't play for Team Canada in the famous series against the Russians a few months later. Had Orr played, Paul Henderson wouldn't have become a legend because Canada wouldn't have needed his historic series-winning goal with thirty-four seconds left in the last period of the last game. If Bobby Orr had played, Canada would have wrapped it up long before then.

▮▮▮▮

During the 1971 Stanley Cup finals *Hockey Night in Canada* invited the coach and general manager of the St. Louis Blues, Scotty Bowman, to be the analyst for a game in Montreal. We were making small talk on our way up to the booth when Scotty suddenly said, "I'm finished in St. Louis."

I said, "Are you serious?"

"Yep," he replied. "I'm finished, and that's it."

For me, the Scotty Bowman era in Montreal started then and there. A couple of weeks later the Blues made it official that Scotty would no longer coach in St. Louis. Sam Pollock wasted no time. A couple of weeks later, Bowman was the coach of the Canadiens.

Bowman was a native Montrealer who could speak passable French. His signing wasn't really fair to Al MacNeil, who had persevered through so much turmoil and adversity to coach the 1971 Stanley Cup winner. But Pollock knew, and so did MacNeil, that there was no way the Montreal Canadiens could ever again have a unilingual English coach.

MacNeil, a good guy and a faithful employee, went back to coach the American League Voyageurs, now relocated to Halifax. He would coach again in the NHL with the Flames, in both Atlanta and Calgary. Tommy Gorman, Mike Keenan, and even Scotty Bowman are examples of coaches who were fired or moved to another team after winning the Stanley Cup, but Al MacNeil is the only Cup-winning coach to start the next season in the minor leagues.

■▓■

Scotty Bowman's career in Montreal got off to a decent start, but the Canadiens were just one of three strong teams in the Eastern Conference. The loss of Jean Béliveau was felt, and the media hype around the "next Béliveau," Guy Lafleur, was somewhat distracting. Lafleur scored twenty-nine goals, the most he would get in his first three seasons. The Canadiens finished with 108 points, good enough only for third place behind Boston and New York, and lost to the Rangers in six games in the first round of the playoffs.

About halfway through the season I asked Frank Mahovlich, "How's the new coach doing?" The Big M replied, "Struggling." Frank never used two words when one was enough. I guess that's why he's in the Senate today, and not the House of Commons.

Montreal didn't struggle much in the 1972–73 season. When Scotty Bowman's coaching career in Montreal is assessed, the emphasis is always on his teams that won four straight Stanley

Cups in the late 1970s. The '72–73 team is often overlooked. Montreal had fifty-two wins, one more than Boston, but finished thirteen points ahead of the defending champs because they tied sixteen games while the Bruins tied five. Montreal's total of only ten losses in the seventy-eight-game season was the lowest since the league went to a sixty-game schedule in 1946–47.

In early January the Canadiens called up a tall, gangling young defenceman from Halifax. He played his first NHL game at the Forum, against Minnesota, and made his first NHL road trip the next day. I was sitting across from him on the plane. The big kid from the Ottawa Valley couldn't keep still, couldn't keep a smile off his face. He was in seventh heaven. Seeing the pure joy he was experiencing I was pulling for him to make the team. He did. The kid was Larry Robinson.

In the series against Philadelphia, Robinson scored his first playoff goal. It came at the Forum, in overtime in the second game, a screened shot from the point. He didn't see the puck go in the net but he saw the red light go on. I have seen some excited players after they scored in overtime and Larry's reaction to that goal is right up there with the best. He went nuts. It was a big goal because the Flyers had surprised the Canadiens with an overtime win in the series opener. The Canadiens won the next three, and then defeated Chicago in six games in the finals.

The final series matched goaltenders Ken Dryden and Tony Esposito, who had shared the duties with Team Canada against the Russians the previous September. They were the two best goaltenders in hockey, yet the most talked-about game in the series ended with a final score of 8–7. It was the fifth game, at the Forum, and with a win the Canadiens would take the Cup. The team's management was so confident of a victory it booked a room at the Queen Elizabeth Hotel for a post-game party. Instead of partying, however, they scrambled to book plane reservations back to Chicago, where they did win the Cup two nights later. The score in that game was 6–4. In the last two games of a very long hockey year that began with them playing in the Summit Series, the two best goaltenders in the game gave up twenty five-goals.

When it finally was over Scotty Bowman had his first Stanley Cup and Henri Richard his eleventh, more than any player ever had or ever will have. And it was number eleven of *my* twenty-six.

■ ■ ■ ■

It's a bit strange for a hockey pacifist, as Don Cherry calls me, to rate the '70s as my favourite decade. People today who complain hockey is too violent should take a look at some videos from the 1970s. A lot of the violence today is in the form of cheap shots. In the '70s, especially in the middle of the decade, it was for real. Helping make it that way were the World Hockey Association and the Philadelphia Flyers.

The NHL didn't believe a rival league would become a reality. Larry Pleau was a player from the Boston area who went to Montreal, where he played junior hockey and then played for the Canadiens. In 1972, when the WHA was starting up, Pleau was offered a contract by the New England Whalers, advised the Canadiens, and was told by Sam Pollock, "They'll never play a game." The next day Larry Pleau became the first player announced as signed by the new league and he played for New England all seven years the WHA lasted.

The NHL's cavalier attitude helped the WHA start up and cost them several players, including one superstar, Bobby Hull. But classy players like Hull and Pleau were the exception rather than the rule. It was said that while 3 or 4 per cent of players on NHL teams were goons, in the WHA it was more like 90 per cent. My former broadcast partner John Garrett was a goaltender for the Birmingham Bulls. Among his teammates were legendary tough guys Steve Durbano, Gilles "Bad News" Bilodeau, and Dave "Killer" Hanson. One of John's favourite WHA stories is about a game his team played in Cincinnati.

"It was Thanksgiving eve. To give you an idea of our game plan, I didn't start because our other goalie was Wayne Wood, who was 6'2" and weighed over two hundred pounds. Our coach, Glen Sonmor, said Wood would start because he was sure there was going to be a brawl. Just before the game a minister came on the ice and offered a prayer for Thanksgiving and thanked the Lord for the fine group of sportsmen who would be playing that night. He called for a display of true friendship and sportsmanship. About twenty seconds after the minister gives his prayer they drop the puck, and another ten seconds later Robbie Ftorek clobbers Durbano and the gloves are off. Everybody on the ice got into the fight and they were all thrown out of the game."

Meanwhile, back in the NHL, the Philadelphia Flyers were slowly building the toughest, and best, team in the league, one that would soon be known as the Broad Street Bullies. But there were setbacks along the way, and one of them resulted in a very funny radio broadcast. Well, funny if you weren't a Flyers fan.

I could pick up the station carrying the Flyers' games through a bit of static and I listened to their last game of the '71–72 season. Philadelphia was playing Buffalo and needed a tie to clinch the final playoff spot in the east. With a couple of minutes to play the game was tied, nothing much was happening, and the Flyers seemed in control.

The Flyers' announcer, the late Gene Hart, began a countdown. "The Flyers are two minutes away from the playoffs," said Hart. A bit more play-by-play, then, "The Flyers are ninety seconds away from the playoffs."

Hart's countdown had reached "The Flyers are ten seconds away from the playoffs" when Buffalo's Gerry Meehan lofted a fairly long shot towards Philadelphia goalie Doug Favell that somehow ended up in the Flyers' net.

Hart said, "Shot, score, Gerry Meehan. 3–2 Buffalo with four seconds left. The Flyers are out of the playoffs for the second time in three years." Hart's voice had cracked when he said "score." He turned away from the microphone and, while I didn't pick it up through the static, people who got a clearer signal said you could faintly hear Hart mutter, "Son of a bitch."

■▮▮■

Two years later, the Flyers didn't need a tie in the last game of the season to make the playoffs. They were first in the West, first in penalty minutes, a guaranteed sellout everywhere they played, and Stanley Cup champions. Philadelphia won the Cup again in 1975, after a season in which the toughest of their tough guys, Dave "The Hammer" Schultz, spent 472 minutes in the penalty box, still a record. (By comparison, the penalty leader in the 1999–2000 season was Tyler Nash, of the St. Louis Blues, with 150 minutes. In 2000–01 it was Matthew Barnaby with 265.)

At a time when bench-clearing brawls were still allowed, the Flyers raised thuggery to new levels. Police got into their act after brawls in Toronto and Vancouver. Andy van Hellemond, perhaps the best referee ever, said, "If you got out of one of their games with maybe eight majors – that's four fights, a major for slashing, a major for high sticking, maybe a head-butting and a gross misconduct, plus a bunch of minor penalties, that would be a normal night's work. They would go after teams and intimidate the daylights out of them and everybody accepted it as part of the game."

The intimidation factor was there, all right. There was a virus going around the league in those days called the "Philadelphia flu" that once in a while kept a player or two from suiting up against the Flyers, especially in Philadelphia. It was in the form of a groin pull, or sore shoulder, or a chill that struck its victims without any warning, except from the schedule that said their team was playing the Philadelphia Flyers.

∎∎∎∎

The best example I saw of the Bullies at work was on a Sunday afternoon at the Forum. It was a rough game with a lot of what Danny Gallivan called "milling about" after almost every whistle. Dave Schultz and Montreal defenceman John Van Boxmeer tangled and the gloves were dropped. Van Boxmeer didn't have nearly as much practice dropping gloves as his opponent and Schultz knocked him out with one punch. That was the signal for the benches to empty and, for the Flyers, it was business as usual.

When the fight broke out, Larry Robinson was in the Montreal dressing room having some equipment repaired. When one of the trainers burst in to tell him what was going on, Robinson charged out onto the ice, his skate laces still undone, and headed straight for Schultz. Dave Schultz didn't lose many fights but Larry laid it on him pretty good that day.

Referee Art Skov once called a delayed penalty on Schultz. When the play stopped, Skov looked for the Hammer but couldn't find him on the ice. What happened was, when he saw the referee's arm go up, Schultz skated straight to the penalty box while the play was still going on. That's where Skov found him, sitting there already serving his sentence, like a good little boy. They tell me that was one of the few times Dave Schultz laughed when he was in his office, a.k.a. the penalty box.

The Flyers had a great mix of talent during their Cup-winning years. They had skilled players like Reg Leach, Rick MacLeish, and Tom Bladon, skilled and tough players like Bobby Clarke, Bill Barber, and Gary Dornhoefer, and the steady, solid types like the Watson brothers, Joe and Jim, and Ross Lonsberry. And of course the tough guys including the Hammer, Don "Big Bird" Saleski, Andre "Moose" Dupont, and Bob "Hound" Kelly, who would lead the team into Dodge with guns blazing.

They made a perfect line-up for the time, yet the Flyers wouldn't have won Stanley Cups without goaltender Bernie Parent. I covered a lot of Philadelphia playoff games in 1974 and '75, and I had never seen a goaltender play as well as Parent did in those years.

On the Sunday afternoon in Philly when the Flyers beat the Bruins 1–0 for their first Cup, I did the HNIC broadcast with Bill Hewitt. Late in the game Bobby Orr hauled down Bobby Clarke and was penalized by referee Art Skov. Orr went ballistic and his teammates had to restrain him from attacking the referee. The memory of Maurice Richard in Boston in 1955 flashed through my mind, and I was glad for Orr's sake, and hockey's, that cooler heads prevailed.

When the game was over, the outpouring of emotion in the Spectrum was as overwhelming as that experienced when Orr scored the Cup-winner in the Boston Garden four years earlier.

I was in Buffalo when the Flyers won again in '75, with Parent shutting out the Sabres 2–0. In the final minutes the fans in Buffalo started chanting, "Bernie! Bernie!" the way they did in Philadelphia. It was quite a tribute to Parent who, again, had been magnificent in the playoffs.

During that time somebody in the Flyers' front office got the bright idea of using Kate Smith's recorded version of "God Bless

America" once in a while instead of the American national anthem, "The Star-Spangled Banner," at the beginning of games at the Spectrum. Kate Smith was an American music legend who had been out of the limelight for years. But her rendition of Irving Berlin's "God Bless America" had become a classic.

The Flyers seemed to win every time they used Kate Smith's recorded voice, so they brought her in a few times to sing it in person. I was there for one of her live appearances and she was marvellous. If Kate didn't send shivers up and down your spine, there was something wrong with you.

The third game of the 1975 finals was played on a hot, humid night in Buffalo. The Memorial Auditorium became full of fog and the game was held up several times. During one of the fog breaks a bat arrived on the scene, swooped down low over the ice, and had the rough, tough hockey players ducking for cover. Jim Lorentz, a Buffalo forward, took a swipe at the bat with his stick, made contact, and killed it. It wasn't exactly Lee Harvey Oswald and Jack Ruby, but *Hockey Night in Canada* received a barrage of complaints from animal lovers. Lorentz quickly acquired the nickname "Batman."

The fans in Buffalo used to come up with some great signs. When the fourth game was played two nights later there was a big one hanging from the upper deck that read, "THE FLYERS HAVE KATE SMITH, AND WE HAVE AN OLD BAT TOO."

∎▌▐∎

In the next four years the Stanley Cup was won by the Montreal Canadiens, and in the years since I have conducted many interviews with the members of those teams for books, television shows, and radio programs. They talk about the second, third, and fourth ones if you ask them, but they talk about the first one even if you don't. The first was in 1976, the year the white hats swept the black hats four straight to prove the Stanley Cup could still be won by skill, not goonery. It's pretty well been that way ever since. To hear the Canadiens tell it, they began taking the Stanley Cup away from the Flyers the previous September, during an exhibition game at the Philadelphia Spectrum when they changed their usual style of play, for one occasion only.

Scotty Bowman's Canadiens had matured into a very talented team. Young players like Doug Risebrough, Steve Shutt, Bob Gainey, and Doug Jarvis were ready to win, as hockey people say. But were they tough enough to beat Philly? Scotty decided to answer that question even before the season began.

The teams had scheduled back-to-back exhibition games, with the first at the Spectrum. Bowman identified every tough guy in the Canadiens' training camp and included them on the team that went to Philadelphia. Steve Shutt described the game:

"We started to get the upper hand on them when we had a big brawl in the exhibition game in Philly. Doug Risebrough started it when he and Bobby Clarke had a bit of a tussle. Clarke said, 'Wait till I get you back in Montreal.' Dougie said, 'Why wait till then?' and he smacked him and cut him for about ten stitches. Then it started. We had a lot of tough guys from our farm team in that game, like Glenn Goldup and Sean Shanahan. And we had Rick Chartraw and Pierre Bouchard. Our tough guys took on all of their tough guys and just pummelled them. I would say that was about the last fight we had in games with the Flyers for about four years."

Another Canadiens star, Jacques Lemaire, said the brawl with the Flyers was a major turning point. "It's tough to play against a team that tries to intimidate you," Lemaire said, "but they didn't beat up on us that night. We knew we could do it against them, and we did. I don't think we lost to them in the next four years."

■I■I■

It may have been necessary to establish that kind of turf against the defending champions, but another game played a big part in the making of Scotty's dynasty in Montreal. It was the first game of the previous season, and it was all about Guy Lafleur.

I have mentioned Lafleur's rather disappointing NHL debut. His goal totals in his first three years were 29, 28, and 21. In his third season Lafleur was a non-factor, so much so that Sam Pollock seriously thought of trading him. Bowman and Claude Ruel, then Scotty's assistant, talked him out of it. Sam signed Lafleur to a new contract, no doubt feeling that this time the kid has to produce, or else.

The Canadiens opened the 1974–75 season at home against the New York Islanders, and when the game began there was one noticeable change in the look of the team: Guy Lafleur was playing without a helmet for the first time in his life. Not only that, he was playing in a style that prompted the question, "Who's that wearing number 10?" Lafleur was flying, starting with his first shift, and he continued flying for the next six years. He went from 21 goals and 56 points in his third season to 53 goals and 119 points in his fourth. I'm sure Don Cherry feels Lafleur's discarding the helmet had something to do with it. Whatever, the era of the Flower was underway at the Montreal Forum.

Guy Lafleur's breakthrough season would be Henri Richard's last. Richard fractured a leg early in the season, returned for the playoffs, where the Canadiens lost to Buffalo in the semifinals, then retired. He still had a year left on his contract, but his relationship with Bowman wasn't the best, he had played a team-record 1,436 league and playoff games, and the young guard was taking over. It always seemed to be like that with the Canadiens. A star would leave just when another was ready to take his place.

I have plenty of memories of Henri Richard, both on and off the ice. Here's just one. During the last few years he played I was a regular on the Canadiens' charter flights. At one time Bowman ruled that each player could have one beer on the plane after a game. Henri found out I didn't drink, which was good news to him. From then on I would ask for a beer, leave it on the edge of the tray, and the Pocket Rocket would casually walk down the aisle and grab it without breaking stride.

■ ■ ■ ■

My mother might not have agreed, but perhaps the best way to sum up the Canadiens' four-straight Stanley Cup dynasty of the late 1970s is with some statistics. In the three seasons starting with 1975–76 the Canadiens lost 11, 8, and 10 games. That was 29 defeats in 240 games. Add the playoffs and you have 213 wins, 34 ties, and 34 losses in 281 games. In the fourth season, 1979–80, they lost 17 games, and the spoiled fans in Montreal were asking, "What's wrong with the Canadiens?" They recovered to win their fourth straight Stanley Cup.

The goaltender, Ken Dryden, and Big Three on defence, Serge Savard, Guy Lapointe, and Larry Robinson, have all been elected to the Hockey Hall of Fame. So have forwards Jacques Lemaire, Guy Lafleur, Steve Shutt, Bob Gainey, and Yvan Cournoyer. The coach, Scotty Bowman, is in the Hall and so is Sam Pollock, the general manager in three of the four seasons of the dynasty.

It's interesting to see how many from the four Stanley Cup rosters stayed in hockey after their playing careers ended. As I write this, halfway through the 2000–01 season, ten are employed by NHL teams as either a scout, assistant coach, head coach, general manager, or team president. Jacques Lemaire and Larry Robinson have coached Stanley Cup–winning teams in New Jersey. Bob Gainey was general manager of the Dallas Stars when they won.

Steve Shutt and Yvan Cournoyer were assistant coaches with the Canadiens, and Serge Savard and Réjean Houle were general managers in Montreal. Pierre Bouchard and Murray Wilson work on broadcasts of Canadiens games, while Brian Engblom is an analyst and interviewer on ESPN hockey telecasts in the United States.

Guy Lafleur has never coached, and likely never will. Like Bobby Orr, who worked briefly as an assistant in Chicago, Lafleur would be asking too much of players who lack his talent and, especially, his intensity. Like Maurice Richard, Lafleur played on instinct, reacting to the moment. Scotty Bowman gave up trying to practise planned power plays because, as Larry Robinson put it, "The Flower would screw everything up." So Scotty just put him on the ice and let him do his thing.

Also like the Rocket, Guy Lafleur does not have a photographic memory of games and goals. When Don Cherry had his television show, *Grapevine*, he would tape two or three episodes on the same day at one of the bars bearing his name. I was a guest when Don also taped shows with Lafleur and with Don's boyhood hockey hero, Ken Reardon.

During Lafleur's taping I was sitting with Don's wife, the late Rose Cherry, and their daughter, Cindy. Don was rolling along in his usual style, talking with Guy about the two Cup finals his Bruins played against Montreal in 1977 and '78. "Okay, Guy,"

Grapes said, "let's take a look at the replay of the overtime goal you scored on Cheevers that really killed us."

I remembered it well. Lafleur fired the puck from the right wing and it went just inside the post, whereupon Gerry Cheevers bolted out of his crease and off the ice without even looking back into the net. But when Don went to the tape I cringed, fearing Guy would have no recollection of the play. He didn't. Like me, Don doesn't like to rehearse, but had I known about that replay I would have strongly suggested to him that Guy see it before the show began.

During the five or six years he was the best player in the world, Guy had a passion for the game. He never let up. Whether the Canadiens were playing their toughest opponents like the Bruins or the Flyers, or weak teams like Cleveland or Kansas City, Guy Lafleur played the same way every night, home and away, game after game after game. It was amazing.

However, fame does have its hazards. After a reception in Los Angeles in the late 1970s, Red Fisher and Guy Lafleur caught a ride with me back to our hotel. When we got in the car, Red said, "Guy, tell Dick what happened the other night in Vancouver." After their game against the Canucks, several of the Canadiens had dropped in at a night club. Guy picked up the story.

"This girl came up to me and said I was her favourite hockey player, that I was the best player she ever saw, and stuff like that. I signed an autograph for her. Then she asked me if I wanted to dance. I said I wasn't interested. She kept asking me and I kept saying I just wanted to have a little relax. Finally she said, 'You're sure you don't want to dance?' I told her I was sure, and she said, 'Well then, go fuck yourself!'"

Guy Lafleur is still involved with the Montreal Canadiens, working, along with Henri Richard, Yvan Cournoyer, and Jean Béliveau, as a good-will ambassador. When the sale of the team was announced early in 2001, the *Globe and Mail* ran a front-page picture of Lafleur putting a team sweater on the prospective new owner. With the Canadiens then near the bottom of the NHL standings, the prospective owner likely wished he could have put a sweater on the Flower, and signed him up to play.

■ ∎ ∎ ∎

The Canadiens of the late 1970s had a love-hate relationship with their coach, Scotty Bowman. Several years after the dynasty ended, Steve Shutt told me, "The key guy on our team was Scotty. He realized that the only team that could beat us was ourselves. We had such a good team that petty little grievances could develop that might bring the team down. So what Scotty did, he made himself the focal point. The one thing we had in common was that everybody hated Scotty." In the same quote Bowman goes from being "the key guy" to someone "everybody hated."

Rewind now to 1979. The Canadiens had just won their fourth straight Stanley Cup under Bowman, who was rumoured to be leaving Montreal for the job as coach and general manager of the Buffalo Sabres. I was golfing with Shutt and asked him, "What do you think Scotty's going to do?" Steve replied, "I don't know, and I don't care. I just hope he goes somewhere else."

A couple of months into the next season the Canadiens were floundering. That's when Shutt told me, "I never knew how much Scotty meant to us, until now."

■ ∎ ∎ ∎

Scotty Bowman is one of a kind. I often remind him he is my second all-time favourite coach, and as strong as the family tie is to my favourite, I have no problem saying Scotty Bowman has been the best coach in hockey history.

When Scotty was in the process of setting every coaching record worth setting, including wins and games, the coach he kept knocking out of the record book was my father. The first one that drew attention was most wins. Scotty was coaching Buffalo and I used to kid him about it. He'd say, "Don't worry, I'm retiring soon. Your father's records are safe." I'd say, "Yeah, sure, Scotty." That was back in the 1980s. When the millennium arrived he still hadn't retired, and my father's records were long gone. Scotty even passed Dick Sr. in a category that isn't official: the oldest man to coach in the NHL.

As I write this, Scotty is tied with Toe Blake for most Stanley Cup coaching victories. Scotty never says much about his milestones, but I'm sure that a ninth Stanley Cup is one he really wants. I think he'll keep coaching as long as he is with a team he feels has a chance to win. If it happens, it wouldn't surprise me if, like Toe Blake, Scotty retires moments after the final game is over. In case you've forgotten, the losing coach when Toe Blake retired right after his final Stanley Cup–winning game, back in 1968, was Scotty Bowman.

▌▐▌▌

Not only his players, but also the media and pretty well everybody who has dealt with him is ambivalent about Scotty Bowman. If you're off balance, that's exactly where he wants you. When Scotty was coaching the Pittsburgh Penguins to a Stanley Cup in 1992, one of the players said to me, "You were with him in Montreal. What can you tell me about him? I can't figure him out at all."

One thing everyone agrees on about Scotty Bowman is that he is in a class by himself when it comes to handling a team during a game. With assistant coaches, bench management is different today, but during his dynasty years in Montreal he worked alone.

Ken Dryden told me how the players would marvel at how Scotty changed his lines. Ken said, "Players who really didn't want to say a lot of nice things about Scotty at other times, when we'd be in a playoff series against the Bruins and Don Cherry, or the Flyers and Fred Shero, or the Leafs and Roger Neilson, they'd be shaking their heads in the dressing room saying they just couldn't believe how he had control, how he could do the things he did during a game."

One story that made the rounds, one I've used in the odd speech, is about Scotty doing a real number on the opposing coach. When the game got going he had left wingers playing right wing, right wingers playing left wing, different line combinations jumping over the boards every thirty seconds, the whole ball of wax. Late in the period he yelled, "Lemaire's line next!" Steve Shutt yelled back, "Who's on it?"

During his last three seasons in Montreal I did a five-minute radio show with Scotty before every game. It wasn't as easy as it might sound. I mean, what do you ask a coach whose team never loses? Scotty bailed me out all the time. No matter who they were playing, or how long an unbeaten streak his team was on, he always came up with a fresh angle. He obviously was able to do the same thing with his players.

■ I ■ I ■

It's hard for a coach to keep a good team good over a long period of time, and it's even harder to keep a great team great. But that's what Scotty Bowman did in Montreal. But his enthusiasm for the task waned noticeably in his last season because he didn't get Sam Pollock's job when Pollock retired in the summer of 1978. Pollock recommended one of his executive assistants, Irving Grundman, and he got the job. Bowman was crushed.

Jean Béliveau had a vote in choosing Pollock's successor. In his autobiography, *My Life in Hockey*, Big Jean explains that he didn't approve of the way Scotty would complain to Pollock about certain players and try to have them traded. In Béliveau's opinion, with Bowman as general manager the team would, as he put it, "Change dramatically from year to year, if not hour to hour." He voted for Grundman. Béliveau knew Scotty was bitterly disappointed, and gave him full marks for staying and coaching the team to another Stanley Cup.

After the 1979 Stanley Cup was won, Scotty Bowman went to Buffalo, where he spent almost seven years without any great success. One highlight was when the Sabres swept the Canadiens in the opening best-of-five playoff series in 1983. Buffalo goalie Bob Sauve had shutouts in the two games played in Montreal.

There was a garage in the Montreal Forum that had space for two or three cars belonging to members of the Canadiens' management. A few years after Scotty went to Buffalo, the Sabres were visiting Montreal and I was walking with him through the garage before the game. Scotty was talking in his usual fashion when we passed Irving Grundman's car. He pointed to it and, without breaking verbal stride, said, "That should be my car," then went right back to his original topic.

Obviously, it continued to bother him. Maybe it still does.

"Don't You Know All the Players?"

....

O nce upon a time, from coast to coast in Canada, the broadcasting of hockey games was a straightforward exercise. It started with radio. In Toronto a station carried the games of the Maple Leafs. In Montreal two stations aired the games of the Canadiens and the Maroons. In time, Foster Hewitt's broadcasts from the gondola at Maple Leaf Gardens became a national institution, every Saturday night.

When the CBC got into the television business in 1952, it was pretty much the same on Saturday nights, only with pictures. In Ontario you saw the Maple Leafs, in Quebec the Canadiens. Fans who lived in Victoria, or Saskatoon, or Charlottetown saw a game from Toronto one week, Montreal the next. Over the years they began to show the playoffs in their entirety as a bonus, and that was it. Thanks for watching. See you next season. But times have changed.

William Houston, a columnist for the *Globe and Mail*, special-
izes in writing about sports media. Here's an excerpt from his
column of December 1, 2000.

> CTV is assured cable carriage for its new category 1 digital
> channels, such as the Women's Sports Network, but there's no
> guarantee that cable will be available to category 2 digital chan-
> nels. Each channel will need to pitch its product to the cable
> operators.
>
> CTV and TSN own the rights to several category 2 channels.
> They include a CTV regional news service, plus the TSN lineup
> that includes Classic Sports, The Hockey Network, Coaches
> Network, Multilingual Sports and Sports Talk TV.

Hello? Are you still with us? The good old CBC still brings you
Hockey Night in Canada. But the oldest established permanent
hockey telecast now has plenty of newcomers in its neighbourhood the other six nights of the week.

There is now a plethora of sports networks, with an accompanying long list of hockey shows, panel discussions, analysis, and
expertising by people advertised as experts. Clarence Campbell
once told me that the office of president of the NHL, now the
commissioner, would always have to be occupied by a lawyer. You
might sometimes think that, in order to be a TV sports panellist
these days you have to be a lawyer, what with the preponderance
of talk about contracts and money. There's much more talk about
what's happening off the ice than on it. Sometimes I feel that if I
hear the phrase "unrestricted free agent" one more time I'll throw
something at my television.

I live in Montreal, where fans once eagerly awaited their
Saturday-night hockey fix. They still do, but it's not such a big
deal any more. If the Canadiens are playing in, say, Nashville on a

Monday, or San Jose on a Wednesday, the game could be on RDS, the all-sports French-language channel. But if it's not on RDS, that means it's on TQS, another French-language station. Radio-Canada still handles Saturday games and, to double our pleasure sometimes, the Canadiens show up on TSN or the CBC once in a while, with English commentary. The team plays eighty-two games in a season, and all eighty-two are available, somewhere, on television. It's pretty well the same thing with the Maple Leafs in Toronto, the Flames in Calgary, the Senators in Ottawa, and so on. Staunch hockey fans who can't afford today's box-office prices have no shortage of hockey in their lives, as long as they subscribe to the right cable service.

There's tremendous competition among the various outlets. It's almost comical to hear the announcers boast that their network broke a story first. They risk dislocating their elbows from so much patting themselves on the back.

In Montreal, a media frenzy attends the Canadiens, no matter if the team is in first place or last. Some players, who were initially happy to play for the storied franchise, are happy as hell when they are traded away. The pressure, the cameras, and the constant coverage can be oppressive.

Jean Béliveau once said to me, "Imagine your dad, or Toe, coaching today, with all the press conferences, especially when they'd lose." Toe Blake didn't like the press around even when its size was minuscule compared to today. He used to tell guys like me what we could do with "that little black box," meaning a tape recorder, when we'd come looking for an interview. I'm not so sure about Dick Sr., though. He was a bit of a ham, which I guess can be hereditary.

Dad enjoyed the company of most of the newspaper reporters on the beat and often used them to stick a few needles into the opposition. He was holding court the morning of a game at the Forum when the Maple Leafs were in town. He said to a group of Toronto writers (which, I recall, included Scott Young) that was with him in the Canadiens' dressing room, "There's the Rocket's jockstrap hanging over there. You guys should go over and take a good look at it. It's the closest you'll get to a great player as long as you're covering the team you're writing about." His words were duly reported, much to his delight.

The coach of the Montreal Canadiens is never free of media scrutiny. That's why Joel Quenneville, who coaches the St. Louis Blues, told me he thinks coaching the Canadiens is the worst job in hockey. Here's how it works.

Say the Canadiens play a home game on Monday night. After the game the coach is marched to a press room where he answers questions, in both languages, from fifteen or twenty reporters. He has no choice. It comes with the territory.

The next morning the team leaves for a road trip on a 9:00 flight. The coach arrives around 8:00, and is immediately surrounded by the reporters making the trip. There he is with cameras and microphones pointing at him, and pencils scribbling, about ten hours after he talked with the media after the game the night before. What in the heck happened between then and 8:00 the next morning? The coach went home, went to bed, got up, and took a taxi to the airport. That's what happened. Come to think of it, I don't think Dick Sr. would have liked it, either.

Enrico Ciccone, a journeyman defenceman for a few years in the NHL, started the 2000–01 season with the Canadiens. He had some injuries, and retired after playing only three games. The day he showed up at the Molson Centre to pick up his things, there were fifteen reporters waiting to interview him. The guy had played three games for the Montreal Canadiens. That media group did not include the fifteen who were with the team, in Ottawa, for a game that night.

∎❘∎❘∎

For the first ten years I worked for *Hockey Night in Canada*, the set-up in Montreal had Danny Gallivan and me in the broadcast booth, with a host in the studio downstairs. During that time there had been a few hosts, including Dan Kelly, Ted Darling, Mike Anscombe, and Dave Reynolds. Just before the start of the 1977–78 season the top boss of HNIC, Ted Hough, asked me for a favour. They were looking for a new host in Montreal but had been unsuccessful. Would it be all right if I did both jobs for a few games until they found one? It took them longer than a few games. I handled both jobs until they found the new host, seven years later.

I call that period of my career "Upstairs, Downstairs." The format for opening the telecast was pretty much the same as it is now, although there wasn't a thirty-minute pre-game show. When the famous HNIC theme had run, the host would welcome the viewers and do a brief scene set. There might be a short interview, live or on tape, and then a commercial. The host would fill until the opening faceoff or, as was the case in Montreal, until Roger Doucette gave his marvellous renditions of the national anthems.

What was different in Montreal was that the host – me – then had to go upstairs to work alongside Danny as the colour man. I'd arrive in the booth a couple of minutes after the game, or a period, had started, and I'd leave the booth a couple of minutes before the period ended to head back downstairs to host the intermissions and the post-game show. This routine led to some interesting experiences.

There was always a third man in the booth, and one night it was former referee Red Storey. I remember arriving upstairs after the second period had started to see that Red and Danny, both great tellers of tales, were engrossed in conversation about something that had happened in the good old days and were paying no attention at all to what was happening on the ice. I was walking to my spot when a big cheer went up because the Canadiens had scored. HNIC had three guys in the booth, and not one of us had seen the goal go in. No sooner had I sat down when Danny, always a quick thinker, leaned back and said, "Well, Dick, tell us all about that one."

Montreal defeated Detroit 4–2 in a playoff game in 1978. All six goals were scored in either the first two or the last two minutes of a period. I didn't see any of them.

I was halfway down the stairs to the studio when Don Cherry's Boston Bruins were called for having too many men on the ice late in the third period of the seventh game of the 1979 Stanley Cup semifinals. To recap, the Bruins were ahead 4–3 and in control. The penalty call was followed by the tying goal, scored by Guy Lafleur, which was followed by the series-winning goal in overtime, scored by Yvon Lambert. The Canadiens went on to defeat the New York Rangers easily in the finals, as Boston would have done. I agree with Don when he says the penalty cost him a Stanley Cup and I was sorry I didn't see that bit of hockey history. Grapes was very, very sorry he did. Mind you, he's made a million out of the story since then.

■ ■ ■ ■

I am sometimes asked about my relationship with my broadcast partner for seventeen years, Danny Gallivan. Truth to tell, there wasn't much of a relationship, off the air. There's nothing sinister in that. Danny and I were good friends and kept in reasonable touch until the day he died. But once the hockey games were over we went our separate ways.

Danny loved golf and we both were members of golf clubs in the Montreal area, but we only played together once. We never had lunch, or dinner, except during road trips in the playoffs. Even those occasions were few and far between. We used to call Danny "Room Service," because nobody saw very much of him on those trips.

Danny Gallivan hated meetings, and there is always a meeting before an HNIC telecast involving the producer, director, and the announcers. Danny never showed up, and there wasn't any real reason for him to be there. When he arrived at the rink he would head straight for the booth. In the years I was the host that meant I didn't see him until the game had started, and we never had the chance to chat even during intermissions. When the game ended and I was doing the post-game show, Danny was in his car and halfway home before I signed off.

I was reminded of this when I was writing *Behind the Bench*, a book about coaches. I wanted to interview Gary Green, who was then the analyst alongside Jim Hughson on TSN's coverage of NHL games. Gary had been the youngest head coach in professional sports history when he took over the Washington Capitals in 1980, at the age of twenty-six.

I caught up with Gary at the Forum the morning of a TSN telecast in Montreal. I told him about my project, that I would like to interview him, and suggested we meet just after lunch. He said, "I can't do it then. That's when Jim and I get together on game day to go over the line-ups and talk about the show." He said it normally took them about two hours.

There's absolutely nothing wrong with that, and I'm sure their telecasts were much better for it. But in the seventeen years

Danny and Dick worked together, we never met for as long as two minutes to discuss line-ups and telecasts. If we had, it would have been two minutes too long for Danny.

∎∎∎∎

When I joined HNIC there was only one microphone in the booth, and Danny had it. He gave it to me whenever he saw fit, which at times wasn't very often. But that was all right. Sometimes rookies in the booth try to say too much, too soon, and Danny orchestrated my arrival at just the right pace. (I got my own mike in my second season.)

The microphone in use then was what is called a stick mike, which is hand-held. In 1974 the CBC decided to go high-tech and supply us with headset microphones. Look, Ma, no hands! This seemed like progress to everyone except Danny, who fought the idea tooth and nail.

Danny Gallivan had been broadcasting hockey games for many years in his native Nova Scotia before he came to Montreal in 1952. A hand-held microphone was part of him once the puck was dropped, and he didn't want to give it up. Danny and the producers had a couple of pitched battles before they agreed on a compromise. Danny would wear the new "contraption," as he called it, and they would let him hold a fake mike in his hand. When the 1974–75 season began, Danny was wearing a headset that was wired up to the outside world, and holding a stick mike that wasn't wired up to anywhere. It was just a piece of metal, but it was his security blanket and he felt comfortable.

The Canadiens played the New York Islanders in the season opener at the Forum, the same game in which a non-helmeted, new-look Guy Lafleur took off on his way to superstardom. Things were going along just fine until, midway through the second period, Danny had to clear his throat. In his broadcasting career before then, that meant holding the microphone at arm's length away from his body and coughing out his problem into thin air. And that's what he did that night. But Danny forgot one important detail, that the microphone he was holding at arm's length was dead, and the one still attached in front of his mouth was live. Coast to coast, viewers heard Danny hacking away, followed by "Faceoff in the Islanders' zone." Danny had no idea what had happened. It was the only time in thirty-three years in the HNIC booth I was laughing so hard I had to take off the headset and walk away for a minute to regain my composure.

■ ■ ■ ■

I have been conducting interviews on radio and television for almost forty years. I thought I had done my last one when I retired from the HNIC booth, but early in the 2000–01 season, after a Saturday-night game at the Molson Centre, they had me tape a post-game interview with Trevor Linden, which ran during the second game of that night's CBC double-header.

When I joined the business in 1961, the first interview Brian McFarlane assigned to me was with two professional soccer players. I had never seen a professional soccer game. My second, conducted on live TV, was with two Australian cricket players. I had never seen a cricket game, and still haven't. The third, also live, was with a promising young Montreal swimmer of international calibre, Dick Pound, who today is well known as a top executive of the International Olympic Committee.

I always conducted interviews on *Hockey Night in Canada*, and that duty was increased when I became the Montreal host. I was the straight man the night Howie Meeker first appeared on HNIC as an analyst and, I believe, the first to talk with Don Cherry when he became an ex-coach. An unsuspecting nation wasn't prepared for either one when they showed up with opinions blazing, and they became fan favourites right from the start. So did Harry Neale, whom I interviewed the first night he joined the show, in 1984.

The Hartford Whalers joined the NHL in 1979–80. Early that year they played, and won, in Montreal. The Whalers' Mark Howe was named first star and was brought into the studio for a post-game interview. I was already on the air when Mark arrived and sat down beside me. I had never met Mark Howe, so live on air I said, "Mark, I'm Dick Irvin," and we shook hands. In the days that followed I couldn't believe how many people who had seen the show said to me, "Don't you know all the players?" I sure didn't then, and as the NHL expanded over the years it didn't get any better.

There are too many teams, and too many players. During the season some teams don't even play once in some cities. I was a season's-ticket holder in Montreal for the 2000–01 season and didn't get to see stars like Paul Kariya, Teemu Selanne, Brett Hull, and Mike Modano because their teams weren't scheduled at the Molson Centre. Steve Yzerman, Brendan Shanahan, Jeremy Roenick, and Keith Tkachuk showed up once. I could discuss how Gordie Howe and Bobby Hull each used to be in town seven times a season, but I've already done that. At least we got Mario Lemieux in Montreal, the only Canadian city he visited after he became a player, as well as an owner, in Pittsburgh.

Randy Holt was a tough guy who racked up hundreds of penalty minutes for several teams in the 1970s and '80s. Holt was playing for Calgary when he scored the winning goal against Philadelphia in a 1981 playoff game. I was hosting the show and he came in for a post-game interview. While we were waiting to start I said, "It must feel good to be named a star and get on *Hockey Night in Canada*." Holt replied, "How should I know? I've never been a picked as a star, and I've never been asked on *Hockey Night in Canada.*"

I am always impressed how calm, cool, and collected players are when they are interviewed after a game, especially goaltenders, and especially in the playoffs. You'd think the last thing they'd want would be to drag themselves off the ice after three or four hours in the pressure cooker and be asked questions. But they always showed up. Goalies like Gilles Meloche, Ken Dryden, John Garrett, and Andy Moog were always amazingly relaxed moments after a big game. As often as not their answers were better than my questions.

■I■I■

I nervously interviewed Bob Hope in 1976, but there were other celebrities who were just close calls. Before a playoff game in Chicago the HNIC gang was gathered in a lobby area of the old Stadium when Leo Durocher, of baseball fame, came in. Durocher was then managing the Cubs, and was arm-in-arm with a gorgeous brunette who was obviously much younger than he was. Our producer, Ralph Mellanby, was a big baseball fan and said to me, "There's Durocher. I'll get him. He'll be a great guest for you."

Ralph walked up to Durocher and said, "Excuse me, Mr. Durocher. I'm Ralph Mellanby of . . ." That's as far as he got. Durocher snarled "NO!" and kept right on walking. So much for Leo the Lip on the big show. Ralph got even by not taking any camera shots of him during the game, despite my complaint that it would be worth it just to give the viewers a glimpse of the brunette.

Hollywood star Kirk Douglas was in Montreal shooting a movie that was produced by a good friend of Danny Gallivan. Danny said Douglas would be at the Forum for the upcoming

Saturday game and his friend would deliver him as an intermission guest. I am a bit of a movie buff, old movies mainly, and was quite excited by the prospect of interviewing a Hollywood legend. Sadly, Saturday night came, and went, and Mr. Douglas didn't show.

Red Fisher filled in. After we solved the NHL's problems in our three-minute interview I thanked him, then added, "You know, Red, you don't look a bit like Kirk Douglas." The audience didn't have a clue what that meant, but we had a good laugh. A few days later Red's wife, Tillie, told me that her husband might have been a bit upset because he thought he did look a bit like Kirk Douglas. She was kidding. I think.

People who appear on camera in the television business sometimes go through an identity crisis. The public is almost always nice, yet at times confused. "I know who you are, but what's your name?" In my case I am often called "Danny," even though Danny Gallivan's last broadcast was in 1984. Every time it happens it proves to me just what a powerful impression he and his wonderful voice made on hockey fans in Canada.

I was in Toronto for the Hall of Fame weekend in November 2000. A man saw me outside the Air Canada Centre and said to his young son, "This is the announcer on *Hockey Night in Canada*." He paused, then said, "This is Foster Hewitt." Not quite. "Oh no. Danny Gallivan." Wrong again. Then I was Brian McFarlane. By now I wasn't in a mood to help him out and he stopped following me. But he caught up a moment later. "Now I know, Dick Irvin." Maybe he had called Regis for a lifeline.

A few years ago, after the Hall of Fame ceremony, which I had emceed on TSN along with John Wells, two fans who obviously had stopped for a few minutes at one of the bars breathlessly asked, "Can we have your autograph, Howie?" The funny part was that the real Howie, Mr. Meeker, was standing about thirty feet away. I signed "Howie Meeker," and the fans went away happy.

Ron MacLean tells of the time he was making another triumphant (he thought) return to his native Alberta and was having dinner in Calgary. Ron was impressed at the fuss the maitre d' and the waiters made of him all evening. When he was leaving the waiter said, "It's been very nice serving you, Mr. Cuthbert."

In my case, the name confuses people. In the mid-1990s, on a hot afternoon in July, I received a call from a chap in Chicago who said he was writing a book on the history of the Blackhawks. He asked if he could ask me a few questions. I didn't think I could help him, but agreed.

First question: "What was it like playing hockey in Chicago in the 1920s?"

I answered, "If the man you think you are talking to was here to answer you, he would be 102 years old."

The caller replied, "You know, I wondered how someone who played in the '20s could be broadcasting in the '90s."

It gets better. In early February 2001, when the Montreal Canadiens were in the process of being sold, I got a call from a nice-sounding lady at CBC News in Toronto. She asked if I would be available to do an interview. I said that, being retired and away from the scene, I didn't think I was the right one for them to talk to. She was persistent, and finally said, "We had a meeting this morning and everyone thought you would be perfect for the interview. You know so much about the history and tradition, because you coached the Montreal Canadiens and the Toronto Maple Leafs."

I wonder how the rest of the meeting went.

A Dynasty on the Island

······························

I have always considered the hockey game played at the Hartford Civic Center on April 11, 1980, to be one of the most significant I ever worked on.

For starters, two of hockey's all-time greatest players, Gordie Howe and Bobby Hull, played their final game that night. Gordie had retired in Detroit in 1971 at the age of forty-three. After two boring years of shaking hands as a PR man for the Red Wings he unretired and joined his sons, Mark and Marty, with the Houston Aeros of the WHA. It was a true feel-good story, and the old guy could still play. In his third WHA season he had 102 points.

The Howes moved to the New England Whalers in 1977. Harry Neale was the coach and he tells a great story about the father playing with the sons:

"We were in Quebec. Gordie was on right wing and Mark on left wing and Mark is heading up the ice, right in front of our bench. The boys always called him Gordie when they were around the team. Anyway, on this rush, when Gordie got the puck, one of their defencemen fell down. Mark yelled for the puck. I guess he was excited because he yelled "Dad!" instead of "Gordie!" Gordie looks up and hits him with a perfect pass, right on the tape, and Mark skates in and scores. The players on the bench had heard it. I never thought guys like Dave Keon and Johnny McKenzie were all that sentimental, but they had a look on their faces that showed they knew they had seen a moment very few people experience. They talked about it and it was lovely, just lovely."

The New England Whalers became the Hartford Whalers when they joined the NHL in 1979 and Gordie had his last hurrah. He appeared in the All-Star Game, which just happened to be in Detroit. When he was introduced, Gordie received the loudest, longest, and warmest ovation I had ever heard, until the one given Maurice Richard the night they closed the Montreal Forum. The 1980 All-Star Game was Gordie's last, and Wayne Gretzky's first.

Gordie played in all eighty games in 1979–80. He had fifteen goals and twenty-six assists. The Whalers met the Canadiens in the first playoff round, a best-of-five series. Montreal easily won the first two games at the Forum, 6–1 and 8–4. Because of a prior CBC programming commitment for an awards show, where a lot of CBC people got a lot of awards, the second game was not televised. I did it on radio and called the play-by-play of what turned out to be Gordie Howe's last goal. Two nights later, in Hartford, the Whalers were eliminated. It was Gordie's 1,924th, and last, NHL game, played eleven days after his fifty-second birthday.

Bobby Hull had also retired, sort of, after playing just four games for the Winnipeg Jets in 1978–79. He came back with the Jets the next year, halfway through their first NHL season, played eighteen games, then was traded to the Whalers. He played nine regular-season games for Hartford, getting two goals and five assists. He failed to get a point in the three playoff games.

When the game in Hartford went into overtime we were scrambling, as usual, for intermission guests. They said they'd try for Hull, a long shot because in those days teams rarely allowed players on TV before an overtime period. The Canadiens were paranoid about their players going on the show at any time during the playoffs. Anyway, during the first commercial break, in came Bobby Hull for the interview. Hockey's all-time greatest left winger had twenty-nine seconds left in his career, because that was how long it took for Yvon Lambert to score in overtime to eliminate the Whalers.

It was kind of full circle for Bobby and me. I was present the first time he was on the ice with the Chicago Blackhawks, at their training camp in 1955. Bobby was sixteen years old and trying out for the Hawks' junior team in St. Catharines. The Hawks' coach, Dick Sr., recruited him as a referee for a practice game. Bobby was my first interviewee when I began broadcasting NHL games, and I did the last of the hundreds of interviews he gave as a player.

I did another interview that night that, in my experience, was unique. I can't remember the guest's name, and that's the truth. I'm not trying to cover up for the guy, who was a Hartford player not in uniform. When he sat down beside me it was obvious he had enjoyed a few "pops," as Grapes would say, during the evening. It's the only time I interviewed a player on HNIC, in or out of uniform, who was slightly tipsy. Notice I said "player."

The Hartford Civic Center was the scene of a broadcasting incident with similar overtones. In the WHA days, and through the first few years of the NHL Whalers, the radio-broadcast location was in the seats, not upstairs in a catwalk as it was later. The announcers sat in the back row of the lower section of seats, with standees right behind. There was no privacy at all. Once in the middle of a game, a play-by-play man, who shall remain name-less, said something like, "The puck is cleared into the Hartford zone . . . both teams are changing on the fly, and . . . Hey! Somebody stole my beer!"

The game in Hartford in April 1980 also marked the beginning of the end of Guy Lafleur's career. From the moment he was bodychecked by Hartford's Pat Boutette and injured a knee, the Flower was never the same.

The Canadiens were still a good team in 1979–80, good yet not quite the same. Scotty Bowman had moved to Buffalo. Ken Dryden and Jacques Lemaire had retired. You knew the Canadiens had a chance to win the Stanley Cup, but it wasn't a sure thing.

Bowman was replaced by a legend from the team's past, Bernie Geoffrion. I don't know why the Boomer took the job, because he didn't want it in the first place. After a few games he said to me, "Junior, I don't know why I'm here. I don't have to put up with all this stuff." Although he was coaching a team with names like Lafleur, Shutt, Robinson, Gainey, and Savard in its line-up, the Boomer didn't put up with whatever "this stuff" was for long. He quit two months into the season.

The faithful Claude Ruel took over behind the bench. Geoffrion quit the day before the team flew west for games in Edmonton and Winnipeg. Flights with the Canadiens had always been fun, the team full of confidence, the atmosphere totally positive. I couldn't believe how quiet and depressed the players were on that one. They were whipped by both the Oilers and the Jets.

The game with the Jets was on Saturday night, and it was Tuxedo Night at the Winnipeg Arena. Fans were asked to dress formally for the Jets' first appearance on *Hockey Night in Canada*. Up in the booth we were decked out in rented tuxes, and it was a fun night for everyone except the Canadiens and Bobby Hull, who was supposed to begin his comeback that night.

Hull got crossed up by an early starting time because of TV and arrived when the teams were already warming up. The Jets had rules about things like that which applied to everybody, including Hull, who was a minority owner. The Jets' coach, Tom McVie, didn't let Hull suit up. Hull's absence caused a stir in the Arena when the game began, but was forgotten in the euphoria of the home team's big win over the mighty Montreal Canadiens.

In the stands that night was a twelve-year-old Bobby Hull fan, Kevin Todd, whose father had brought him to the game so he could see his hero play for the first time. When it was announced Hull wasn't in the line-up, the kid cried. Ten years later Kevin Todd was playing for the New Jersey Devils, and Tom McVie was the coach. When they met, Todd said, "So you're the guy who wouldn't let Bobby Hull play that night."

■ ■ ■ ■

The Canadiens recovered from the western trip and had a good season, finishing with 107 points, third overall. Lafleur had 50 goals and 125 points, behind only Marcel Dionne and a kid named Wayne, who tied for first with 137.

Lafleur scored three goals in the first two playoff games. When Boutette hit him he was through for the night. I sat with him briefly in the hotel coffee shop after the game and he said his knee was "a bit sore." It was more than a bit. The Canadiens played Minnesota in the second round, which went seven games, and the Flower couldn't play. The North Stars won it, mainly on the strength of fabulous goaltending by Gilles Meloche, a fugitive from the beloved Oakland Seals. They haunted us still.

When Scotty Bowman's Canadiens were winning four straight Stanley Cups, Guy Lafleur scored thirty-six playoff goals. In the last twenty-eight playoff games of his career, he scored three. The Flower was in decline, and so was the team. Their Cup win in 1979 was the tenth for the Montreal franchise in fifteen years. In the next twenty-two years the Montreal Canadiens won the Stanley Cup twice, and both times the victory was considered a surprise.

There was a television moment during the 1980 playoffs that, to me, was an omen of things to come on HNIC. Don Cherry worked a few games during the Canadiens' series with Minnesota, both in the booth and in the studio. One of the games in Montreal ended early and we had a lot of time to fill. The Minnesota coach, Glen Sonmor, joined Don and me to talk about the game, and other things. Glen's a good talker and, as his team had won the game, he was in fine form. I let Glen and Don take over, although once those two got going I didn't have much choice. It was a great bit, and Don was the most relaxed he had been since he had started with HNIC. I thought then and there this guy might have a future in a TV studio. But at one point during the series, he wondered if maybe he had done his last game. Naturally, it was because of something he said.

Both coaches, Sonmor and Claude Ruel, had lost the sight in one eye as players. Don was in the booth with Danny and me when they took a split-screen shot that put both coaches on at the same time. Don said, "There's a good look at the two coaches. but I don't think they're seeing eye to eye tonight." Rose was sure they'd fire him for that one.

HNIC assigned me to the 1980 Stanley Cup finals between Philadelphia and the New York Islanders. The Flyers, under coach Pat Quinn, had finished first overall, thanks mainly to an incredible thirty-five-game unbeaten streak that began October 14 and ended January 6. The Flyers won twenty-five and tied ten. They eliminated the Rangers and the North Stars in their first two

series, losing only twice in the process. The Islanders ousted
Boston and Buffalo, losing only three games. We looked forward
to a good final series, and we weren't disappointed.

For the previous year or two the New York Islanders had been
a steadily improving team that, as the cliché goes, wasn't ready
to win the big one. In 1978 they had been upset in the first round
by Toronto, Lanny McDonald scoring the series-winning goal
in overtime in the seventh game. In 1979 they finished first
overall, edging Montreal by one point, then lost to the Rangers
in the semifinals. The key to that series was the goaltending of
the Rangers' John Davidson. That's right, the same J.D. who has
been a regular participant in hockey telecasts on a variety of networks for the past several years.

When the Islanders managed only twelve wins in their first
season, 1972–73, nobody thought they'd be Stanley Cup champions
seven years later. Two men were key to the transformation:
general manager Bill Torrey, and coach Al Arbour, who almost
didn't make it. After the Islanders' first season Torrey offered
Arbour the coaching job, which he turned down because he was
turned off by the words "New York." He didn't want to live in the
big city.

Arbour had been fired by the St. Louis Blues. As he tells it,
"We went to Florida and I bumped into people from Long Island.
They were telling me how nice it was to live there, that it was
another world when compared to Manhattan. I called Bill and
asked him if the job was still open. He said it was, and it was mine
if I wanted it. We went to Long Island and saw that it was a very
nice area. I took the job, and the rest is history."

Gradually some future Hall of Famers became Islanders: Mike
Bossy, Denis Potvin, Billy Smith, Bryan Trottier. Added to the
mix were good players like Clark Gillies, Bob Nystrom, Butch

Goring, and Ken Morrow. It added up to four straight Stanley Cups, beginning in 1980.

As was often the case where the Flyers were concerned, the officiating was a controversial factor in the series. In the first game, in Philadelphia, Andy van Hellemond called a penalty on the Flyers' Jim Watson early in overtime. A minute later Denis Potvin scored the first overtime power-play goal in Stanley Cup history. Van Hellemond became an instant villain in Philadelphia, but was replaced in that role later in the series by linesman Leon Stickle.

The Islanders led what had become a tough, emotional series 3–2 and were on home ice for the sixth game. With the score 1–1 in the first period Stickle missed an offside call at the Flyers' blueline and the Islanders scored. In the years that have followed Leon has always admitted he blew the call. The next season was half over before he was assigned to a game in Philadelphia, and it seemed to him the Philadelphia fans never forgot it. He retired in 1997 after twenty-five years as one of the best linesman ever. Yet having interviewed him for my book *Tough Calls*, I know the play on Long Island still haunts him.

I was in the booth with Jim Robson and Gary Dornhoefer for the "Stickle game," with Jim calling the Cup-winning goal by the Islanders' Bob Nystrom, at 7:11 of the first overtime period.

If the Islanders won the Cup that afternoon I was to go down to the ice and interview the Conn Smythe Trophy–winner. So a couple of minutes after Nystrom's big goal there I was, slipping and sliding through a mass of humanity, trying to find Bryan Trottier. They can't do it now, but back then fans would climb over the glass and onto the ice for the celebration, and confusion reigned at the Nassau Coliseum. When I found Bryan, I saw the director who was with me frantically signalling for me to start the interview. I immediately told Bryan he had won MVP honours, went into a spiel about how far he had come from his home town of Val Marie, Saskatchewan, and he reacted with great glee, as you might imagine. However, as I found out later, we had a problem. We weren't on the air. Back in the studio Dave Hodge and whoever was with him were talking and somehow the cues got mixed up. Hodge kept talking. Trottier and Irvin never made it.

∎∎∎∎

My personal Stanley Cup–final streak ended the next year, 1981. I had worked all, or part, of fourteen straight Cup finals going back to 1968, and had seen the Cup won a total of eighteen times. There were eight more in my future.

An early highlight of the 1981 playoffs came when the upstart Edmonton Oilers defeated the Montreal Canadiens in straight games in the opening round. Wayne Gretzky had won his first scoring championship with a record 164 points in a freewheeling season that saw twelve players get more than one hundred points. But we all thought the Oilers, who had finished fourth in their division with 74 points, were too young to be a serious threat to the Canadiens, who had finished first in theirs with 103. The Canadiens seemed to think so too. That was the only time the team I had covered for many years appeared cocky and overconfident going into a playoff series. They paid the price.

The Oilers started an unknown goaltender, Andy Moog, who had played in only seven NHL games. Shades of Ken Dryden. Moog, and the Oilers, shocked the fans at the Forum with 6–3 and 3–1 victories in the first two games. I flew to Edmonton with the Canadiens the next day. I mentioned earlier how down they were on the plane ride west the season before in the wake of the Bernie Geoffrion disaster, but that trip was like a New Year's Eve party compared to the one to Edmonton in '81. If ever a team were convinced it was going to lose, this was it. The next night the Oilers swept the best-of-five series by thrashing the Habs 6–2. Claude Ruel quit as coach right after the series and resumed scouting. Ruel didn't speak to the Montreal media for years after, because he felt his work had been unfairly criticized.

Mickey Redmond had joined HNIC as an analyst, and worked with us on the Oilers-Montreal series. Mickey was one of the players the Canadiens traded to Detroit to get Frank Mahovlich in 1971, and had a good career with the Red Wings. He was a natural in the booth, and for the past several years has been the TV analyst on all Red Wings games. After the last game in Edmonton, Mickey and I took the red-eye back east and broadcast a Nordiques game against Philadelphia the next night in Quebec City.

Danny and I worked part of the Oilers' next series, against the Islanders. Brian McFarlane was the host. Before a game on the Island, Brian talked to a nineteen-year-old rookie Edmonton defenceman and asked him if he would like to be an intermission guest on the show. The kid's eyes lit up. *"Hockey Night in Canada?* You're kidding! Wow!"* He was still starstruck when he was Brian's guest that night, but as the years passed he got used to it. The kid was Paul Coffey.

The Minnesota North Stars were a rough-and-tumble bunch who made it to the finals against the Islanders in 1981. Their coach, Glen Sonmor, had a reputation for handling tough teams. On February 26, 1981, Sonmor's North Stars were involved in what became known as the "Boston Massacre." Their game against the Bruins that night produced four single-game penalty-minute records that still stand, including the game total of 406. And, like the WWF, it was all planned. One of the linesmen, Gord Broseker, talked about it in my book *Tough Calls*:

"I was skating around before the opening faceoff and a player for Minnesota, Tommy Younghans, said to me, 'Gord, did you work out at the Y today?' I told him I hadn't because Kevin Collins and I had just flown in. He said, 'Well, you should have.' I asked him why and he said, 'You'll find out.' Glen Sonmor was coaching Minnesota and I don't think they had ever beaten the Bruins in Boston. Bobby Smith and Steve Kasper were the starting centremen. Dave Newell dropped the puck and Smith jumped Kasper. It just went on from there. The first period was unreal [sixty-seven penalties were called]. At one point we had thrown out Craig Hartsburg and Brad McCrimmon and they got into a fight in the hallway. We ended up shoving Hartsburg into our dressing room, and locking the door. The game started at 7:30, and ended at 12:20 the next morning."

I didn't work the finals in '81, but I don't think Bobby Smith jumped Bryan Trottier at an opening faceoff. The Islanders won the series, and their second straight Stanley Cup, in five games.

▮▮▮▮

The season of 1981–82 belonged to Wayne Gretzky. That was the hockey year when he broke Phil Esposito's long-standing record of 76 goals in a season, finishing with 92 goals and 212 points, two numbers that are in the NHL record book to stay. That must have been the year they started calling him "The Great One."

I was travelling with the Canadiens, and when I'd hit the hotel coffee shop for breakfast I'd check the papers for the previous night's NHL scores, and to see what Gretzky had done. If some of the Montreal players were nearby I'd mention that Gretzky got three goals, or four or five points, and I wouldn't get much response. It took a while for me to realize that these were players who were happy if they got four or five points in ten games, never mind in one. They weren't too thrilled hearing about somebody doing things they weren't capable of doing. I know they appreciated Wayne's talents. They just didn't need a guy like me talking about him at breakfast.

The Oilers lost only seventeen games in 1981–82, but a marvellous season for Gretzky and his teammates came crashing down in the playoffs when the Los Angeles Kings did to them what they had done to the Montreal Canadiens the previous year. The Kings had finished forty-eight points behind Edmonton, yet upset them in a wild, goal-filled first-round series. The teams scored a playoff record eighteen goals in the opener, which the Kings won 10–8. In the third game, in L.A., Edmonton led 5–0 after two periods. The Kings' owner, Dr. Jerry Buss, was so disgusted he left the building. Big mistake. He didn't see his team score five unanswered goals in the third period to tie the game, and win it early in overtime on a goal by Daryl Evans. Los Angeles won the best-of-five series with a 7–4 win in the fifth game, in Edmonton.

The Oilers were not treated kindly by the local press. Columnist Terry Jones gained some notoriety by calling them a bunch of "weak-kneed wimps." To his credit, Gretzky headed overseas and played for Canada at the World Championships in Finland, and led the scoring with fourteen points in ten games.

∎∥∎∥∎

When a team is on its way to becoming a dynasty, that means they're winning Stanley Cups. As with the Canadiens before them, the Islanders were turning the regular season into a long exercise in redundancy. Everybody knew that, unless a serious glitch developed, they'd win in the end. In 1982, after finishing first in their division, their path to the Cup became smoother when the other three division winners, Edmonton, Minnesota, and Montreal, were upset by fourth-place teams. The Islanders got a scare when Pittsburgh took them to overtime in the deciding game in the first round, but after that they lost only twice in fourteen games to win their third straight championship.

Mike Bossy was the playoff MVP in '82. He had scored sixty-four goals in the regular season, a feat barely noticed in the wake of Gretzky's ninety-two. Bossy grew up in Montreal and played junior hockey for a team in neighbouring Laval and broke Guy Lafleur's Quebec Junior League scoring records. When Bossy became available in the 1977 draft, Scotty Bowman and his assistant, Claude Ruel, tried their best to persuade Sam Pollock to pick him. But Pollock's scouts, Ron Caron in particular, claimed Bossy was timid. Sherbrooke had a team full of goons, and Caron and the scouts would say to Pollock, "He can score, but wait till you see him play in Sherbrooke." Bossy was available when the Canadiens' turn came in the draft, but they chose Mark Napier. Napier became a good player, but he was no Mike Bossy.

The Vancouver Canucks made the finals against the Islanders and were victimized by two great goals scored by Mike Bossy. HNIC split the crews doing the finals and I was assigned to work the games on Long Island. Harold Snepsts was a Vancouver defenceman I appreciated because of his work ethic. There was a game in Montreal during that era when the Canucks were beaten 10–1, and Snepsts was the only Vancouver player who kept trying. In the opener of the finals it was 5–5 in the dying seconds of the first overtime period. Snepsts had the puck deep in his own zone. All he had to do was clear it around the boards and the buzzer would sound. But for some reason he shot it up the ice. Poor Harold. The puck was picked off by Mike Bossy, of all people, who fired it into the Vancouver net and the game was over, with two seconds left in the period.

The Islanders won four straight. In the fourth game, in Vancouver, Bossy scored what he says was his greatest goal. He shot the puck right after he had been checked off his feet. Bobby Orr flew through the air in 1970 after he had put the puck into the net. Bossy was flying through the air before he shot the puck past Richard Brodeur.

In the 1982 playoff year, Roger Neilson set off the white-towel craze in Vancouver. Harry Neale was the Canucks' coach and general manager, and Roger was his assistant. Harry was suspended late in the season for slugging an obnoxious fan in Quebec City. Roger took over, and the team did so well with him behind the bench that Harry kept him there when his suspension ended.

Neilson became upset with the work of referee Bob Myers during a semifinal game, in Chicago, and waved a white towel as if he were surrendering. Fans in Vancouver picked up on it, and white towels became the team's new symbol for the rest of the playoffs.

In recent years, Roger Neilson has been battling cancer. In the 2000–01 season he was an assistant coach with the Ottawa Senators, and was in Vancouver shortly after undergoing more treatments. The Canucks' management showed a lot of class by handing out white towels for the fans to wave as show of support for their former coach.

■ ■ ■

The next season, 1982–83, more of the same. Gretzky won the scoring championship, finishing seventy-two points ahead of Peter Stastny. He could have won without scoring a goal. The Great One had 125 assists. Stastny had 124 points.

The Oilers finished first, again, but the Islanders didn't. They were second in their division, ten points behind Philadelphia. But the Flyers were upset by the Rangers in the first round, and again the Islanders' path to the finals was made easier. This time the old pros would be up against the new kids on the block. Glen Sather's Oilers were getting closer to knowing how to win, and they reached the Stanley Cup finals for the first time.

I wasn't assigned to the series, but after the Islanders won the first three games, Ralph Mellanby called me to go to Long Island for the fourth. He wanted me to do some interviews and cover the champagne party in the Islanders' dressing room should they win, which they did. Maybe they were jaded after four straight wins, as it was a relatively quiet scene. Nobody threw champagne in my eyes. It was my twentieth Stanley Cup, but I remember more about a conversation I had before the game than the interviews I did after it.

When you travel with a team on a regular basis you get to know people in the various rinks around the league. There was a group of season-ticket holders at Islanders games who sat near the broadcast location. Before the 1983 Cup-clincher, I saw them in the coffee shop of the Marriott Hotel across the street from the Nassau Coliseum and sat down to chat.

A sideshow attached to the finals that year was the effort by a group from Saskatoon to buy the St. Louis Blues. Ralston Purina owned the Blues and the deal seemed set, pending league approval. The Saskatoon group was to make its presentation to the NHL Board of Governors that week in New York. There was a large media contingent on hand from the west, including Lloyd Saunders, who had been one of my sportscasting heroes when I was growing up in Regina.

My Long Island friends had heard the story and their reaction was: "What's all this about a place called Saskatoon? Where is that? Who would want to see a team from there?"

I chipped in, "You people are paying good money to see your team play Edmonton tonight. Do you know where Edmonton is?"

The guessing began, and they didn't have a clue. The closest anyone came was "I think it's near Montana."

"So," I said, "what difference would it make if Saskatoon was playing here tonight? You don't know where Edmonton is, and you've been coming to see them play for four years."

Bill Hunter, the long-time hockey promoter, was behind the Saskatoon bid and was, as usual, full of confidence the deal would go through. He talked to me about becoming the team's broadcaster, the same way he talked about it to a lot of others, including Dan Kelly.

There were rumours Don Cherry was seriously considering a coaching offer from Hunter. Don was being made up in the studio before the game when I walked in and said, "It's all set for us in Saskatoon. I'm going there as the broadcaster and you and I are going to have a weekly TV show, and a radio show before every game." Don looked surprised and didn't have one of his usual comebacks, which made me think there was something to the rumour.

Grapes never got behind a bench, and I never got behind a microphone, in Saskatoon. But I might have been tempted, and we would have had a blast.

The Cup Goes West

······························

When Wayne Gretzky scored ninety-two goals in the 1981–82 season, he reached the fifty-goal mark in his thirty-ninth game, scoring five times against the Philadelphia Flyers on December 30. Pete Peeters, who is from the Edmonton area, was with the Flyers then, and I was pleased to see Pete in the audience when I spoke at a Special Olympics fundraiser, in Edmonton, in October 2000.

I acknowledged Pete, and had some fun by saying that he and I were at the Nassau Coliseum on Long Island when Bob Nystrom scored what I called "a rather historic goal." I said I was a broadcaster at the game, and that Pete was also working there that day. I didn't say he was the Flyers' goaltender Nystrom scored on, but it was obvious the sports-savvy audience knew what I meant, and were getting a chuckle out of it.

When the affair was over, Pete told me I could also have mentioned he was in goal for the Flyers the night Gretzky hit the fifty-in-thirty-nine mark, and told me quite a story about that game:

"We were down 6–5 with about a minute to go and our coach, Pat Quinn, wanted to pull me for the extra skater. Gretzky had scored four to get to forty-nine. I told Pat if he took me out, for sure he'd score and that wouldn't be right. He should get his fiftieth against a goalie, not into an empty net. Pat didn't agree, so I sat on the bench and, sure enough, the fiftieth went into the empty net. I made some real good saves off Gretzky that night. He could have had six or seven.

"But here's the best. He gets a breakaway and he's coming in on me but he's not looking at me. He's looking past me at the glass. I wondered if maybe there was a good-looker sitting there I had missed, but what he was doing was looking into the glass to see if anyone was chasing him. I'm serious. That's exactly what he was doing, looking at the reflection in the glass. And, yeah, he scored."

The Wayne Gretzky legend grew quickly, and the stories and images accumulated too. For instance, when he was a teenager in the WHA the referee-in-chief was once called in to the dressing room to look at the kid's battered body. Old pros in the league had been hammering him, especially in the faceoff circle. The league immediately put in a new rule about faceoff interference.

There was a still very young Gretzky the diver, with the crowd in Edmonton howling for a penalty every time he hit the ice. Veteran referee Bill Friday had had enough one night and told the Edmonton captain, Al Hamilton, "You tell Mr. Gretzky that this swimming pool is frozen and the next time he does that I'm gonna whistle his butt for ten." The next time Wayne took a faceoff he sheepishly said to the referee, "It won't happen again, Mr. Friday." And it didn't.

There was Gretzky the magician, toying with Mike Vernon when he was a rookie goalie with Calgary, flipping the puck from behind the net and over it to a waiting Mark Messier, who promptly scored.

There was Gretzky the television pitchman, taping a commercial in which he was shooting pucks into a net. During a break while they changed tapes in the camera, he kept shooting. One shot rang off the crossbar and the director said it would be neat if he happened to hit it while they were taping. "You want me to hit the crossbar?" They resumed taping, the shooter took a shot, and the puck hit the crossbar.

And there was Wayne, before his first game at the Montreal Forum, doing a taped interview with the host of *Hockey Night in Canada*. While it was being set up the kid was saying "Mr. Irvin" this and "Mr. Irvin" that. The host, obviously sensitive about his age, said, "Please call me Dick. If you call me Mr. Irvin in the interview, I'll have them stop and we'll do it again." When the camera rolled he didn't call the host anything. As he was leaving the studio, young Wayne said, "So long, Mr. Irvin. See you in Edmonton next week."

When Mr. Irvin visits the Hockey Hall of Fame he never fails to stop by the Wayne Gretzky exhibit to look at his favourite item of Number 99's memorabilia. It's the summary sheet of every game he played in the 1971–72 season for a novice team, in Brantford, Ontario, when he was wearing number 9. The sheet shows eighty-two games played, and 378 goals scored. I'm sure there were parents of some of his teammates sitting in the stands complaining that the Gretzky kid was hogging the puck, and likely he did on occasion. The sheet with the 378 goals, and a picture taken around the same time of the kid with Gordie Howe, are fascinating.

When the Edmonton Oilers reached the Stanley Cup finals for the first time, it was the beginning of great run for the two NHL teams in Alberta. Starting in 1983, either the Oilers or the Calgary Flames were in the finals eight straight years. Their record was six wins, two losses, with the Oilers getting five of the six victories.

Their first was in 1984, when they finished first overall with 119 points, fifteen ahead of the New York Islanders and the Boston Bruins, who tied for second. Gretzky got back above the 200-point mark again with 205, which left him an unbelievable seventy-nine points ahead of the field. The runner-up was his teammate Paul Coffey, whose point production as a defenceman was bringing back memories of Bobby Orr.

It was fitting the Oilers and the Islanders would meet in that year's final series, the new kids on the block again up against the defending champs. Both had close calls on the way to the summit. Edmonton needed a seventh game to defeat Calgary in the division final, while the Islanders went into overtime to eliminate the Rangers in the deciding game of their first-round match-up. Ken Morrow scored at 8:56 of the first overtime, which had been a spine-tingling end-to-end masterpiece, the emotion heightened by the bitter rivalry between the two New York teams and their fans. Bob Cole and I did the game for HNIC, and when it was over we both thought it was the best 8:56 of overtime hockey either one of us had ever seen.

The Islanders lost the first two games of the conference final, in Montreal, then won the next four to advance against Edmonton. That series marked the end of one of the greatest eras in hockey broadcasting when the Islanders won the sixth game, on home ice, 4−1. When our HNIC broadcast ended, Danny Gallivan had called his last game.

Danny was a private man and, typically, nobody but he knew it would be his last game. We were scheduled to work the final series, which was opening on Long Island five days later. When the Canadiens' charter landed we walked to the parking lot, making small talk.

"See you next Tuesday," I said when we got to our cars.

"No you won't," he replied. "That's it. I've done my last game."

I confess I didn't take him seriously. Danny had been fighting a cold and he was tired. We all have moments like that. There were a few times when I was convinced I had done my last game before I finally did it. But Danny was serious. I was at the Nassau Coliseum for the opener five days later, but he wasn't. The man many, including me, still say was the best ever had indeed done his last game. When I talked with him about it later all he would say by way of explanation was, "It was time."

The Danny and Dick show ran for seventeen years. I still meet people who tell me how much they enjoyed our work, and how much they still miss it. After Danny left I showed up in the HNIC booth for another fifteen years. When I decided it was time, I had something in common with Danny. We both retired a couple of months after our sixty-seventh birthdays.

■I■I■

Edmonton fans caught a break in the '84 finals. The schedule had the first two games on Long Island, the next three in Edmonton. The Oilers won the first 1–0, or I should say Grant Fuhr won it 1–0. He was remarkable. Although the Islanders won the next game 6–1, and even though the Oilers had been outplayed, you had the feeling they were heading home in control. They were, and they won the three games, and the Stanley Cup, by scores of 7–2, 7–2, 5–2.

The Stanley Cup was won on a Saturday afternoon, Gretzky sealing it with a breakaway goal that was vintage 99. A few of the HNIC gang were at the Edmonton bench a couple of hours before game time. Edmonton tough guy Dave Semenko, dressed in his hockey underwear, came out of the dressing room and joined us. As we chatted, he was shaking with excitement. I mean, really shaking. It was kind of scary.

When the game ended, another image: Mark Messier, in the midst of the Cup-winning bedlam on the ice, leaning over the boards bawling his eyes out after learning he had won the Smythe Trophy as the playoff MVP. Gretzky had thirty-five points in the Oilers' nineteen playoff games.

The losers had had a great run. Before dropping that series, the New York Islanders had won nineteen straight playoff rounds. That, and the fact that the Islanders were in the finals five straight times, are two more entries on my list of things I don't think we'll see happen again.

∎∥∎∥∎

A couple of heated provincial rivalries were in full bloom in the 1980s. In the west it was Calgary and Edmonton, and that one is still going strong. In the east it was the Quebec Nordiques and the Montreal Canadiens, a rivalry that sadly is no more.

I had plenty of exposure to the Battle of Quebec, which was intense right from the first faceoff in 1979. The western teams were both newcomers to the NHL, but in the east it was the old guys against the new guys. The atmosphere was charged, and at times bizarre.

The Quebec media, especially on the French side, was a big part of the show. At times some of the writers and broadcasters thought they were the whole show. There were a few based in

Montreal who were closet Nordiques fans, and some who weren't in the closet. I doubt if there was a Canadiens supporter anywhere in the Quebec City media.

On one occasion, when the Canadiens were in Quebec City, the local morning paper had nine pages of coverage on the day of the game. There were twelve pages the day after it was played. That game was the first of the season between the teams, and was played in early October.

I attended a game-day skate one morning in Quebec City and counted twenty-one media people in the seats at the Colisée, while a few more were likely waiting by the coffee machine for the players to come off the ice. When the teams met in the playoffs, that number was even bigger. By contrast, I was at dozens of similar game-day workouts in places like Pittsburgh, Long Island, Tampa Bay, and San Jose where the total media turnout might have been ten or twelve, with only two or three from the home city. The Canadiens' large travelling entourage accounted for the rest.

In 1999 I covered a playoff game in Dallas, where the St. Louis Blues were the visitors. On the morning of the game there were two media people at the Blues' practice, me and a reporter from a Dallas TV station. Nobody from St. Louis covering the series bothered to show up.

A sportswriter from Chicago, Jerome Holtzman, wrote a book titled *No Cheering in the Press Box*. That didn't apply when the Canadiens played the Nordiques. In Quebec City, the visiting and home radio-broadcast locations were side-by-side. I will never deny that my voice on radio didn't leave much doubt as to who my home team was, but – and trust me on this – I never jumped up and cheered and high-fived when the Canadiens scored. There was plenty of that around the home-team microphones at the Colisée when the Nordiques scored a big goal on the Canadiens.

At least one journalist once wrote that the way some of his col-leagues behaved when covering games between the two Quebec teams was a disgrace to their profession. In 1993 the teams met in the first round of the playoffs, with the Nordiques winning the first two games on home ice. After the second game, a smiling Quebec City radio reporter, who had never spoken to me before, poked his head into the HNIC booth's doorway and said, "I guess you'll be going to the Expos games early this year," and quickly walked away. The Canadiens won the next four games, and the series. When it was over I waited for another visit from my smiling Quebec City friend, but he didn't show up.

■ ▮ ▮ ■

At the height of the Canadiens-Nordiques rivalry the players rose above the surrounding nonsense and played some great games. After finishing dead last in their first NHL season, the Nordiques quickly improved. The Stastny brothers were spirited out of their native Czechoslovakia and their arrival in Quebec gave the team instant credibility. Peter Stastny was the NHL's second-highest scorer, after Wayne Gretzky, in the 1980s. Other good players, including Dale Hunter and Michel Goulet, filtered into the line-up, enabling the Nordiques to make the playoffs seven straight years after their poor start.

The two Quebec rivals met four times in six years in the play-offs. In 1982 the Nordiques won a best-of-five series when Dale Hunter scored twenty-two seconds into overtime in the deciding game. The Canadiens won in six games in 1984, with the decid-ing game remembered as the Good Friday Massacre. The teams had a huge brawl at the end of the second period, and a bigger one before the third began. In 1985 Quebec won in seven games when Peter Stastny scored the series-winner in overtime. In 1987 it was Montreal in seven.

The Nordiques fell on hard times after that and didn't make the playoffs until 1993, when the Canadiens beat them in six. It was the last series between the two teams. Three years later, several players from the 1993 Quebec Nordiques won the Stanley Cup, but by then the franchise had become the Colorado Avalanche.

The two organizations got into the act off the ice as well. For example, when the teams played there were almost always pre-game ceremonies, one trying to outdo the other. If a Quebec athlete did well at the Olympics or another high-profile international competition, the teams would compete to see which one would get him or her to drop the puck at a ceremonial faceoff. Pop stars, former NHL greats, and a variety of high-profile Quebecers were constantly being introduced at centre ice before games.

Early in the rivalry, with the Nordiques' ambitious president, Marcel Aubut, the instigator, the media were the big winners in a competition to see which team served them the best pre-game meal during the playoffs. It began one year when a series between the teams opened in Montreal, where the Forum press room featured its usual pre-game fare of hot dogs (best in the league, mind you), hamburgers, potato chips, and Mae Wests. When the series switched to Quebec City, the Nordiques surprised the media freeloaders, and the Canadiens, by serving full-course meals, complete with waiters in tuxedos, wine, and strolling violinists playing Québécois folk tunes.

As soon as the Canadiens' brass heard about the menu and the music in the Colisée's press room they hit the panic button and, while the game was going on, held an emergency meeting to decide what they would serve the hungry horde of journalists when the series went back to Montreal. As a result, back at the

Forum we enjoyed lobster, served by uniformed waitresses and eaten with fancy silverware. However, I can't recall any music. This sort of thing kept up whenever the teams met in the playoffs. If the Canadiens won the series and the Nordiques were no longer involved, the bill of fare in the Forum press room immediately reverted to hot dogs, hamburgers, potato chips, and Mae Wests.

On the ice, in the press box, and in the press room, there was never a dull moment in the Battle of Quebec.

The Unseen Hand Strikes Again

....

The Edmonton Oilers didn't put on the kind of show the Nordiques and Canadiens did in their press rooms at playoff time, but they had a much better team on the ice once the games began. The Oilers hardly broke a sweat to win their second straight Stanley Cup in 1985. Their 109 points placed them thirteen ahead of the second-place Winnipeg Jets in the Campbell Conference. The Philadelphia Flyers, under rookie head coach Mike Keenan, were first in the Wales Conference with 113 points. (Writing the names of the two conferences reminds me how dumb it sounded back then when we would broadcast "the Wales against the Campbells" in the All-Star Game.)

Wayne Gretzky won his fifth straight scoring championship with 208 points, seventy-three ahead of his teammate Jari Kurri. In the playoffs the Oilers lost just three games, easily defeating Keenan's Flyers in five in the Stanley Cup finals.

In 1985–86, when Edmonton finished first overall with 119 points, Gretzky had a new, but still distant, rival when Mario Lemieux started making a few miracles for the Pittsburgh Penguins. But the Great One made sure we all knew he was still the greatest by finishing seventy-four ahead of Mario in the scoring race, 215 to 141. When the Oilers swept the Vancouver Canucks in the first round of the playoffs, outscoring them 17–5 in three games, it seemed nothing would stop them from winning their third straight Stanley Cup. But something did, something my favourite hockey coach called "The Unseen Hand."

The Oilers and the Calgary Flames met in the Smythe Division final, a terrific series that turned on a well-remembered play. Neither team won two straight games, and it boiled down to a big showdown, game seven, in Edmonton. In the third period, with the score tied 2–2, Oilers defenceman Steve Smith had the puck at the side of his net. He attempted a pass but miscued and it hit goalie Grant Fuhr and caromed into the net. Smith dropped to the ice and lay there for several seconds, not believing what had just happened.

The more I see the replay, the more I think it's unfair to put the onus entirely on Steve Smith. I feel goaltender Fuhr has to shoulder a fair share of the blame because, to me, he seemed to lose his concentration for that historic split second. They both fouled up. The high-scoring Oilers still had time to tie the game, but they didn't. From Steve Smith's standpoint, where were Wayne and Mark and Jari when he really needed them? Final score: 3–2, Calgary.

In his many years in hockey my father saw plenty of that kind of thing. Hit goal posts and crossbars, deflections into the net (see Tony Leswick, 1954), the myriad sudden, unexpected, and unexplained things that happen in a hockey game. My dad grew philosophical, and would refer to them as the work of the Unseen Hand. The press picked up on it and the term was linked to him for years. In 1986, long after Dick Sr. had left the scene, it seems the Unseen Hand was still lurking in the shadows of the NHL. It's too bad it picked on a good guy like Steve Smith.

There's no doubt in my mind that Edmonton would have won another Cup had they beaten Calgary. Add that to those won the previous two years, and the Cups they won the next two years, and Glen Sather's Oilers would have tied the record set by Toe Blake's Canadiens, five in a row. I can't see another team coming that close. That record's etched in stone.

■■■■

Meanwhile, back east, the Montreal Canadiens were, for a change, enjoying playoff success. A few new faces were making it happen. One was the coach, Jean Perron, who had been hired out of the University of Moncton in 1985 as an assistant to Jacques Lemaire. Perron had coached two national champions at Moncton, and was Dave King's assistant with the 1984 Canadian Olympic team.

In his first year with the Canadiens, Perron was in the background, and was used mainly as a spotter in the press box. About halfway through the season, in a hotel lobby in St. Louis, Guy Carbonneau pointed to him and asked me, "What does he do?"

"You're asking me?" I answered. "You play for the team. I don't." After the season ended, Guy's question was answered when Perron became the head coach after Lemaire suddenly quit.

Starting in 1940, the Montreal Canadiens had two coaches in twenty-eight years. Extend that to 1979, and they had five coaches in thirty-nine years. One, Al MacNeil, worked for about half a season. With most teams constantly spinning their coaches through revolving doors, the Canadiens were uncommonly stable. But times changed, and Jean Perron was the fifth coach in seven years.

Perron had an uneasy relationship with his players, especially the veterans, and the team experienced a mediocre season. There were predictions he would be fired a couple of days after the playoffs. Instead, a couple of days after the playoffs Jean Perron was riding in a Stanley Cup parade through the streets of downtown Montreal.

Fifteen years after a rookie goaltender led the Montreal Canadiens to an unexpected Stanley Cup, it happened again. Ken Dryden's playoff debut in 1971 was replayed by Patrick Roy in 1986. While Dryden had played just six regular-season games before he began his playoff heroics, Roy had been with the Canadiens the entire season. His first NHL start was on his twentieth birthday, the season opener in Pittsburgh. He was beaten for a soft goal early, after which old pro Larry Robinson told him, "Okay, relax. Things are gonna get better. I'm gonna get one." A few minutes later, Robinson fired the puck past Gilles Meloche and the kid thought, "Wow, this guy is something."

Roy played half the Canadiens' games that season, with Doug Soetaert and Steve Penney splitting the rest. Perron showed confidence in the rookie and the rookie showed promise, but he wasn't a threat to win the Calder Trophy. He started the playoffs against Boston, as Dryden had, and was brilliant, as Dryden had been. The Canadiens swept the series three straight. In 1971, Ken Dryden started to become Ken Dryden in a first-round series against Boston. In 1986, Patrick Roy started to become Patrick Roy in a first-round series against Boston. Later, in the third game of the conference final, against the Rangers, Roy made thirteen saves in the first nine minutes of overtime. Claude Lemieux scored on the Canadiens' second shot, and Montreal took a 3–0 lead in a series they won in five games.

Roy barely spoke English when he broke in. The Canadiens' physiotherapist, Gaetan Lefebvre, served as his interpreter with the press and got plenty of work in the playoffs. During the season Patrick had developed the habit of staring intently at his goal net after the national anthems were played. During the series against the Rangers, a New York reporter asked him about it, and the cocky kid goalie replied, "I'm talking to my goal posts." The reporter said, "Do they answer you in French?" After Lefebvre's translation, Roy said, in English, "Do you have another question, sir," with emphasis on the *sir*. Roy claims he looks at the net and imagines it smaller than it really is, but the story about him talking to the goal posts is much more prevalent, and a lot more fun.

The Rangers had upset the first-place Flyers in the first round, leaving the Wales Conference wide open. The Canadiens, with a solid group of veterans, including Robinson, Bob Gainey, Ryan Walter, Rick Green, Bobby Smith, Guy Carbonneau, and Mats Naslund, were playing well. Naslund, one of my all-time favourite players, had a 110-point season. No Canadien has reached a hundred points since.

The Montreal team was enjoying a fine playoff, but I was in a slump. The Canadiens won the division final against Hartford in the seventh game in overtime. I was doing the play-by-play and blew the big call. Claude Lemieux shot the puck past Mike Liut, and it came back out of the net immediately. I saw Lemieux take the shot and I thought it went in, but then I saw it out of the net and Liut was acting as though the play was still alive. I was sputtering away, totally confused, until I noticed the red light had gone on. Bad call, Dick. Since the English guy blew it, whenever HNIC replays the goal they use the French version, which incidentally contains a lot of cheering in the broadcast booth.

My slump continued, after a fashion, when the conference final against the Rangers ended and I was told I wouldn't be working the first two games of the finals in Calgary. They said they didn't have the budget, and I would work only the games in Montreal. Funny, I thought, they've got the money to fly Dave Hodge from Toronto to host the show, but the only Montreal guy on the crew can't go, and it's his home team that's playing, not Hodge's.

My ego had taken a hit and I complained, but the Stanley Cup finals started without me on HNIC. With the exception of playoffs between the Maple Leafs and the Canadiens when the Montreal crew didn't work in Toronto, the opening game of the 1986 Stanley Cup finals was the first Montreal Canadiens playoff game that didn't have either Danny Gallivan or Dick Irvin in the HNIC booth since the CBC began televising the playoffs in 1953.

I showed up in Calgary just the same, and broadcast the games on CFCF Radio. When I got back home, Danny called me. He was furious about what had happened and urged me to boycott the rest of the series. Danny had sat out the finals one year because he refused to share the play-by-play duties with Dan Kelly, who was working for an American network that had made a deal to simulcast the games with the CBC. The Montreal *Gazette* carried a photo on the front page the morning after the series opener showing Danny sitting at home watching the game on television.

When he said I should do the same thing I replied, "That's easy for you to say. You're Danny, but I'm Dick. After you sat out, you were still a legend. If I don't work tonight, I'll be unemployed tomorrow." I eventually would walk out on HNIC during a playoff series, but that hassle was still a few years away.

The teams had split the first two games in Calgary, but when the Canadiens won the next two at the Forum HNIC told me I'd be going to Calgary for the fifth game. I dutifully went along with it, knowing full well they wanted me there to do the dressing-room interviews if Montreal won the Cup. The Canadiens won, I did the interviews, and got totally soaked with champagne in the process. I wondered how many Edmonton Oilers were watching.

∎❘∎❘∎

Some stubborn old-timers, like me, might claim the Edmonton Oilers of the 1980s don't qualify as a dynasty because they didn't win the Stanley Cup more than two consecutive years. But after the Unseen Hand struck them down in 1986, Glen Sather's team won again in 1987, 1988, and 1990. I guess it's time for me to concede that five Stanley Cups in seven years is good enough.

I was present for only one of the five, the first one, in 1984. In 1987, after finishing first overall, the Oilers breezed through the playoffs until they were taken the full seven-game distance by the Philadelphia Flyers in the Stanley Cup finals. That was the year Philadelphia's goaltender, Ron Hextall, joined a small group of players chosen MVP of the playoffs while playing for the losing side.

The next season the Calgary Flames had more regular-season points than Edmonton, but the Oilers let the Flames know they were still the best by sweeping them in the division finals. Another difference that season was that, for the first time since 1980, Wayne Gretzky didn't win the scoring championship. He finished second to Mario Lemieux. Mario was in his fifth season, but despite his play the Pittsburgh Penguins missed the playoffs for the fifth straight year. In his first seven seasons, Lemieux was in the playoffs only once.

Edmonton lost only two games in the 1988 playoffs, and that year the Unseen Hand did their fans a big favour. With Edmonton leading the final series 3–0 over the Boston Bruins, the fourth game was halted in the second period when the Boston Garden was hit by a power failure. The game was replayed, in Edmonton, two nights later, giving the hometown fans a chance to see their team win the game 6–3, and the Stanley Cup for the fourth time in five years.

Wayne Gretzky gave us his usual share of magic moments during those playoff years. One was a rush up-ice late in a period when he looked at the clock to see if there was enough time for him to engineer a goal. There was, and he did. It might have been on that play, or on another, when he made an unbelievable pass to set up Paul Coffey, who scored. The camera zoomed in on Coffey in time for us to read his lips as he looked at Wayne and said, "What a pass!"

■▮■

In the summer following the Oilers' 1988 Stanley Cup victory two important things happened to Wayne Gretzky: he got married, and he got traded. On the day of the trade, August 9, 1988, I was in my office at CFCF when the news broke. CTV set up a line to its affiliates from the scene of the news conference in Edmonton, and I watched everyone gathering for the announcement on a monitor in my office.

Hockey writer Red Fisher was on holiday in Portugal, so I thought I should alert my long-time travelling buddy. It wasn't easy, but I tracked him down. When he got on the line I said, "Red, it's Dick. Don't worry, nobody died, but I want you to know that I'm sitting in my office watching a TV feed from Edmonton where they are about to announce that Wayne Gretzky has been traded to the Los Angeles Kings."

Red swore.

"What's wrong?" I asked.

"I had that story," he growled. "Bob McCammon [an Oilers assistant coach] told me at the meetings in June it might happen.

I started to write it, but changed my mind. It was in my machine two months ago."

I said, "Well, it's happening. Here they come. There's Wayne, Peter Pocklington, Bruce McNall. You shouldn't have changed your mind."

Red Fisher, who began covering the Canadiens in 1955 and still is, doesn't suffer missed scoops lightly. I felt rather bad that I had spoiled a day of his expensive vacation.

It might have been the Unseen Hand again, but the 1989 All-Star Game was played in Edmonton, where Wayne's presence dominated the festivities. He also dominated the game and was named MVP.

I was assigned to the game by HNIC, and the Oilers invited me to emcee the gala All-Star Dinner. Our daughter, Nancy Anne, was in her first year at the University of Alberta, so I had a great date and we had a great time. I particularly enjoyed ending my part of the program by introducing, "for your dancing pleasure," a big band led by well-known Canadian musical personality, Tommy Banks.

When I gave Tommy the big intro I felt I had come full circle from when I first attended hockey games at Maple Leaf Gardens in the early 1940s. That was the swing era in popular music and between periods they would play recordings by the top big bands. Two Glenn Miller hits, "Moonlight Serenade" and "Elmer's Tune," were the ones I recall being played most often.

That may have been when I developed an interest in big-band music. I'm still a fan. In the mid-1980s I began producing and hosting a big-band music show on Montreal radio. It was quite a departure for me and, to my surprise and great satisfaction, it lasted fourteen years. I had more positive reaction to my music show than to anything I'd ever done in broadcasting, and, yes, that includes the Stanley Cup finals.

The end of my career as a disc jockey came when the station carrying the show made some management changes. The new program director was a young-looking chap, and I wondered if he had ever heard of Glenn Miller or Benny Goodman. I told Wilma that, even though the show had good ratings, I had a hunch it might be in trouble. I was right. Not long after taking over, the new PD phoned to tell me he was taking all music programs off the air and replacing them with talk shows, so *Dick Irvin's Bandstand* was gone. That meant he also got rid of a Sunday-night classical program that had been on the air longer than any show of its kind in the history of Canadian radio. I guess the guy had never heard of Bach or Beethoven either.

■ ▌ ▌ ■

While the Edmonton Oilers were winning Stanley Cups, and trading Wayne Gretzky, the team I was covering, the Montreal Canadiens, weren't going very far in the playoffs, except in 1989, when they lost to the Calgary Flames in the finals. After their unexpected Cup win, in 1986, seven years would go by before their next one, and that too was unexpected.

The Canadiens were involved in a couple of wild and bizarre incidents in the late '80s. In the Good Friday mess, in 1984, they had engaged the Quebec Nordiques in big brawls at the end of one period and before the start of the next. In 1987 they went one better: they had a brawl with the Philadelphia Flyers before the game even started.

The teams met in the conference finals and the Flyers were ahead 3–2 going into the sixth game in Montreal. Sometimes the men who play the boy's game of hockey can look pretty stupid, and they sure did that night.

The silliness had started early in the series when two Montreal players, Claude Lemieux and Shayne Corson, made a habit of being the last ones on the ice when the pre-game warm-up was over. They'd shoot pucks into the Philadelphia net before leaving. The Flyers didn't like it. Before game six two Philadelphia players, goalie Chico Resch and Ed Hospodar, waited them out. Corson and Lemieux finally left but, like little boys playing hide and seek, waited in the corridor until the two Flyers were gone. Then they skated back on the ice to take their last shots, only the two Flyers hadn't really left. See what I mean by silly? Chico Resch explained it this way:

"Lemieux and Corson left, but we knew they were coming back. They had a lookout to tell them when. We made the mistake of going to our bench. They jumped over the boards and raced to the net and Lemieux had a puck. I came back on the ice and threw my stick to try and knock the puck away from him. I was still in the mood that it was just fooling around.

"Hospodar took a different approach. He charged at Lemieux and jumped him and started pounding him on the back. I yelled at him, 'Ed, what are you doing?' Lemieux looked up at him and said, 'Yeah, Ed, what are you doing?' By then word had reached the dressing rooms about what was happening so here were all the other guys pouring out onto the ice. Some even came running out in their bare feet. It was one of the biggest brawls I'd ever seen."

Me too, Chico. Certainly it was the biggest I had ever seen before the game had started. When the game ended the Flyers had won and were on their way to the best-of-seven final series against Edmonton.

■ | ■ |

In 1987–88, the Canadiens had their best season under Jean Perron, finishing just two points behind the league-leading Calgary Flames. Following the playoffs, in which the Habs had been eliminated by Boston in the second round, the Canadiens' management rewarded their coach for his team's 103-point season by telling him he was fired.

The New York Islanders finished first that season in their division. The Canadiens were the visitors for the home opener at the Nassau Coliseum the following year when they raised a banner honouring the Islanders' division championship in 1988. I mentioned to Marc de Foy, one of the beat writers in Montreal, that the Canadiens never raised a banner when they won their division.

"No," said Marc, "they fire the coach instead."

After Perron left, the Canadiens called a cop. Pat Burns was a police officer in Hull, Quebec, who left the force after sixteen years to become a hockey coach. He coached the Hull Juniors when Wayne Gretzky was the owner. With Luc Robitaille in the line-up, Burns led the team to the Memorial Cup finals. The Canadiens hired him for their American League farm team, in Sherbrooke, and a year later he replaced Perron with the big team. Burns was a bit in awe of the Forum, and the team he was to coach there.

"Six years before that I had bought scalper's tickets to see the Canadiens play at the Forum," he told me for my book *Behind the Bench*. "I sat in the blues [the cheapest seats] and watched Bob Gainey, Larry Robinson, Bobby Smith, and Mats Naslund. Then six years later, I'm behind their bench."

After a shaky start when they won only four of the first twelve games, the Canadiens got back on track and had a very good season. They lost only five of the last thirty-seven games and finished with 115 points, which for the second straight year left

them two back of the overall-leading Calgary Flames. Burns was
named coach of the year.

I travelled with the Canadiens the four years Pat Burns was
their coach. On a charter ride home after a game in St. Louis I
happened to overhear Pat do something few, if any, coaches do:
he admitted he had a bad night. A losing coach's post-game
quotes usually deal with the shortcomings of his players, and
especially with the ineptness of the referees, whose work obviously cost his team the game. But they never blame themselves.

Pat had one of his assistants, Charlie Thiffault, grade each
player after every game. The game in St. Louis had ended 6–6.
Brett Hull scored three for the Blues and, from a broadcaster's
standpoint, the high-scoring game had been great. On the plane,
as Charlie was working on his grades, I heard Burns say to him,
"Give me a D tonight, Charlie. I coached like a dink."

In the 1989 playoffs, Montreal advanced to the Stanley Cup
finals by sweeping Boston, then beating Hartford in five games
and Philadelphia in six. The Philadelphia series was rough. Chris
Chelios, who won the Norris Trophy that year as the league's best
defenceman, set the tone early in the first game when he bodychecked Philly forward Brian Propp into the boards. Propp's head
hit the glass, then the ice, and he suffered a concussion. From
then on the series often was a war zone.

The Canadiens took a 3–2 series lead into the sixth game in
Philadelphia. Late in the third period Montreal was leading 4–2
and it was all but over. They would receive the Wales Trophy (as
opposed to the Campbell Bowl) when the game ended. With five
or six minutes remaining I left the booth and went downstairs to
host the trophy presentation in a makeshift studio we were using
next to the Montreal dressing room.

Waiting there to make the presentation was Gil Stein, an
NHL vice-president, and the league's legal counsel. Stein was

from Philadelphia and became involved with hockey when he joined the Flyers, as their legal counsel, in 1972. In 1992 he succeeded John Ziegler as president of the NHL, a position he held for just over seven months. Stein left office amid allegations he had tried to orchestrate his own induction into the Hockey Hall of Fame.

There were a couple of other league officials in the studio, and everyone was watching the game on the monitor. With about a minute to play, Chelios was involved in an offside at the Flyers' blueline. The play was whistled down and Chelios turned and flipped the puck to the linesman. Philadelphia's Ron Hextall, the most-penalized goalie in the NHL, decided to get even with Chelios for his controversial hit on Propp. Hextall raced out of his net and charged into Chelios, and a full-scale brawl ensued. It was just like the bad old days at the Philadelphia Spectrum. (As a result of what happened, Hextall was suspended for the first twelve games of the following season.)

Back in the studio, Stein, a league official but seemingly still a Flyer at heart, started beefing that the incident was all the Canadiens' fault. He was ranting that Chelios shouldn't have been on the ice, that the Canadiens knew the Flyers were looking for revenge, and if they'd kept him on the bench the fight wouldn't have happened, blah, blah, blah. I was listening to a vice-president of the NHL claim one of the teams should have kept its best defenceman on the bench, in the final minutes of a series-clinching game, to avoid a fight breaking out in, of all places, the Philadelphia Spectrum.

It seemed to me that, while he likely passed his bar exams with flying colours, Mr. Stein obviously had flunked Hockey Strategy 101. The fight lasted so long, HNIC ran over its allotted time and signed off quickly when the game finally ended. That meant the VP from Philadelphia didn't get to present the coveted Wales

Trophy to Bob Gainey, the captain of the Montreal team the VP
said had caused the brawl.

∎∎∎∎

The Calgary Flames kept the Alberta beat going by defeating the
Canadiens in a six-game final to win the Stanley Cup. In 1986
the Canadiens won the Cup in Calgary, then in 1989 the Flames
won in Montreal. It was the only time the Canadiens lost a Cup-
winning game on home ice in the seventy-two years the team
played at the Forum.

Players like Al MacInnis, Joel Otto, Joe Mullen, and Doug
Gilmour were terrific in the finals. I thought Gilmour and
Mullen were the difference. But the player who received the most
post-series attention was Lanny McDonald.

Lanny had become one of hockey's most popular players
during his career with Toronto, Colorado, and Calgary. During
the Flames' Cup-winning season, his last regular-season goal
was the five hundredth of his career. But coach Terry Crisp sat
Lanny out on several occasions, including a game the Canadiens
played in Calgary that he watched from a seat a few feet away from
our radio location. Had I been a good reporter, digging for a
scoop, I would have put him on the air and on the spot with
probing questions like "How do you feel sitting out?" and "Are the
Flames being fair to you?" But I was never that kind of a reporter,
and besides, Lanny looked so forlorn behind his famous mous-
tache I didn't have the heart to ask him. He was obviously having
a problem, as most players do, coming to grips with the approaching end of his career.

McDonald was in uniform three times in the six-game final
and scored a big goal in the Cup-clinching game. It was his only
playoff goal that year, and became the best remembered, and

most replayed, of all the goals the Flames scored in the 1989 playoffs. It was Lanny McDonald's last goal, his last game, and his only Stanley Cup. One of hockey's truly good guys retired on a high note.

∎❚❚∎

The Stanley Cup stayed in Alberta when the Edmonton Oilers won again in 1990. By then Wayne Gretzky was in Los Angeles and Glen Sather was in the front office full-time. John Muckler led the team behind the bench, and Mark Messier led it on the ice.

The Oilers' fifth championship meant that in fifty years only eight different teams had won the Stanley Cup. Two, Chicago and Calgary, had just one win. But the era of dynasties was over. In the nine years after the Oilers' win in 1990, seven different teams won the Stanley Cup. This is not a bad thing.

Wayne, Elvis, and Other Celebs

....

I have been singularly fortunate to have done what I have done for most of my working life. There is really no carry-over in the sports and news business. Every day, and every game, is a new beginning. Along with all the Stanley Cups I broadcast there were Olympic Games, Grey Cups, Canadian Open golf and tennis championships, and many other events. Yet one of my most memorable experiences took place in a sixteen-thousand-seat hockey arena when I was the only person in the stands, and there was only one skater on the ice.

On January 2, 1993, the Montreal Canadiens played the Kings in Los Angeles in a game I broadcast back to Montreal on radio. On the morning of the game the teams held their usual game-day workout, visitors first, home team second. Wayne Gretzky hadn't played yet for the Kings that season because of a back injury he suffered during the 1992 Canada Cup series, but by then he was just about ready to return.

I watched both teams work out, and taped a couple of short interviews for use on our show that night. Gretzky had been on the ice with the Kings in full uniform. He'd casually drifted around the ice, passing the puck out from the corners for shooting practice once in a while, but wasn't part of his team's basic workout.

When I left the dressing-room area I walked by the Zamboni entrance and, for some reason, looked out at the ice and thought I saw Number 99 skate by. I walked into the arena and, sure enough, there he was. I went up a few rows into the seats and sat down. It was weird, but I was the only person watching. There was nobody else in sight, not even a maintenance worker. Wayne was the only skater, but now he wasn't just gliding, he was working. And how he was working.

In the otherwise silent L.A. Forum there was only the sound of his skates – *chomp, chomp, chomp* – as he drove himself as hard as he could, up one way, down the other, back and forth, back and forth. He was sweating buckets. I was fascinated.

Wayne finally took a breather at the Kings' bench. He spotted me and waved his gloved hand. I waved back but stayed where I was. After no more than a thirty- or forty-second respite he was back on the ice. *Chomp, chomp, chomp,* back and forth, back and forth, legs pumping, sweat pouring. There was still nobody else in the seats, nobody else on the ice.

I was wishing every young hockey player with dreams of playing in the NHL could have been there. I would have said to them, "Take a good look at that guy, because that's how you get to be hockey's greatest player. He doesn't need this. He could quit tomorrow and never have to work another day. But he loves the game too much to leave it now. That's why he's out there, doing what he's doing. That's why he's the Great One."

I left while I was still the only spectator, with Wayne still on the ice, punishing himself so he could play hockey again. A week later he came back, and in his shortened season had sixty-five points in forty-five games. In the playoffs, Gretzky led every offensive category with fifteen goals and twenty-five assists, for forty points in twenty-four games, and the Kings reached the Stanley Cup finals for the first time in franchise history.

■|■|■

Wayne Gretzky is hockey's all-time celebrity. Some have been big, but he's the biggest. He was big in Edmonton, and bigger still in Los Angeles. Nobody else could have done for the game what he did, or handled the media pressure the way he did, especially once he joined the Kings. Hockey had been on the back burner in the L.A. media. You'd usually find it buried three or four pages into the sports section of the *L.A. Times*, and NHL scores rarely appeared on late-night sportscasts. That changed when Wayne arrived.

On the bus ride down Century Boulevard from the L.A. airport to the hotel the first time the Canadiens were there after the trade, we saw a picture of Gretzky as the main part of an ad for a cable-TV company. The ad simply said, "No Cable, No Gretzky." Suddenly, a Kings game became in on the celebrity scene. The atmosphere at Kings home games, which had been blah for many years, became charged. Only one guy could have done it.

Celebrities started to show up regularly at the games. These included Goldie Hawn and Kurt Russell, Michelle Pfeiffer, James Woods, and celebrity lawyer Robert Shapiro. I was told Rocky Balboa, a.k.a. Sylvester Stallone, was at a Canadiens game there, but I couldn't find him. He was likely a big Philadelphia Flyers fan. Ronald and Nancy Reagan sat rink-side at the two Stanley Cup final games played in L.A. in 1993.

It's not easy being Wayne Gretzky. When I had a show called *Hockey Magazine* on CFCF-TV, I would tape interviews with visiting players in a nice quiet spot on the second level of the Forum. We'd go there, do the interview in privacy, and that would be that. When I interviewed Wayne Gretzky in that setting, we had to call security to keep a horde of fans from disrupting things.

In the early 1990s I was working on the Canadian Open golf tournament for CTV at the Glen Abbey course in Oakville. Wayne showed up one day and his agent, Mike Barnett, who has been a good friend for years, invited me to join them for lunch in the clubhouse. I got a kick out of Wayne grilling me about the Canadiens and who they might have that would help the Kings in a trade. He was acting like the general manager. Maybe, by then, he really was.

It was pro-am day at the Open, and Mario Lemieux was in the field. After lunch, Wayne said, "Let's go watch Mario." But the word was out that Gretzky was in the clubhouse, and when we walked out the front door the area was jammed with people waiting for him. The media was there, the autograph hounds, the cameras. It was a mob scene. A few fairly big-name golfers passed by, including Ben Crenshaw and a recent PGA champion, Bob Tway, and nobody looked sideways at them. Mike and I got down the stairs, unmolested, and waited for Wayne so we could "go watch Mario." Mike kept waiting, of course, but I gave up. I watched Mario play a few holes on the back nine. Wayne and Mike never made it.

From my perspective, in the years I was on the hockey media scene, Wayne was always the same Wayne. He called me "Mr. Irvin" right to the end. At the 1999 All-Star Game in Tampa, Wayne arrived along with the other players, all of whom headed straight for the dressing rooms. Wayne spotted Mr. Irvin and Jim Matheson of the *Edmonton Journal* hanging around the coffee and doughnuts table and came over to say hello. It was going to be his last All-Star Game, and I thought he looked exhausted. Wrong again, Dick. He put on a terrific show, with a last shift that was absolutely awesome, and won another car as the MVP.

Not everyone is a Wayne Gretzky fan. Among those who have reservations, perhaps, is Bobby Smith, a former player and a good guy, who was general manager of the Phoenix Coyotes for several years, and did a good job under tough circumstances. In February 2001, ownership of the team changed hands. Gretzky was part of the new group and was put in charge of the hockey operation. Less than two days after the sale was finalized, Gretzky fired Smith, replacing him with Cliff Fletcher.

Some Wayne Gretzky critics surfaced after he retired as a player. He was knocked, sometimes severely, by some commentators and writers for doing too much product endorsement in print and on TV. Those same critics would have set world records grabbing for a pen had they been offered the same deals. No chance of that, of course, so they were brave about throwing barbs from afar.

I always thought that when Mario Lemieux retired he would head straight for the first tee and never be seen around hockey again, while Wayne would never get away from the game. Mario fooled me, first by becoming the principal owner of the Pittsburgh Penguins, then, amazingly, returning to the ice as a player. Wayne didn't fool me. He stayed in hockey, with the Phoenix Coyotes, and became manager of the Canada's 2002 Olympic hockey team, and various other projects. There had to be a message in there somewhere when Numbers 99 and 66 were still among the biggest stories in hockey after their playing careers had ended, in Mario's case, his first playing career. The people running hockey, at all levels, had better hope they hang around for a long time.

■❙■❙■

When you grow up with a father who is also a celebrity in his field and get the chance to mingle regularly with his fellow celebrities, I guess you take a lot of it for granted. When my father returned home to Regina after the hockey season, he would be invited, as a celebrity, for an interview at a local radio station, CKCK. I usually tagged along and was always fascinated by the studio, the microphones, and the announcers, who were local celebs in Regina. I've always thought those experiences were why I became interested in broadcasting at an early age.

As a hockey broadcaster I routinely dealt with the biggest names in the game and, believe me, I realize how lucky I was to have done so. I didn't even have to leave the HNIC booth at the Forum to hobnob with some of them. Once they started using a third man with Danny and Dick upstairs, our broadcast partners included Gordie Howe, Bobby Hull, Bobby Orr, Don Cherry, Scotty Bowman, and others too numerous to mention. Sometimes they even asked me for some broadcasting advice.

Because of my association with hockey I had the occasional brush with non-hockey celebrities, including some pretty big movie and television stars. The first one came the second night I did radio play-by-play, in Los Angeles, in February 1969.

I had made the trip to California and did my first broadcast the night Minny Menard and the mighty Oakland Seals whipped Jean Béliveau and the Montreal Canadiens. We flew to Los Angeles after the game on a short commercial flight that was the roughest I ever experienced when travelling with the hockey

team. The plane rocked and rolled and several passengers, including a couple of the players, became airsick. Toe Blake was in his
first year of retirement but still made trips with the team in
his role as a consultant to the new coach, Claude Ruel. When we
landed and were waiting for our luggage one of the beat writers
on the trip, Pat Curran, said to Blake, "Pretty rough trip, eh, Toe?"

Blake, still a fierce competitor and very upset by the loss in
Oakland, replied, "I wish the fuckin' thing had crashed!"

During the first period of the game the next night, the Kings'
PR Director, Jon Washington, came by and asked, "Would you
like Lorne Greene as a guest in the first intermission?" I guess so.
Lorne Greene was a Canadian and I had grown up listening to
him read the national news on CBC Radio. He turned to acting,
landed in Hollywood, and became a star as Pa Cartwright on the
long-running TV series *Bonanza*. He was an original member of
the Kings' board of directors, and attended most of their games.

The period ended and Greene arrived, a bit out of breath. I welcomed him and said how fitting it was that he was appearing on
CFCF Radio, the oldest station in the world, during the year it was
celebrating its fiftieth anniversary. He replied, "Happy fiftieth
anniversary, CFCF." Luckily, someone back at the station was taping
the interview. Lorne Greene's anniversary greeting ran hundreds
of times as a station promo from then to the end of the year.

Halfway through the second period, Jon Washington came by
again. This time he asked, "Would you like Jim Brown and
George Kennedy as guests in the second intermission?" By then
I was having trouble concentrating on the game and was wondering, "Is it always this good out here?" Brown, the greatest
fullback in NFL history, had recently retired to become an actor.
George Kennedy had won the Academy Award for best support-
ing actor the previous year for his role in *Cool Hand Luke*. So two

more Hollywood names were booked for my show, but they almost didn't make it.

The second period ended with no sign of Brown and Kennedy. There was a French Canadian Club in Los Angeles, and that night the Radio-Canada broadcast of the game had arranged for its members to appear during the second intermission. There were a lot of them and they lined up to say their name and hometown over the air. Ralph Mellanby, my HNIC boss, happened to be in Los Angeles and sat with me and Red Fisher during the game. I was muttering about the two Hollywood guys being no-shows when suddenly Ralph said, "There they are!" It was comical, because Kennedy and Brown were patiently standing in line with the members of the French Canadian Club, waiting to be interviewed. They'd asked where "Canadian" radio was located and had been sent to the French broadcast position. Ralph hustled down and quickly returned with my guests in tow.

It turned out that George Kennedy was a big hockey fan. When he was growing up, in New York, his father often took him to Madison Square Garden to see the Rangers and Americans play. On the other hand, Jim Brown had never seen a hockey game until that night. After the usual "what do you think of the game?" routine, I asked him questions about football. I wonder if he ever saw another hockey game.

∎∎∎∎

I don't know how long Paul Newman has been a hockey fan, but he got plenty of exposure to the game when he starred in the 1977 movie *Slap Shot*. A few years later, Newman was in Montreal for several weeks during the winter, shooting a movie. He and his wife, Joanne Woodward, showed up at the Forum one Saturday night as guests in a private box. The press was advised that Mr. Newman insisted there be no interviews, and no photographs. He wanted complete privacy as he sat in the crowd of eighteen thousand, and as far as I know he got it.

A couple of weeks later I arrived in the radio-broadcast booth at the Forum for a mid-week game. As I negotiated my way down the narrow space between the seats and a wall I saw Paul Newman sitting with two local goons hired to be his bodyguards. As I walked past them one of the goons recognized me, stood up, grabbed my arm, and grunted, "Don't talk to him." I shrugged, and kept going, but every time I think of the incident I wish I'd said, "Don't talk to who?" I always think of the right answer at the wrong time.

Another Hollywood legend, Gregory Peck, was much more pleasant. In 1997, Wilma and I attended *An Evening with Gregory Peck*. It began with a montage of highlights from his movies, after which he came onstage, told stories, and took questions from the audience. He was eighty-one years old at the time and he was marvellous.

Microphones were positioned around the theatre, and I was one of many who had a question for him. My favourite Gregory Peck movie is *Twelve O'Clock High*, which was released in 1949. It's the true story of General Frank Savage, played by Peck, who takes over command of a dispirited American bomber squadron in England during the Second World War. By applying strict, and at first unpopular, discipline, the general whips the squadron into shape and it proudly flies its way to success. The main theme of the movie was how tough the general was on his men, and how it paid off in the long run.

I asked my question and, in finishing his answer, Peck said, "I'm very pleased that movie is still being used by many companies as a motivational tool." That gave me an opening to tell him a story.

"Mr. Peck, when that movie came out, my father was coach of the Montreal Canadiens hockey team." As soon as I said that people applauded, and so did Gregory Peck! He might not have known much about the Montreal Canadiens, but he realized what I said meant something to an audience in Montreal.

I proceeded with my story, about how Dick Sr. had been so impressed by the movie, and its message about discipline, he rented the theatre for a morning and, instead of holding a practice, he took his players to watch *Twelve O'Clock High*. His message was, "If you think I'm tough, watch this guy."

I once told that story to Bob Gainey, then captain of the Canadiens. Bob's take on it was, "Do you think that would work today?" I knew from the way he said it, it wouldn't.

■ ❘ ■ ❘ ■

Another movie legend who made it to our HNIC studio was Bob Hope. It was during the playoffs in 1976, the year the Summer Olympics were held in Montreal. Hope was in town to tape a TV special with an Olympic theme at the Forum. Bing Crosby was with him and the original plan was for me to tape an interview with Hope and Crosby at the hockey game the night before their show. After our producer, Don Wallace, told me they were coming, I was a basket case the rest of the day. At showtime Crosby wasn't there, but Hope was. In all my years in showbiz, that was the only time I had sweaty palms. All I can say about it now is that the interview got done. Hope was fine. I was terrible.

■ ❘ ■ ❘ ■

Elvis Presley gave a concert at the Oakland Alameda County Coliseum the night before the Canadiens played there sometime in the early 1970s. It was another trip to Oakland where I flew out on my own, not with the team, and when I checked into the hotel I learned that Elvis was staying there. The place was crawling with security, even though the star was a couple of miles down the highway giving his concert. Something about young girls trying to get into his room.

The next morning there was a limo parked at a side entrance waiting to take the King across the bay to San Francisco, where he was to appear that night. So, like a groupie, I waited for him to show up, which he did around ten o'clock. Even at that early hour he was dressed in a tight-fitting black outfit, complete with a red-and-black cape that would have looked good on Batman.

This was before Elvis got fat, and he was smaller than I had imagined. Perhaps he seemed small because he was surrounded by four bodyguards, all of whom looked like fugitives from the offensive line of the Oakland Raiders. But it was a good thing they were there to hold back the unruly crowd of me and three young housewives. He was only about ten feet from where I was standing when he walked by, and I stayed until the limo pulled away. Then I knew for sure that Elvis had left the building.

■■■■

Paul Anka, the music man from Ottawa, once dropped the puck before a Canadiens game in Detroit. It was at the old Olympia, and Anka stepped onto the ice sporting a deep Las Vegas tan and wearing skates. He was shaky on his pins, very shaky, but he wobbled out to centre ice and did the honours.

During the first period, Alex Delvecchio, the long-time Detroit star who was then the Wings' general manager, came by our radio booth and asked if I wanted to interview Anka between periods. I did, of course, and found out he was very much up on the hockey scene. Anka was happy to do the interview because he was on tour and scheduled to perform in Montreal a week later, and I was happy to let him plug his show.

■■■■

In 1989, a few days after the Calgary Flames defeated the Montreal Canadiens to win the Stanley Cup, I took part in a charity golf tournament in Barrie, Ontario. The tournament was organized by Len Bramson, a long-time family friend. The out-of-towners stayed in Toronto and Len arranged limos to drive us to the event. My fellow passengers were Jean Béliveau, president of the Montreal Canadiens Ronald Corey, and actor Hal Linden. Best known for his starring role in the TV series *Barney Miller*, Linden, a golf nut, was in Toronto appearing on stage in *Show Boat*.

I'm pretty sure neither Corey nor Béliveau knew who Hal Linden was. Linden certainly didn't know me or Corey, and showed no sign of recognition when he was introduced to Jean Béliveau. That didn't stop him from regaling the strangers in the limo with several show-business stories, including one about Gary Crosby, the alcoholic son of the legendary singer and actor Bing Crosby.

Linden told of the time Gary Crosby attended a party in London, England, where he became totally drunk and couldn't remember where he was staying. One of the guests took pity on him and brought him home for the night. When he was crawling into bed Crosby started to cry and said to his host, "You have no idea what it's like to be the son of a famous father." The drunken Crosby obviously had no idea that the person who had come to his rescue and was putting him to bed was Charlie Chaplin, Jr.

■■■■

I have found myself alone with some fabled sports heroes. There was Wayne Gretzky in the L.A. Forum, and Kareem Abdul-Jabbar in a hotel elevator in Kansas City. If Elvis looked small among his bodyguards, I must have looked like a midget alongside the seven-feet-plus basketball legend.

And there was the time I was all alone with Muhammad Ali in the lobby of the Royal York Hotel in Toronto. He was still Cassius Clay then, and I had just seen him win a fifteen-round decision at Maple Leaf Gardens against a courageous George Chuvalo. I was in Toronto to tape a sports hot-seat program with Johnny Esaw and had seen the fight at ring-side courtesy of Brian McFarlane, who again got me a press pass to a big event. Brian and I went out for a bite after, and it was around 12:30 when he dropped me off at the Royal York.

The champ and his large entourage were staying there, and had booked an entire floor. I was waiting for an elevator to take me up to my room when who comes slowly up the stairs from the street, surprisingly all by himself, but Cassius Clay. There wasn't another soul in the lobby. I forgot about my up signal, and walked towards him.

"I saw you fight tonight, Champ," I said. "Congratulations," Then I reached out to shake his hand.

"Can't shake," he said in a tired, but very familiar voice. "Hand's too sore. Too sore."

Then there was Michael Jordan. Between the third and fourth games of the 1992 Stanley Cup finals between Pittsburgh and the Blackhawks in Chicago, it was golf day for the hockey crowd at the nearby Kemper Lakes Course, where Payne Stewart won the PGA championship in 1989. Bob Murray, a former Hawks player who was still working for the team, was a part-time assistant pro there and he set it up. I went with Bob Cole and Ron

MacLean, and when we arrived the buzz was that Jordan was on the golf course.

We arrived at a green somewhere on the first nine, and spotted His Airness getting set to drive off a nearby tee. When he did, we could see he had a pretty good swing. Bob walked over and said something to him, then I called out, "Michael, they just took a poll in Canada about the most-recognizable pro athlete. Gretzky was first, and you were second."

Jordan, by now in his golf cart, said, "Canada? Ain't never been," and drove away. That changed, but at the time we had yet to see a Raptor or a Grizzly.

▌▐▌▐

I had an interesting few words about sports broadcasting with golf great Lee Trevino. In 1988 I worked on the CTV telecast of a Skins Game at Glen Abbey, which involved Trevino, Dave Barr, Arnold Palmer, and Curtis Strange, who had just won the U.S. Open. My partner in the tower was Jim Nelford, who had easy access to the golfers, being a PGA player himself, and I tagged along one morning when Jim joined Trevino for a coffee.

At that time Trevino was working as an analyst for NBC. The talk got around to broadcasting, and I mentioned that golf commentators usually made excuses for the players rather than come right out and say somebody had made a bad shot or a mistake in judgement.

Trevino said, "That's the way I do it. You'll never hear me say anything bad about any of my guys."

I pointed out that, in Canada, hockey announcers were criticized if they didn't criticize, and asked Trevino why he treated "my guys" the way he did.

He replied, "Hey, they've got wives and kids out there. I don't want them hearing any bad stuff about their husbands and daddies."

It's interesting when athletes who have not been co-operative with the media end up in a broadcast booth themselves. Curtis Strange is a good example. Media types used to call him "Discourteous" Strange, and that was a fitting way to describe him during our Skins telecasts. Now that he's a regular analyst on ABC, I wonder what he thinks of golfers who treat the media the way he often did.

Celebrities can be in awe of other celebrities. Scotty Bowman met Tiger Woods at a *Sports Illustrated* awards show early in 2000. Woods is a hockey fan, and recognized Scotty immediately. In July, Scotty was at Pebble Beach working as a scorer during the U.S. Open golf championship, which Woods won by a record-shattering fifteen strokes. On the final day he walked with the twosome of Woods and Ernie Els. I watched the telecast and spotted Scotty a couple of times, striding along with the golfers. I also saw him standing behind them in the scorer's truck when they were verifying their cards.

Two days later Scotty called to tell me about his experience at Pebble Beach. He was talking a mile a minute and I finally said, "Scotty, I've been with you for six of your eight Stanley Cups, and I think you're more excited now than you were then." He just kept talking.

What impressed him most was Tiger Woods's total focus on his game. When it was all over and the scorecards had been signed, Woods turned around, saw Scotty, and said, "Scotty Bowman. What are you doing here?" Through the entire four hours they spent at close proximity on the golf course, Woods had never acknowledged Bowman simply because he had never seen him. Scotty called it "amazing" the way the world's greatest golfer could shut out everything around him. I'm sure the coach tried to get that message across to his players in Detroit the next season.

∎∎∎∎

For the last twenty-four years I worked at CFCF, the station sponsored the annual Montreal Sports Celebrity Dinner, in aid of the Montreal Children's Hospital, and I was the chairman. It was a rewarding but nerve-wracking experience. I would line up ten or twelve head-table guests every year, and put together a video package of each to show at the dinner. Each athlete would speak for a minute or two, which was fine with them, and then there would be a guest speaker. It was a big undertaking, and I worried my way through it every year.

I made sure hockey was front and centre. We always had a Canadiens player at the head table. Paul Henderson was there after his big goal in 1972, and Mario Lemieux after his Canada Cup winner in 1987. Over the years Bobby Hull, Gordie Howe, Bobby Orr, Jean Béliveau, Don Cherry, and the Rocket sat at the head table, and so did the Stanley Cup. It was there in 1986, the year the Canadiens weren't supposed to win it, but did. We never had Wayne, because the Edmonton Oilers were never in town when the dinner was on.

The Expos were always represented. Hank Aaron was a guest, as were Pete Rose, Brooks Robinson, and Don Drysdale. Canadian amateur athletes often drew the biggest response in the wake of victories on the Olympic and international scene. These included skier Nancy Greene, swimmers Victor Davis, Alex Baumann, and Elaine Tanner, and figure skater Donald Jackson.

One of Canadian football's best-remembered plays happened when the Montreal Alouettes' Chuck Hunsinger fumbled late in the 1954 Grey Cup game, and the Edmonton Eskimos' Jackie

Parker picked up the ball and ran for the game-winning touch-down. The two had never met until I got them together at the dinner twenty-five years later. That same year we had Ralph Branca and Bobby Thomson, the pitcher and the hitter involved in perhaps baseball's most-famous home run, when the New York Giants beat the Brooklyn Dodgers to win the pennant in 1951.

One of the biggest names we had, and the one who sold the most tickets for us, was Joe DiMaggio. The dinner usually drew crowds of around eight or nine hundred, but the year DiMaggio was the headliner there were twelve hundred in the room. DiMaggio arrived a couple of days early, with a pal of his whose expenses we also had to pay. He did everything we asked him to do, including visit the Children's Hospital, which was kind of sad, because none of the kids knew who he was. But by the time it was all over, DiMaggio had been defensive, demanding, and generally a pain in the ass. It's disappointing to learn one of your boyhood heroes has a bit of clay on his feet.

■ ❙ ■ ❙ ■

Through all of my years on HNIC my work received very little mention in the print press, which was probably a good thing for my ego. But write a book and everybody gets into the act. It seems like every paper in every city and town has a book reviewer who can be nice, or not so nice. I can honestly say most have been nice, but there were exceptions.

My book *The Habs* was, as you might guess, about the Montreal Canadiens. You can also guess what kind of a critique it got from the reviewer who began with, "I've hated the Montreal Canadiens all my life."

My favourite review appeared in a Vancouver paper. I think it was also a review of *The Habs*, but I'm not sure. Anyway, the first half of what the reviewer wrote was all about what a terrible hockey announcer I was, how he turned down the sound every time I came on, and so on. He finally got around to a grudging acknowledgement that the book wasn't too bad, and then threw in one of my all-time favourite lines: "The best thing about this book is that you don't have to listen to Irvin talk."

I hope the guy never finds out how many times I've used that line. He might send me a bill.

A Few Highs and a Low

....

I spent a good portion of the 1989–90 season as the HNIC play-by-play man for Canadiens games and, on most occasions, my colour man was Scotty Bowman. Scotty and the Sabres had parted company three years before, and shortly after that he began working on the show. He had been a quick study in the booth, which didn't surprise me, and we had a pretty good thing going. At the same time a lot of us were baffled because hockey's all-time winningest coach couldn't land a job in the NHL. Once he did, he won three more Stanley Cups in the space of seven years.

When he had been the coach in Montreal, Bowman had ruled the roost, but on the show I was in some ways his mentor. One night, before a game in Long Island, Scotty was holding court in the press room with some newspaper reporters when I interrupted and said, "Come on, Scotty, we're late. Let's go." Red Fisher was there and said to me, "You've been waiting a long time to talk

228

to him like that. You must love it." I wouldn't say I loved it, but for sure our relationship had changed.

The Canadiens played Buffalo in the first round of the 1990 playoffs. Scotty and I were assigned to do the series, which suited him fine because he was still living in the Buffalo area. The teams split the first four games. Ed Milliken was producing our shows, and the night before the fifth game, in Buffalo, he called with what sounded like disturbing news. Toronto was playing in St. Louis that night and, if the Leafs lost, they were out of the play-offs. Ed advised me that if that happened, Bob Cole would come to Buffalo and take over the play-by-play for the rest of the series, and I would become the third man in the booth. The decision had been made in Toronto by the show's executive producer, Ron Harrison.

Through most of my hockey broadcasting career I was a play-by-play man on radio, and a colour man on television. Most of my television play-by-play work came the first few years after Danny retired. On several occasions I did play-by-play in the first playoff round, and colour after that. That never bothered me, but the prospect of being replaced during a series did. I told Ed that if it worked out that way, I would prefer to step aside completely rather than become the third man. I spent the evening cheering for the Maple Leafs to win. They didn't.

Ed called me early the next morning to confirm that Bob Cole was coming to Buffalo. I said, "Fine. Have a good show."

A few minutes later the man who made the decision, Ron Harrison, called me to confirm Ed's confirmation. I said, "Ron, tell me one thing. What have I been doing wrong? Nobody has said anything about my work."

He replied, "There's nothing wrong with your work, but I have no choice. I have to do it." That's all the explanation I ever received, which did nothing for my bruised and battered ego. I can only assume somebody up there in the CBC didn't like my play-by-play.

I'm glad I was never asked, or ordered, to take over from a fellow announcer during a playoff series. I like to think that, if I had a choice, I would not have agreed. Bob likely had a tough time with it, although he never said a word to me about the situation, then or later, and I never asked him. Bob worked with Scotty that night, and I switched over to the CFCF Radio booth. The Canadiens won the game 4–2, and I had become the first, and still only, HNIC play-by-play man to be replaced during a playoff series.

Back in Montreal I found myself in the middle of a bit of a backlash against *Hockey Night in Canada*. Mike Boone, the television critic for the Montreal *Gazette*, wrote that I had been treated in a "shamefully shabby" fashion. I received a lot of calls of support, or should I say sympathy. The first was from Danny. Ron Harrison's two immediate predecessors, Ralph Mellanby and Don Wallace, both called, and so did a few broadcasters from around the league, including John Davidson and Jiggs McDonald. I wasn't accustomed to that much attention.

I attended a Canadiens practice and ran into Réjean Tremblay, an influential columnist for *La Presse*. I had even made the French papers. Réjean was a separatist before there were separatists and he said to me, "You know how to avoid something like this, don't you?" I laughed and said, "Yeah, I know. Separate." The next day he wrote a short piece about my situation, claiming replacing the Montreal Canadiens' announcer with the Toronto Maple Leafs' announcer was another insult to Quebec from the hated Rest of Canada, especially Toronto.

When I walked into the press room at the Forum before the sixth game, Bob Cole was sitting at a table with John Garrett, who had flown in from Vancouver to be the colour man. There was no sign of Scotty Bowman. Apparently, according to what John had

Learning to put on a TV smile with the cast of *Carte Blanche*, my first TV show.
Left to right: Marge Anthony, who did the weather, host Jimmy Tapp, and newscaster Art Leonard.

The first program I hosted was *Pinbusters*, a kids' bowling show, in 1961.

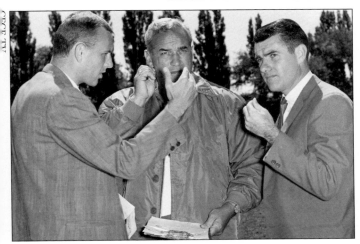

Long-time HNIC producer Ralph Mellanby and I go back a long way. Here we are in 1965 during the taping of a weekly show on CFCF with Montreal Alouettes head coach Jim Trimble.

Having fun in the broadcast booth at the Forum with Howie Meeker. I was the first to work with Howie when he burst onto the HNIC scene.

Canadiens' tough guy John Ferguson was in the booth with Danny and me for the classic 1975 New Year's Eve game between the Canadiens and the Soviet Red Army.

Jean Béliveau was the first hockey player I interviewed. Here we are a few years later in the broadcast booth at the Forum.

I joined *Hockey Night in Canada* in 1966. Ralph Mellanby was producing the Montreal shows and Brian McFarlane was the host.

The young coach of the St. Louis Blues, Scotty Bowman, was working as an analyst in Montreal during the playoffs in 1971. A few weeks later, he became coach of the Canadiens.

A moment from my other life as a disk jockey. I hosted a big band TV special that starred singers Buddy Greco and Ranee Lee.

Lambert Mayer, on the left, was my predecessor as the official scorer at the Montreal Forum. With us at a banquet in 1984 were two of my best friends, Danny Gallivan and Red Fisher.

With Brian McFarlane, Dan Matheson, and Bob Cole before a CTV broadcast of an exhibition game between the Canadiens and a Russian team in the early 1980s.

The Selke and Irvin families together again at the party to celebrate the Canadiens' 1986 Stanley Cup win. Left to right: Frank Selke, Jr., his sister Blanche, Wilma Irvin, and her husband, Dick.

Centre ice on a game night at the Forum in 1988 with Danny Gallivan making a presentation on behalf of the Canadiens in recognition of my selection to the Hockey Hall of Fame.

A great family moment. Nancy Anne, Wilma, and Doug were with me in Toronto when I was inducted into the Hockey Hall of Fame Media Section in 1988.

Three of my favourites getting together at the Forum: Danny Gallivan holds court with Don Cherry and Ron MacLean.

One of the highlights of my career was being co-host of the closing ceremonies at the Montreal Forum, March 11, 1996, more than fifty-five years after I first was in the building.

Watching from the podium as Jean Béliveau passes the torch to Henri Richard during the emotional closing ceremonies at the Montreal Forum, March 11, 1996.

Flanked by my HNIC bosses, John Shannon (left) and Alan Clark, who organized my retirement party, September 22, 1999. I'm holding the seven wood from the set of golf clubs they presented to me.

Colin Campbell(left) and Jim Gregory of the NHL present me with a Milestone Award from the league at my retirement party.

The HNIC gang all showed up. Left to right: Scott Russell, Chris Cuthbert, Harry Neale, and Kelly Hrudey.

With Don Cherry in a corner of one of his bars after guesting on his TV show. Grapes looks happy with the result.

Eight of Maurice Richard's former teammates served as pallbearers at his funeral, May 31, 2000. Clockwise from left: Elmer Lach, Ken Mosdell, Butch Bouchard, Jean Béliveau, Dickie Moore, Ken Reardon, Gerry McNeil, Henri Richard.

With a couple of greats from the glory years of the Habs, Bernie Geoffrion and Guy Lafleur, in Montreal, 1999.

been told, he was there because Scotty had to deal with a family problem. So the entire crew in the booth was different from the one that had started the series, another first for HNIC. The Canadiens won the game 5–2, and the series was over.

The next morning I was in the CFCF record library preparing a big-band show when the phone rang. I picked it up and heard a familiar greeting: "Dick, Scotty."

"Where are you?"

"I'm in Florida."

"I hear there's a problem in your family. Anything serious?"

"There's no problem. I figured if that's the way they're going to treat a faithful employee, I didn't want to work any more. So we came down here for a few days."

Scotty didn't have to do that, and shouldn't have done that. But under his often gruff exterior there's a pretty soft heart, and I was touched by what he did. A year later, in his speech when he was inducted into the Hockey Hall of Fame, Scotty made mention of his work with HNIC and thanked me for helping him. I was touched then too, although any help I gave Scotty Bowman didn't begin to compare with what I learned about hockey sitting beside him in a broadcast booth for a couple of years.

After what I had done in Buffalo, Ron Harrison could have told me to take the rest of my career off, but he didn't, and I was back in the booth when the Canadiens played Boston in the second round. I really wasn't in the mood, and when the Bruins won the series in five games my season was over, which was a good thing. Bob Cole did the play-by-play and, while I can't recall who the second man in the booth was, it was my fault that crew wasn't a Happy Gang. It was a long time, like maybe two weeks, before I started looking forward to the next season.

∎∎∎

The controversy was quite uncharacteristic of me. I was never one to rock the boat, which is maybe why that isolated incident is just about the only real downer I had in thirty-five years on *Hockey Night in Canada*, and in forty years of broadcasting. (One of my employees once stabbed me in the back when I was sports director at CFCF Radio, but I won't count that.) Oh, there were times I complained, after a fashion, usually about not having a contract when the season began, but there was never anything major. Ralph Mellanby would ask me, "Did they call you about a new jacket?" I'd say yes, and he'd laugh and say, "That's all you need. If they call you about a jacket, you're back on the show."

I could have argued once in a while for more money, but I had to remember that the CBC allowed me on their air even though I had a full-time job at a CTV station, and vice versa. That happy, and unique, situation lasted twenty-four years until I retired from CFCF in 1991. Put the two incomes together and compare it with what other sportscasters in Canada were earning and, well, let's just say I was doing all right.

When I signed a contract with HNIC to do some features during the 2000–01 season, it marked my thirty-fifth straight year on the show. I've asked a few CBC types and they can't name anyone, other than Fred Davis and Pierre Berton on *Front Page Challenge*, who had that long a run on the same show at the CBC. It will likely never get mentioned in a history of the corporation (especially one written in Toronto, as Réjean Tremblay might say), but I'm proud of it.

∎▮∎▮

After 1990 there would be four more Stanley Cup–winning broadcasts in my future, and some playoff play-by-play as well. Certainly Cups twenty-three through twenty-six rank among my

HNIC broadcasting highs, and I have Mario Lemieux to thank for the first two.

In 1990–91, six teams finished the regular season with more points than the Pittsburgh Penguins, two in their own conference. Lemieux, the best player in the game when healthy, wasn't healthy that season because of his chronic back problems, and appeared in just twenty-six games. But he missed only one game in the playoffs, racked up sixteen goals and twenty-eight assists for forty-four points in twenty-three games, and accepted the Stanley Cup at centre ice when it was all over.

The Minnesota North Stars were the big surprise of the 1991 playoffs. Before the season the moribund franchise had hired Bob Clarke as general manager and Bob Gainey as coach, but the team continued to struggle. Around the halfway mark the Canadiens played there and only five thousand or so fans bothered to show up. But somehow the Minnesota team turned things around, sneaked into the final playoff spot, and defeated Chicago, St. Louis, and Edmonton on their way to the finals against Pittsburgh.

After Boston eliminated Montreal in the second round, HNIC assigned me to work the Wales Conference final between the Bruins and Pittsburgh. In the sixth game, in Pittsburgh, the Penguins' notorious hitman, Ulf Samuelsson, kneed Cam Neely in the thigh and put him out for the rest of the game, which the Penguins won 5–3 to clinch the series.

Neely had been great in the playoffs and had scored sixteen goals. As he lay on the ice after the hit, Boston coach Mike Milbury went berserk behind the bench, slamming a stick against the glass and screaming blue murder at Samuelsson. Much like what happened to Guy Lafleur after the hit he took from Hartford's Pat Boutette in the 1980 playoffs, the incident in Pittsburgh was the beginning of the end of Cam Neely's career.

Several years later, Tie Domi of the Toronto Maple Leafs was suspended for knocking out Samuelsson with a sucker punch. The following summer Domi attended the Cam Neely Charity Golf Tournament in Boston, and at the dinner they showed the video of him KO'ing Samuelsson. The next night Domi was at a dinner I spoke at in Barrie. He told me what had happened the night before in Boston: "When the video ended everybody stood up and they cheered for two minutes. That's the longest standing ovation I ever got."

■|■|■

A unique character, Bob Johnson, was coaching the Penguins. Known as "Badger Bob" because of his fifteen years as the coach of the University of Wisconsin Badgers, where his teams won three U.S. national championships, he was also known for his favourite saying: "It's a great day for hockey." That meant every day as far as Bob was concerned.

Johnson became coach of the Calgary Flames in 1982 and spent five years there. After a Canadiens game in Calgary, I ran into him leaving the Saddledome with a stack of videotapes under his arm. "Going home to figure out how to beat Edmonton," he said. But through most of his tenure with the Flames, Badger Bob never quite managed to do that. The 1986 playoffs were an exception, but Bob Johnson's Flames were never quite as good as Glen Sather's Oilers. Johnson left Calgary in 1987 to become executive director of USA Hockey. Two years later the Flames won the Stanley Cup, with Terry Crisp coaching. Johnson returned to the NHL in 1990 with the Penguins.

Bob Johnson loved to talk hockey with anybody, anywhere. During the 1991 finals, post-practice press conferences were set up for the two coaches. Johnson would arrive early, talk until the last reporter had left, and then wait a bit longer in case anybody else showed up. In contrast, Bob Gainey never appeared. I ran into him in a hallway one morning and said, "Aren't you supposed to be at a press conference?" Gainey replied, "If they want me, they know where to find me."

After three games of the 1991 finals the North Stars had a 2–1 lead. Was the sixteenth team in the sixteen-team playoff field going to win the Stanley Cup? Mario Lemieux had missed the third game, in Minnesota, because of his bad back. But he returned for the next game and the hockey world began revolving as it should. The Penguins won the next three games, 5–3, 6–4, and 8–0. During that series Mario scored one of his greatest goals, one that was replayed many times when he retired in 1997, and replayed many times again when he came back in 2000. Jon Casey was the Minnesota goalie. What was never replayed was a save the other Minnesota goalie, Brian Hayward, made off Lemieux on a breakaway. It was one of the best I ever saw, but that tape is lost somewhere in space.

I worked the finals in the booth with Bob Cole and Harry Neale, and was put on dressing-room alert for the sixth game, in Minnesota. It was a blowout, so I headed down early. The first player I interviewed was Pittsburgh defenceman Jim Paek, who was born in South Korea and had grown up in Toronto. Paek spent most of the 1990–91 season with the Canadian national team, then joined the Penguins and appeared in eight playoff games. He was in a state of total excitement as I interviewed him, thanked him, and moved on to the next guest. When it was all over I realized I had forgotten to congratulate him for scoring the Penguins' seventh goal, which I should have done because it was his first in the NHL. There he was, on national television not long after the biggest goal of his career, and the dumb interviewer never mentioned it.

After we signed off I sought Paek out, apologized, and said, "Win the Cup next year and we'll put you on first again, and I'll ask you about all the goals you scored." The Penguins did win in 1992 and we put Jim on first again. He played in nineteen playoff games that year, but I couldn't ask him about his goals because he didn't score any.

My interviews with the victorious Penguins were done in a room adjacent to their dressing room, but I still didn't escape a champagne shower. One of their equipment men started celebrating after the Penguins took a 3–0 lead, in the first period. By the time the game ended he was smashed, and was staggering around dousing anybody within his shaky reach. That included me and whoever I was interviewing at the time. He really soaked us.

■ ■ ■ ■

One of my interviews that night in Minnesota was with Bob Johnson. I had got to know Bob pretty well over the years, and I almost choked up I was so happy for him. Sadly, it was our last conversation. While he was preparing the American team for the 1991 Canada Cup, Bob Johnson was stricken with multiple brain tumours. He passed away three months later.

With Bob Johnson ailing as training camp drew near, the Penguins quietly began making plans to appoint an interim coach, and they had a pretty good candidate already on their payroll. Scotty Bowman. Shortly after he left HNIC to solve a "family problem" during the 1990 playoffs, Scotty finally got back into the NHL, with the Penguins, who gave him the fancy title of Director of Player Development and Recruitment. He spent a season travelling around watching hockey games. Scotty was in Minnesota the night the Penguins won the Stanley Cup, and was genuinely happy.

Bowman took over just before the season began. His coaching style was different from Bob Johnson's, and he wasn't nearly as well liked by his players. As the season went on there were stories of unrest within the ranks, which reminded a lot of us in Montreal of Scotty's tenure with the Canadiens.

It reached a point where the Pittsburgh players held a meeting with general manager Craig Patrick to air their complaints. But as the playoffs approached, things got better. Maybe the players started to realize Scotty Bowman knew something about the game after all, and the Pittsburgh Penguins went on to win their second straight Stanley Cup.

Mario Lemieux missed sixteen games that season but still won the scoring championship with 131 points, eight more than teammate Kevin Stevens, and ten more than Wayne Gretzky. After winning a tough seven-game series against Washington, the Penguins played the New York Rangers in the second round. In game two Lemieux was slashed by Adam Graves, suffered a broken hand, and missed the rest of the series. (Graves received a four-game suspension.) Mario was their best, but the Penguins had more than a few very good players. Stevens, Rick Tocchet, Ron Francis, Larry Murphy, and Bryan Trottier were all part of a fine hockey team. And with Jaromir Jagr, then in his second season, picking up a lot of the offensive slack left by the Lemieux injury, Pittsburgh defeated the Rangers in six games.

Lemieux missed the first game of the next series, against Boston, but returned to help eliminate the Bruins in four straight. That series produced another much-replayed goal by Mario, the one where he twisted Raymond Bourque every which way as he flew past the great Bruins defenceman to score on Andy Moog.

I worked the 1992 finals between Pittsburgh and the Chicago Blackhawks, who were coached by Mike Keenan. The Penguins won four straight, but it was closer than that would suggest. They took the opener 5–4, Lemieux scoring the winning goal on a power play with just thirteen seconds remaining in regulation time. The next two games ended 3–1, and 1–0, and the Penguins hung on to win the Cup clincher 6–5, in Chicago. Lemieux won his second straight playoff MVP award but, in my mind, it could just as easily have gone to Rick Tocchet, who was brilliant, especially in the finals. It was Scotty Bowman's sixth Stanley Cup, and my twenty-fourth.

I attended Mike Keenan's press conference in the bowels of the Chicago Stadium following the last game. When it was over, Mike spotted me, came over and said, "The next time you're here, come to my office. There are a lot of old pictures there and your dad's in some of them." That was very nice of him, I thought, considering the circumstances. But the next time I was there, the following season, Mike wasn't. He'd been fired a few days earlier.

John Davidson had arranged for a group of us to play the famed Oakmont golf course near Pittsburgh, one of the world's best, if the series went to a fifth game. The first time the Penguins played in Montreal the next season I spoke to Mario and, pretending to be serious, said, "I'm pretty mad at you."

He looked puzzled and said, "Why? What's wrong?"

Still frowning I said, "Well, if you had lost that last game in Chicago, I was all set to play Oakmont the next day."

Mario laughed and said, "I was there – Oakmont was in great shape."

In the Penguins' two Stanley Cup–winning playoff years Mario Lemieux played in thirty-eight games, and had seventy-eight points. In the past several years, whenever I have been asked who is the best player I've ever seen, I always reply that I don't have a best player because I've seen so many great ones. But I will say that Maurice Richard is the most exciting player I ever saw, and Guy Lafleur the most exciting I ever described as a broadcaster. And, in the playoffs of 1991 and 1992, Mario Lemieux raised the individual aspect of the game to a level higher than anyone I've ever seen play.

I still feel that way.

∎∥∎∥∎

If Marty McSorley hadn't had an illegal stick in his hands in the 1993 Stanley Cup finals, Wayne Gretzky would have succeeded Mario Lemieux as the Cup-winning captain. At least that's my opinion of what was perhaps the most bizarre incident in a bizarre playoff year, especially for those of us covering the team that won the Stanley Cup, the Montreal Canadiens.

To this day a lot of people say the Canadiens' 1993 win was a fluke. They argue that the team was a far cry from the dynasties of the past when Stanley Cup parades were almost an annual rite of spring in Montreal. That's true, but it's also a bit of a bad rap because, in 1992–93, the Canadiens had 102 points, one of the seven teams that finished the regular season with more than one hundred points. The Penguins, with Scotty Bowman still coaching, led with 119 to finish ten points ahead of runner-up Boston. But the second-place Bruins were only eight points ahead of seventh place Vancouver in the overall standings. The playoff winner was a toss-up if you eliminated Pittsburgh, which is exactly what the New York Islanders did in the second round.

Shortly after Montreal was eliminated by Boston in 1992, their coach, Pat Burns, signed with Toronto. To replace Burns the Canadiens hired Jacques Demers, a two-time coach of the year with Detroit. Known as a good motivator, Demers had spent the previous two seasons doing colour commentary on radio broadcasts of the Quebec Nordiques, who finished dead last in their conference both years. Which reminds me, in the days before blanket radio and television coverage of the NHL, what did coaches do after they were fired? Today, it's almost automatic that they wind up in a broadcast booth or television studio. Some, like Harry Neale, become very good at it, and are happy to be there. As Harry says, "This way I get to the finals every year, and never lose a game."

Between 1944 and 1993 the Montreal Canadiens had not gone more than seven years without winning the Stanley Cup (an impressive achievement that went out the window in the year 2000), and it had been seven years since their last one when they began the playoffs in '93. The first round was a renewal of the Battle of Quebec, the Montreal Canadiens against the Quebec Nordiques.

The Nordiques had rebounded from a 52-point season to a 104-point season, the biggest one-year improvement up to then. (The San Jose Sharks improved by 58 points the following season.) They had patiently developed high draft choices such as Joe Sakic, Mats Sundin, and Owen Nolan. In 1991 they drafted Eric Lindros and his family, but they didn't want any part of Quebec City and never showed up. A year later the Nordiques traded the Lindroses to Philadelphia, receiving proven players like Steve Duchesne, Mike Ricci, and goaltender Ron Hextall in return. All this added up to 104 points in 1992–93, two better than Montreal.

The Canadiens had also improved. The team was still basically homegrown, with players like Patrick Roy, Eric Desjardins, Mike Keane, Guy Carbonneau, John LeClair, and Lyle Odelein having been drafted or signed as rookie free agents. To makes things better, general manager Serge Savard had entered the marketplace in the off-season, trading for Vincent Damphousse and Brian Bellows. He had obtained Kirk Muller a year earlier, and those three scored a combined 116 goals in '92–93. With both Quebec teams strong, the rivalry was back in business, and there were some wild nights at the Forum and the Colisée. For example, in a game on December 17 the Canadiens led 4–0 after the first nine minutes. Then the Nordiques scored three goals in the next three minutes, but before the period ended the Canadiens scored two more in less than a minute. The fans, and the announcers, had a ball.

Six Canadian teams were in the playoffs that year, so the HNIC talent base was spread all over the map. Chris Cuthbert and I broadcast the all-Quebec series, and when the Nordiques won the first two games on home ice, the cheering in the press box reached record proportions.

Quebec had won the first game on an overtime goal by Scott Young, one that normally would be long forgotten by now. But a trivia question makes it memorable: "Who scored the only overtime goal against the Montreal Canadiens in the 1993 playoffs?" The question is out there because, in their remaining nineteen playoff games the Canadiens would go into overtime ten times, and win ten times.

Their incredible string began in the third game against Quebec, Vincent Damphousse scoring for a 2–1 win. After a 3–2 regulation-time victory to even the series, it was overtime again in the fifth game, Kirk Muller scoring for a dramatic 5–4 win.

That fifth game is one I well remember. Early in the second period, with Quebec leading, Patrick Roy was hit on the shoulder by a shot from Mike Hough and his arm went dead. Roy left the game and was replaced by André Racicot, his young back-up who had been dubbed "Red Light" Racicot by my hard-hearted friend Red Fisher. Montreal fans were sure their cause was lost but, after a couple of needles in the arm, Roy returned. His arm started to feel numb again in overtime and Patrick didn't know how much longer he would last. But Muller came to his rescue in the ninth minute of OT.

Players "play hurt" in the playoffs. I went into the Canadiens' dressing room after the game and there were guys all over the room with ice packs on knees and shoulders, arms and ankles. I'd never seen anything like it. Roy had an arm in a sling, as did Muller. It reminded me of the scene in *Gone With the Wind* where Scarlett O'Hara is walking through hundreds of wounded soldiers lying on the ground at the Atlanta railway station. The playoffs were just beginning, and I thought there was no way those guys could last much longer. But they proved me wrong, again.

I went to the Forum the morning of the sixth game and tried to make small talk with Joe Sakic and Ron Hextall. They were polite, but I sensed they knew they were done, and they were. The Canadiens won that night 6–2, and Quebec coach Pierre Pagé lost it. As the score mounted, the cameras zoomed in on Pagé as he screamed at his players on the bench, especially Mats Sundin. It wasn't a pretty picture.

█▌█▌█

The Canadiens played Buffalo next and swept the series in four. All but the first game went into overtime, Montreal winning on goals by Guy Carbonneau, Gilbert Dionne, and Kirk Muller. Chris Cuthbert and I worked that series and then were sent to cover the end of the series between Pittsburgh and the New York Islanders.

Mario Lemieux missed twenty-four games in 1992–93, first because of his back and then because he was diagnosed in early January with Hodgkin's disease, a cancer of the lymph nodes. On March 2, after undergoing his final radiation treatment, Lemieux travelled to Philadelphia and rejoined his team for a game that night. Remarkably, he scored a goal and an assist. When he was forced to leave he had a comfortable lead in the scoring race. When he returned, Buffalo's Pat LaFontaine was ahead of him by twelve points, but from then on LaFontaine never had a chance. Lemieux was awesome, with fifty-one points in a stretch of sixteen games, which included two four-goal games and a five-goal game. He ended his sixty-game season with 160 points, twelve more than LaFontaine, who played in all Buffalo's eighty-four games.

But Mario's magic faded with fatigue in the playoffs, and the Islanders won the sixth and seventh games for a come-from-behind upset of the defending champions. David Volek's series-winning overtime goal ended the hopes of a dynasty in Pittsburgh, and also ended Scotty Bowman's tenuous term as the Penguins' coach. Scotty, who was not happy when the season ended, signed with the Detroit Red Wings a few weeks later.

The Canadiens played the Islanders in the conference final and defeated them in five games, two of which they won in overtime. Stephan Lebeau scored at 6:21 of the second overtime in the second game. Two nights later Guy Carbonneau scored in the first extra period, giving the Canadiens seven overtime wins in eleven games.

In the other half of the playoff draw the Toronto Maple Leafs were the biggest story. The Leafs had enjoyed a fine year in Pat Burns's first season behind their bench, setting team records with forty-four wins and ninety-nine points. (Burns and Dick Sr. are the only two men to have coached both the Maple Leafs and the Canadiens.) The Leafs prevailed in seven games over both Detroit and St. Louis to advance to the conference final against Wayne Gretzky and the rest of the Los Angeles Kings. Gretzky had missed the first half of the season because of a back injury but had returned to his old form in leading the Kings past Calgary and Vancouver in the first two rounds.

When Toronto defeated the Kings in the fifth game to take a 3–2 series lead, fans in Canada were ecstatic. The Canadiens had already beaten the Islanders, and one more Maple Leafs win would mean a Toronto-Montreal Stanley Cup final for the first time since 1967. CBC executives in Toronto were salivating over the prospect of the potential ratings which they thought surely would be the biggest in the history of not only HNIC but the CBC itself. Then the guy wearing number 99 for the Kings spoiled the party.

The Kings won the sixth game when Gretzky scored at 1:41 of overtime and Toronto was forced to a seventh game for a third straight series. It was played at Maple Leaf Gardens May 29 and Gretzky calls his performance that night the greatest of his great career. He had three goals and two assists and the Kings won 5–4. Los Angeles was in the Stanley Cup final and, with their beloved Maple Leafs gone from the nation's television screens, those once-joyful CBC executives were in shock.

Which brings us to Marty McSorley's illegal stick.

▌▐▌▐

In the first Stanley Cup final to begin in June, the Kings stunned the Forum faithful in Montreal by defeating the Canadiens 4–1. They were still in shock late in game two with Los Angeles leading 2–1, and the Canadiens seemingly a beaten bunch. There was a whistle at 18:15 of the third period, at which time Jacques Demers asked for a measurement of the stick being used by Kings defenceman Marty McSorley. Kerry Fraser was the referee, and he described the incident in my book *Tough Calls*.

"One of the most talked-about calls I have ever made was one of the easiest, in the '93 finals, when Marty McSorley got caught with an illegal stick. It was cut and dried, it really was. . . . For any player to go into a third period in a Stanley Cup final with an illegal stick was, to my mind, absolutely asinine. The stick was so illegal, I mean, I just looked at it and said, Holy smokes, we don't need the gauge for this one. But we went through the motions and measured it. It was a brilliant coaching move by Jacques Demers."

Indeed it was. With McSorley in the box, Demers pulled Patrick Roy to give his team six skaters to L.A.'s four. Montreal defenceman Eric Desjardins, who had scored his team's first goal in the first period, scored the power-play tying goal at 18:47 of the third to send the game into overtime. You knew, you just knew the Canadiens would win, which they did fifty-one seconds into OT. There was bedlam in the old Forum when Desjardins scored again to complete a rare defenceman's hat-trick, and tie the series.

I've always thought that had the Kings gone home leading 2–0 the Canadiens wouldn't have come back to win the Cup. But their dramatic victory in game two gave them new life. And who were Demers's spies? Nobody has ever claimed responsibility, but equipment-staff members Pierre Gervais and Bobby Boulanger still get a twinkle in their eyes when you mention the night Marty McSorley got caught with an illegal stick at the Montreal Forum.

■ | ■ | ■

During the Stanley Cup finals, the NHL takes the Stanley Cup to each of the competing cities for public display and it's usually, but not always, a big attraction. In the 1994 final between the New York Rangers and the Vancouver Canucks there were long lines of fans in Vancouver. But at the Hilton Hotel in downtown Manhattan, the security guards were the loneliest guys in town as hardly anybody showed up. In 1993, the Cup was shown off at a hotel in the L.A. airport area and, to the surprise of a lot cynics from the east, including the author, hundreds showed up. It was another example of how Wayne Gretzky had brought hockey to life in La La Land.

It took the L.A. Kings twenty-six years to play a home game in the Stanley Cup finals. In 1993 there were two at the Great Western Forum, and both went into overtime. With former president Ronald Reagan and Mrs. Reagan among the celebrities in attendance, an American playing for the Canadiens scored the winning goal in both games. The Kings battled back from 3–0 and 2–0 deficits to force OT, but both times John LeClair of St. Albans, Vermont, scored the game-winning goal for Montreal.

The two wins in Los Angeles gave the Canadiens ten straight playoff overtime victories. Patrick Roy had shut out the opposition through seventy-seven minutes and five seconds of overtime pressure while his teammates scored ten game-winning goals. In game five, at the Montreal Forum, the Canadiens led 3–1 after two periods and this time the Kings didn't come back. The game ended 4–1, as did the series.

Good old Dick was the dressing-room guy again after the Cup-winning game and, as usual, I left Bob and Harry in the booth and headed downstairs during the third period. The CBC was setting up in the Canadiens' dressing room, but this was one time I wasn't going to get hooked up and then stand there for fifteen or twenty minutes waiting for the players to come in. So I stood in the corridor behind the benches and watched the final minutes of the game, plus the presentation of the Stanley Cup by the NHL's new commissioner, Gary Bettman, to the Canadiens' captain, Guy Carbonneau.

A CBC technician kept pestering me that "they" wanted me in the dressing room to get ready. I'm afraid I was a bit short with him, for which I apologized later. But I stayed where I was because this was my home team, in my home rink, and I wanted to enjoy the moment. There's a lot of hurry-up-and-wait in the television business. I knew there wasn't any hurry. After the Cup was presented I went to the dressing room, a walk of about ten seconds, and they wired me for sound. Then I waited, for ten minutes, until the players arrived.

In 1893 the Stanley Cup was first won by the team representing the Montreal Amateur Athletic Association. One hundred years later it was back again in the city where it had begun its long, fascinating history. The 1993 Stanley Cup victory marked the twenty-fourth for the Montreal Canadiens, but I was one up on them. It was my twenty-fifth.

■|■|■

A couple of weeks after the playoffs, the Montreal Canadiens hold a golf tournament organized by the team's marketing department. Players past and present attend, as do representatives of the team's major sponsors. For a few years I was invited because of my association with the radio station carrying the team's games.

The 1993 event was held at Carling Lake, north of Montreal, where the golfers all posed for pictures on the first tee with the Stanley Cup. Just before I teed off I saw John LeClair, by himself, on the putting green. I walked over and we were chatting when Maurice Richard came by. I called him over and introduced him to John.

"So, you're LeClair, are you?" said the Rocket.

Then I piped up and said, "You guys share a pretty good record. Know what it is?" They didn't, so I explained that they were the only Montreal Canadiens to have scored game-winning overtime goals in two consecutive playoff games. The Rocket

scored his two goals in Detroit, in 1951, on Terry Sawchuk. John
LeClair scored his two in Los Angeles, in 1993, on Kelly Hrudey.

That brief conversation involving Maurice Richard and John
LeClair was, I thought, a small but unique bit of Montreal
Canadiens history, and I was the only one there to see it. For a
nostalgia buff like me, it was a perfect ending to a memorable
playoff year.

Some Fond Farewells

....

A
t 7:25 a.m. on Friday, February 26, 1993, I was sound asleep in my hotel room in Buffalo when the phone rang. My sluggish hello was immediately followed by the voice of Ted Blackman, my boss at the radio station back in Montreal.

"Danny Gallivan's dead," he barked. "You're going on with me and Red Storey in five seconds." Five seconds later I was on with Ted and Red, which is the fastest I was ever on the air after waking up.

The sad news was a complete surprise. Danny had been ailing with a bad cold and had sounded a bit weak the last time we talked on the phone, but his sudden death nineteen days before his seventy-sixth birthday was a shock to his family, friends, and hockey fans across Canada.

I was in Buffalo for the radio broadcast of the Canadiens game there that night. Between Ted's call and when I left the hotel to go to the rink, my phone never stopped ringing. I did nineteen interviews that day for radio, television, and the print press. It was obvious that, almost nine years after our last broadcast, Dick was still very closely linked to Danny.

The following Monday marked another first when I helped broadcast Danny's funeral on radio from the St. Ignatius of Loyola Church in Montreal. Some of Danny's friends kidded me that I was again strictly the colour commentator. The play-by-play, as it were, was provided by a long-time friend of mine, Father Barry Jones.

All of the phone calls, interviews, and tributes proved just how respected Danny Gallivan was, and what an impact he had made coast to coast in Canada. Several interviewers wanted me to talk about his colourful and distinctive vocabulary, which became so much a part of his legend, and I said I hoped that, in the future, hockey broadcasters wouldn't be so bold as to steal from it. To my knowledge, nobody has. I mean, who of us would now dare describe a shot as "cannonading," or a save as "scintillating," or that somebody is "negotiating contact with the puck"?

As Don Cherry might say, I want all you young hockey announcers out there to know that a player whose last name happens to be Savard can never be described as doing a "Savardian spinnerama," even if he does one. I don't want to hear you say that a player has skated "gingerly" over the blueline, and a whistle must never again be blown because somebody has the puck "caught up in his paraphernalia." Those words and phrases belong to Danny Gallivan, hockey's greatest play-by-play broadcaster, and they are now retired. Don't you dare use them.

▋▏▋▏

The Montreal Forum was the scene of many memorable hockey games. I have no idea when the first memorable game was played, but I sure know the date of the last one. It was Saturday, December 2, 1995, the night Patrick Roy, one of the greatest in a long line of great Montreal Canadiens goaltenders, played his last game for the team. His wasn't exactly a fond farewell.

I was in the HNIC booth that night, and I was in the CFCF Radio booth when Patrick Roy played his first game for the Canadiens, at the age of nineteen. The Winnipeg Jets were at the Forum for a rare Sunday-night game, February 24, 1985. Roy, who was with the Granby team in the Quebec Junior League, had been called up as an injury replacement and played the last period. He stopped the only two shots he faced in a 6–4 Montreal win.

Roy made his first NHL start in the first game of the following season on his twentieth birthday, in Pittsburgh, and allowed two goals in the first five minutes. The first was scored by Mike Bullard, the second by Mario Lemieux. Between then and now he has become hockey's all-time winningest goaltender. During his years with the Montreal Canadiens, Roy won the Jennings Trophy three times, and was named to the first All-Star Team three times. The Canadiens won two Stanley Cups, and Roy won the Conn Smythe Trophy as the playoff MVP both times. But even with all of his success in Montreal, one of his best-remembered games there is his last one, and it's remembered for all the wrong reasons.

The Canadiens missed the playoffs for only the third time in fifty-five years in the lockout-shortened 1994–95 season. In the opening game of 1995–96 they were thrashed 7–1 by the Philadelphia Flyers at the Forum. Roy was pulled at the 2:12 mark of the second period with Philadelphia leading 5–0. I don't think I ever heard the Canadiens booed at the Forum the way they were that night. After losses on the road to the Florida Panthers and Tampa Bay Lightning, they were beaten again on home ice by the New Jersey Devils. A couple of days later, team president Ronald Corey fired general manager Serge Savard and coach Jacques Demers.

The New Jersey game had been played on a Saturday night. The Canadiens weren't scheduled to play again until the following Friday, a road game against the New York Islanders. By then Corey still hadn't named anyone to replace Savard and Demers, and the team played the game against the Islanders without a head coach or general manager. That may have been a first in the NHL, and was quite a comedown for the organization long considered one of the most efficient in professional sports. With assistant coaches Jacques Laperrière and Steve Shutt running the team, the Canadiens lost their fifth straight game, 2–0. Predictably, there was panic in the Montreal media. The rumours were wild, and kept getting wilder as the days went by with no replacements in sight.

A high-profile member of the French-language media was a former Canadiens player, Mario Tremblay. A fiery, hard-nosed right winger, Tremblay first played for the Canadiens during the Scotty Bowman era, and retired in 1986 after a twelve-season career. By 1995 he had become a leading radio and TV personality. Mario had a daily talk show on radio, worked as the colour commentator on mid-week telecasts of Canadiens games, and was the French equivalent of Don Cherry on Radio-Canada with a between-period rant on Saturday nights.

On the afternoon of the game in Long Island, I ran into Mario and, jokingly, said, "Hey, Mario, do you want to coach the Canadiens?"

He replied with an emphatic, "Yes, sir. And I wouldn't be afraid of the fuckin' pressure." I laughed, and forgot about it.

On the telecast of the game that night, Tremblay interviewed Islanders assistant coach Guy Charron, and asked him if he was going to be the next coach of the Canadiens. When he was asking Charron that question, and when he had answered mine earlier in the day, Mario Tremblay already knew the identity of the next coach of the Montreal Canadiens. It was Mario Tremblay.

The Canadiens had a home game against Toronto the next night. Corey had lined up Tremblay as head coach, Yvan Cournoyer as an assistant coach, and another former player, Réjean Houle, as the new general manager. Tremblay had never been a coach and Houle had never been a general manager at any level in hockey, so they were starting their careers right at the top. Corey, who craved positive publicity for his hockey club, wanted to hold the announcements until Sunday, when he would stage a big press conference at centre ice at the Forum.

On Saturday afternoon his new coach and general manager told Corey they wanted to start right away. Reluctantly, Corey agreed. When Mario Tremblay was introduced as the Canadiens' new head coach a couple of hours before game time, the players were as surprised as everyone else.

It's tough to keep a secret on the hockey scene in Montreal. There's a joke that reporters follow the players into the men's room in case there's another reporter in there who might get a scoop. But that one, as big as it was, was a secret until just before a hastily-called press conference was held late Saturday afternoon. That night's game was a thriller, the Canadiens winning 4–3 on a goal by Pierre Turgeon at 19:59 of the third period.

The new regime was off to a fine start, and it got better. After the five-game losing streak that began the season, the Canadiens won six straight under new coach Tremblay, with Patrick Roy playing in all six. The back-up goaltender was a raw rookie, Patrick Labrecque, whose only NHL start was in the next game, in Washington. The Canadiens lost 5–2, but with Roy back two nights later at the Forum, against Boston, they won again.

As the Canadiens continued on their roll, Roy was outstanding. He played against Boston in the games before and after his night off in Washington, and was as sharp as I had ever seen him. The Bruins had seventy-five shots in the two games, and scored only twice. The Habs travelled to western Canada for three games and won them all, with Roy giving up just three goals. I went for a walk in Vancouver with Patrick and a few other players, and told him I thought he was playing as well as I had ever seen him, maybe better. Patrick, who will never be accused of being humble, agreed. In his first thirteen starts under Tremblay, Roy had a record of twelve wins and one loss, with the loss coming in overtime.

There certainly wasn't any outward indication of trouble brewing between the coach and his goaltender, but it was. A rumour began to circulate that Roy didn't think much of Tremblay's early efforts as coach. He wasn't alone. Another player told me, "It's a good thing Shutt and Laperrière are here to run the practices. The new guy doesn't have a clue." Even so, no one was prepared for the public display of animosity between coach and goaltender that would end Roy's tenure with the Canadiens.

On November 28, Roy played in a 3–2 loss in Detroit. Earlier in the month, the Canadiens had traded defenceman J.J. Daigneault to the St. Louis Blues for goaltender Pat Jablonski. The night after the Detroit game, Jablonski played in St. Louis, when the Blues won 5–4.

In the fateful game against Detroit on December 2 at the Forum, the Red Wings took a 3–1 lead halfway through the first period and stretched it to 5–1 with two power-play goals in the last two minutes. The natives in the Forum were becoming restless, and their displeasure was directed mainly at Patrick Roy.

Most of us thought Tremblay would put Jablonski in goal to start the second period, but he didn't. The Wings scored two more goals in the first five minutes, yet Tremblay made no move to change goalies. Another Detroit goal, at 10:06 of the second period, made it 8–1, and the boo-birds really were giving it to Roy. That's when he waved his arms at the crowd in what was, as many of us thought, a "fuck you too" gesture. In the HNIC booth I said, "Patrick Roy has just taken the final score off tomorrow's front page." Good thought, Dick, but the best, or worst, was yet to come.

At 11:56, Sergei Fedorov scored another Detroit goal to make it 9–1. That was when Tremblay finally changed goalies. Roy came off the ice and, as he walked behind the bench to take a seat, Tremblay was fiercely glaring at him, almost nose to nose. Roy stopped, turned back, and spoke to Ronald Corey, who was sitting in the first row behind the bench. Corey immediately looked like he had been hit with a sledgehammer because Roy said to him, in so many words, "I've played my last game for the Montreal Canadiens." The final score was 11–1, which equalled the Canadiens' one-game record for most goals against, and widest losing margin.

Roy was not on the ice when the Canadiens practised the next day because he was meeting with Corey and other team officials. His teammates played down the incident and felt everyone would cool off. But nobody cooled off. When the meeting ended it was announced that Patrick Roy had indeed played his last game with the Montreal Canadiens, and the team would grant his wish to be traded.

It all happened too fast. I still think if the Canadiens had said to Roy, "Here are a couple of plane tickets to Florida. Take your wife on a holiday, play some golf, and come back when you feel like it," the thing would have blown over. But there were too many big egos involved, on both sides, and nobody budged. An era was over in Montreal and, with all due respect to those who have taken Patrick Roy's place in the Canadiens' goal crease, things haven't been the same since. Meanwhile, Roy has won two more Stanley Cups and a third Smythe Trophy as the playoff MVP.

The morning after the game my phone rang and I was met with the familiar greeting, "Dick, Scotty." The coach of the Red Wings was back in Detroit, and proceeded to give me his version of the events surrounding his team's 11–1 victory. "It's our fault," he said. "We're gonna pay for this. He's done in Montreal. They'll trade him to Colorado and that's bad news for us." A couple of days later, the Canadiens did trade Roy to Colorado, and in the conference finals that year he was brilliant when the Avalanche eliminated Scotty's Red Wings in six games.

Twelve days later, on June 10, Patrick Roy shut out the Florida Panthers for 104 minutes and 31 seconds before Uwe Krupp's goal gave Colorado a 1–0 win, and a sweep of the Stanley Cup finals. Roy gave up only four goals in the four games.

The Canadiens had been eliminated by the New York Rangers on April 28. After their 1993 Stanley Cup, the Canadiens won just one playoff series in the next eight years. Starting in 1999, they missed the playoffs three straight seasons. Prior to that, the Montreal Canadiens had missed the playoffs only three times in fifty-eight years.

■ | ■ |

On Monday, March 11, 1996, just over three months after Patrick Roy was responsible for the Montreal Forum's last memorable game, the Canadiens played the last game ever in the arena. For many years the three best-known buildings in Canada were the Forum, Maple Leaf Gardens, and the Peace Tower on the Centre Block on Parliament Hill in Ottawa. They don't play hockey any more at the Forum or MLG. The Habs and Leafs have moved into mammoth structures with corporate names that contain dozens of private boxes, expensive seats, and ear-shattering sound systems. When last I looked, the Peace Tower was still there, without an ear-shattering sound system. The politicians are loud enough on their own.

The closing of the Forum became a major story. At almost every home game that season I ran into fans from all over Canada as well as parts of the United States who had made the trip to Montreal so they could say they saw the Forum at least once. I saw the Forum more than once, but have no idea how many times I walked through its doors. I tried a rough calculation and came up with a figure in the area of five thousand but that's probably on the low side.

After I retired from the booth I was often asked what the highlight of my career was. There were two big ones. First, seventeen years in the HNIC booth beside Danny Gallivan. The second was being one of the MCs on the ice for the closing ceremonies at the Montreal Forum. I never missed an assignment beside Danny, but I almost didn't make it to the closing ceremonies.

The Canadiens had kindly asked me to be the English MC. Richard Garneau was my French counterpart. On March 2, nine days before the closing, the Canadiens played in Los Angeles, then had a week off until their next game. Because of this strange bit of scheduling, Wilma joined me on the West Coast and we had a brief golfing holiday in the Palm Springs area. On the second day we were there the Santa Ana winds were howling, and Wilma thought we should stop after nine holes. I disagreed because, wind and all, I was having a good game. We pressed on

and I ended up shooting a seventy-six. Good game, bad decision.
By the time we flew home I could barely talk, the after-effect of
the hot, dry, windy day on the golf course in the desert.

Hockey Night in Canada did its last telecast from the Forum two
nights before the last game, and the closing ceremonies, to the
CBC's chagrin, were shown on TSN. Funny thing about that. HNIC's
Saturday show was terrific, perfectly capturing the mood and the
memories. In the following weeks the HNIC people continually
talked to me about the rave reviews their show had received, while
not once mentioning TSN's show two nights later, where one of
their own had been front and centre. It was as if they couldn't
bring themselves to acknowledge theirs hadn't been the last show
out of the Forum.

I was the third man in the booth on Saturday, and with about
two minutes left in the third period Chris Cuthbert surprised me
by saying, "There's only one way for us to go out of our last show
at the Forum, and that's with Dick Irvin doing the play-by-play.
So, Dick, it's all yours." I wasn't ready for that, and neither was
my throat, but I croaked my way through it and was very grateful
to Chris for his thoughtfulness.

When Monday arrived my throat problem was still very much
with me. I had to be at the Forum by noon for the rehearsal. In
1951, when the Irvins moved to Montreal, we lived in an apartment at 2075 Lincoln Avenue, a couple of blocks from the Forum.
I drove by there on the off-chance there was a parking space available, and there was, directly in front of the door to the building.
So I parked, and walked to the Forum on the same route I had
used forty-five years before. On a day of memories, that was a
good one.

The Dallas Stars played the Canadiens in the game preceding
the closing ceremonies. I worked on the radio for the first half,
with my throat still very weak, then went downstairs to change

into my tuxedo. I had been told the Directors' Room, where team officials and their friends would go before and after the games, would be empty when the intermission was over, but there were a lot of men and women there who couldn't have cared less about the game, which the Canadiens won 4–1. They never left the room, and I changed into my tux in the kitchen. Another glamorous show-business moment.

The list of former players and executives who were introduced was limited to those who had been elected to the Hockey Hall of Fame. There were nineteen players, and all wore Canadiens sweaters. They gathered in the dressing room and, just before the show began, I went there to shake a few hands. The first time I had been in that room, in 1940 when I was eight years old, Elmer Lach and Ken Reardon were there as players. They were there again the last time I walked into the room fifty-six years later. My dad had been their only coach in the NHL. That got to me.

The ceremonies were tightly scripted and timed. There was no chance for Richard or me to do any ad libbing, and that helped make it such a good show. I never understood why they didn't produce a video of that closing night at the Forum. Judging by the positive reaction I got from people all over the country, I'm sure they would have sold a ton of them.

I was scared when I walked out and took my place at the microphone. It wasn't because of the moment, or the 17,959 people in the seats. I was scared because of my throat. It was one thing to talk my way through interviews, or game broadcasts, but it would be another to project my voice more than usual, as you do at a time like that.

Remember my dad's theory about the Unseen Hand? Well, I think it showed up one last time at the Forum to help the coach's kid get through the evening. I was sweating it out when I spoke my first line. but my voice came through loud and clear, and it remained that way for the entire ceremony. (When I woke up the next morning, I couldn't speak a word.)

The ceremony, which was highlighted by the thunderous, emotional ovation given Maurice Richard, ended with a torch being passed through a succession of former captains to the current captain, Pierre Turgeon, who carried it off the ice to mark the official closing of the historic building. The former captains included Butch Bouchard, the Rocket, Jean Béliveau, Henri Richard, Yvan Cournoyer, Serge Savard, and Bob Gainey. Another former captain, Guy Carbonneau, played that night for Dallas and was included. Carbonneau was justifiably upset because the Canadiens sweater they had for him bore the letter A, instead of a C. This hardly noticeable glitch was the only one I know of in what was the last of many memorable ceremonies at the Montreal Forum.

There were some notable absentees, including Bernie Geoffrion. The Boomer had a previous commitment, but he was present the following Saturday for the opening of the Molson Centre. His wife, Marlene, was on the ice when they raised retired sweater number 7 in tribute to her father, the legendary Howie Morenz.

Larry Robinson, then coaching the Los Angeles Kings, was scheduled to be present and his video was prepared for showing when he was introduced. At the last minute, he cancelled.

"We were fighting for a playoff spot," Larry told me, "and had a big game against Buffalo two nights later. I decided the right place for me was with my team. We watched it on ESPN, and my wife cried all the way through. I wasn't far from crying myself."

∎∎∎

A lot of people in Montreal wish the Canadiens still played at the Forum, but as movie mogul Sam Goldwyn once said, "Include me out." The Forum, for all its charm and tradition, was an old building. Too old. Television trucks had to park in the street. There was no basement. Parts of the antiquated ice-making equipment had been there since the building opened in 1924. After a practice at the Nassau Coliseum during the 1993 playoffs, Denis Savard said to me, "This must be the worst ice in the league. It's even worse than the Forum's."

When I saw new buildings around the NHL in places like Chicago, Vancouver, Boston, and San Jose, it was obvious how outdated the Forum was by comparison. Over the more than thirty years I travelled around the league I grew very fond of the old buildings, and I was sorry to see them disappear. But time, and the need for more bucks at the box office, waits for no one, or place.

On the road my two favourite buildings were the Chicago Stadium and the Boston Garden. I saw the Stanley Cup won three times in each one, and the atmosphere in both was terrific. For many years in Chicago, the games started with Wayne Messmer's stirring rendition of the national anthem accompanied by the biggest pipe organ in the world. Eighteen thousand fans would begin cheering with the opening phrase, "*Oh, say can you see . . . ,*" and the noise level would build until it finally drowned out Messmer's final words, "*. . . and the home of the brave.*" They'd keep cheering until the opening faceoff. If a hockey announcer wasn't pumped by then, he was in the wrong business.

Next to the Forum, the rink where I saw the most NHL games was the Boston Garden. Montreal and Boston were always in the same division, and I broadcast fifteen playoff series between the two teams. Boston fans were great, if at times annoying. Danny used to talk about a guy who sat behind him in his early days who had a friend named Ginger sitting somewhere in the building. All through the game the guy would keep hollering, in his Boston accent, "Gingah! . . . Gingah! . . ." Danny never heard Gingah answer back.

It was the same thing in the '90s when Andy Moog was the Boston goaltender. A fan seated right behind the TV broadcast location must have been Moog's number-one fan. All night he'd keep yelling, "Andy Moog! . . . Andy Moog! . . . God-damned Andy Moog!" He used to drive John Garrett crazy.

After the 1994–95 season, the Garden was replaced by the Fleet Center, which was built right beside it. In the fall of 1995 they held a week of nostalgic farewells at the old Garden. They had nights for boxing, basketball, hockey, and so on. The Canadiens were booked for the last hockey game, an exhibition, because the Canadiens were the visitors when the Bruins played their first game there. For years the annual *NHL Official Guide and Record Book* printed the date of the opening games in the various arenas, and the attendance. For the Boston Garden it always read, "November 20, 1928. Attendance not known. Fans broke down the doors."

Our radio station carried only home exhibition games, but my broadcast partner, Dino Sisto, and I convinced them the game in Boston was historic and we should do the game. They finally agreed, and I was glad I was in the Boston Garden the night the Bruins played there for the last time. Several Bruins greats from the past paraded to centre ice after the game. But the most emotional moment was when Normand Leveille was introduced. In 1982 Leveille was nineteen years old, and in his second season in Boston, when he suffered a brain aneurysm during a game in Vancouver that ended his career, and almost ended his life. When he appeared on the ice in a wheelchair pushed by Raymond Bourque, there was hardly a dry eye in the house.

I was in on a few lasts in some other old buildings. I helped broadcast the last game played at the Pacific Coliseum in Vancouver, May 27, 1995. It was a playoff game between the Canucks and

Chicago and ended when Chris Chelios scored in overtime to give the Blackhawks a sweep of the series.

On April 13, 1967, I worked the last playoff game in the old Madison Square Garden, in New York. The Canadiens' John Ferguson ended that one, in overtime. The Rangers moved to the present MSG in January of '68.

I was at the Colisée in Quebec City May 14, 1995, for the Nordiques' last home game. It was the fifth game of a series with the New York Rangers, and the Nordiques, facing elimination, won 4–2. Two days later they were defeated in New York. By then the word was out that the franchise was moving to Denver, where the team won the Stanley Cup a year later. Would the franchise have won the Cup if it hadn't moved? I don't think so, because the Montreal Canadiens never would have traded Patrick Roy to the Quebec Nordiques.

And it was a night of many memories for me when HNIC had me work the last game the Canadiens played at Maple Leaf Gardens, December 26, 1998. The slogan for the final year at the Montreal Forum was "Forever Proud." For Maple Leaf Gardens it was "Memories and Dreams." Stars from other eras were introduced prior to the games as the days dwindled down before the team moved to the Air Canada Centre. That night Maurice Richard was there with Ted Kennedy, a great Leafs captain from the same era. Kennedy received a warm welcome. The Rocket got a standing ovation.

It had been sixty years, seven months, and nineteen days since my folks took me to Maple Leaf Gardens to see my first NHL game. I opened the telecast with Ron MacLean and wondered if there was anyone else there that night who had seen the Maple Leafs play the Chicago Blackhawks in the second game of the 1938 Stanley Cup finals. There might have been and, if so, I hope they have as many great memories of the game of hockey as I have.

Maple Leaf Gardens was always a special place for me. For many years when I would enter the doors on Carlton Street, the first thing I would see was a big picture frame containing individual photos of the 1932 Stanley Cup–champion Toronto team. I'd always look at the one of my dad as a reminder of how he looked the year I was born.

Time to Retire

....

O n New Year's Day, 1997, I broadcast an afternoon game between the Canadiens and the Stars in Dallas. The game drew a capacity crowd, which surprised me, because the Cotton Bowl football game was being played at the same time. It was obvious hockey fans in Dallas were faithful, and their faith was rewarded two years later when the Stars won the Stanley Cup.

We flew to St. Louis after the game, and when I woke up in my hotel room the next morning, I had lived one day longer than my father. He died at sixty-four, one year before he planned to retire. I was still enjoying the job, and the travel, but once in a while had the feeling that the time might be approaching when it wouldn't be fun any more. By the time I finished breakfast I had made up my mind to leave radio at the end of the season. I told my family, but nobody else.

I experienced a weird ending to that part of my career. My last two radio games were on the road, in Long Island and Washington. Everything was normal before the Islanders game. I did the pre-game show and the early part of the first period as usual. My big mistake had been to eat in the press room, known in those days for serving maybe the worst food in the NHL. That night it had been hard hunks of something masquerading as pasta that I now believe was really the insides of old golf balls with red sauce poured on them.

Early in the first period I suddenly felt ill, very ill, something that had never happened to me during a game. I had two regular colour men alternating alongside me that season. One was Jim Corsi, a former goaltender who did not do play-by-play, and the other was Montreal broadcaster Dino Sisto, who did. Luckily, Dino was with me on the trip. I motioned to him to take over the play-by-play and raced to the nearest men's room, where it was quickly confirmed that, yes, I was sick. The golf balls covered in red sauce had done me in.

The Canadiens' travelling secretary, Michèle Lapointe, found the Islanders' team doctor, who, after checking me over, advised me to take the rest of the night off. The way I was feeling, he didn't have to talk me into it, and with Dino in charge, and Stu Hackel moving in to handle the colour, I knew the broadcast was in good hands. Stu is a writer and broadcaster who often worked games with me in the New York area.

That scene brought back another memory of Danny Gallivan. In 1976, during the second period of a playoff game in the same building, Danny suddenly said, "Dick, my throat isn't feeling too good right now. You take over." With that he took off his headset, lit a cigarette, and sat back to watch the rest of the game while I flew solo. Danny hadn't said a word about having a sore throat.

I managed to work the next night, in Washington, knowing it was my last radio broadcast. After fulfilling my obligations to the station during the playoffs, pre- and post-game shows and the like, I informed Ted Blackman that I was retiring. After twenty-nine years, broadcasting close to two thousand games in fifty-one different arenas, and constantly packing and unpacking suitcases, I was ready.

▌▐▌▐

I hung in for two more years with *Hockey Night in Canada*. I had mentioned retirement to John Shannon, who had become the executive producer in 1995. John said it was up to me, that I had a job with the show as long as I wanted to stay. I stayed until 1999.

During my last six years in the HNIC booth, my principal team, the Montreal Canadiens, missed the playoffs twice and reached the second round just once. My employer was very kind in giving me a lot of playoff work elsewhere, but after my last one in 1994, I was never again assigned to work the Stanley Cup finals.

Before the 1998–99 season I told Wilma, Nancy, and Doug it would be my last year on the show. The Canadiens didn't make the playoffs, but I worked a few games in April and May, travelling to Buffalo, St. Louis, Dallas, and Denver. My final assignment was in Buffalo. After I finished an on-camera game wrap-up, John Shannon said to me from Toronto via the headset, "Okay, Dick, you're done." I smiled. He didn't know how true his words were.

A few days after the playoffs I called John and told him I was retiring. His immediate answer: "No, you're not. If you want out of the booth, fine. But I'd like you to do some features. We need more tradition and history and you're the guy who does it best." And that's what I did the following season and, even though John was no longer associated with the show, the season after that.

I was invited to attend HNIC's pre-season seminar, in Toronto, in September 1999. Included on the agenda was a retirement dinner for the "old man on the show," as I was calling myself, who came away from it with some very nice gifts, a lot of great memories, and a contract to stay on the show doing features. So I wasn't totally retired, after all. The CBC has been very, very good to me, lo these many years.

After the seminar's wrap-up the next afternoon I shared a taxi to the airport with Steve Armitage, the long-time CBC sportscaster based in Vancouver. Our ride had barely begun when Steve, ever the intrepid reporter, said, "Okay, what happened? Did you really retire, or did they push you out the door?" I assured him I had made the call and really retired, but I don't think he believed me. It's true, Steve. Honest.

When I interviewed goaltenders past and present for my book *In the Crease*, it was obvious those from earlier eras were self-taught. Gump Worsley, Johnny Bower, and Glenn Hall all said they had never had any coaching on their way to the NHL, nor when they got there. Today, there are goalie coaches and consultants all over the hockey map, and the kids learning to play the position are much better for it.

Looking back on my career, I can relate to the old-timers. I never had any coaching. Nobody ever sat down with me and gave me advice on how to do colour, play-by-play, or interviews. And with very few exceptions, nobody in a position of authority ever critiqued my work. Days, weeks, seasons went by and I would wonder: Is anyone I work for out there, either watching or listening?

The only person who ever passed judgement on my work after a hockey game was me. I'd drive home from the Forum or the Molson Centre and decide if I had done a good job, or otherwise, and there were some nights when it was the latter. What was it Pat Burns said about the job he did one night in St. Louis? "I coached like a dink." There were nights I thought I announced like a dink. But I rarely heard a word, good or bad, except from myself.

I might also add that, despite the odd media shot about hockey announcers being puppets of the teams, in thirty-five years broadcasting games, principally Montreal Canadiens games, nobody ever told me what to say or not to say on the air. Not once. The management of the Canadiens has always been more concerned with the French shows than the English, both radio and television, which is one reason that business about wondering if anybody was listening applied there too. In that particular case, I don't think they were.

∎▮∎▮∎

Now that I am a listener and viewer, I notice some interesting contrasts in styles of hockey announcers. Bob Cole, still the purest play-caller in the business, is from an older school where, with rare exceptions, only the play-by-play man talks while the puck is in motion. I can relate to that. After all, I'm the guy who wasn't even given a microphone when I started to work alongside Danny Gallivan. Times are changing, and it's good to hear the colour man come in once in a while during play, especially when the game is dull. But some talk as much as, and even more than, the play-by-play man when the play is on, and a lot of what they say is superfluous. There has to be a happy medium in there somewhere between the old style and the new.

Television play-by-play is still basically programmed as if it were radio with pictures. In my later years on HNIC it seemed they didn't want a second of quiet time, just like the guys who run the sound systems in the arenas. When there are three passes in five seconds in the neutral zone, does every passer and receiver have to be identified? There has to be a happy medium somewhere there, too.

■ ■ ■ ■

I have an obvious and understandable bias towards *Hockey Night in Canada*, which, despite there being much more competition today than yesterday, is still far and away the best hockey show in the country. This was proven again when Toronto played Ottawa in the first round of the 2001 playoffs. There was a great hue and cry out of Ottawa over a perceived bias of the HNIC announcers in favour of the Leafs and against the Senators. Everybody got into the act, including the mayor of Ottawa. After raving and ranting at the show and the CBC, His Worship somehow managed to find the time to pose for a picture with Don Cherry that was prominently displayed in the local papers.

The playoffs were getting blanket coverage on TSN and CTV. While the many panellists and experts on those networks avoided mentioning the Ottawa–HNIC hassle, which was front-page news for a couple of days all over the country, they were saying some good and at times controversial things. Yet I doubt if anyone was rushing to call the open-mike radio shows because of what they heard on TSN and CTV. And with due respect to some good friends on both networks, the mayor of Ottawa wasn't chasing after any of them for a photo-op. But when Messrs. Cherry, MacLean, Neale, or Cole say something on HNIC the folks don't like, the floodgates open.

It brought back memories for me of the time when fans in Toronto complained that Danny and Dick were biased against the

Maple Leafs, while in Montreal everyone was sure Bill Hewitt and Brian McFarlane hated the Canadiens. One Montreal radio station started referring to Brian as Brian McMapleLeaf. And it always reached a fever pitch at playoff time.

A perfect example of what HNIC means to aspiring young hockey players happened after the opening game of the 1996–97 season in Montreal between the Canadiens and the Ottawa Senators. Nineteen-year-old Ottawa defenceman Wade Redden was playing in his first NHL game, and scored his first NHL goal on his first NHL shot. The final score was 3–3.

It was Saturday and I was working as the local HNIC host. After the game they brought Redden into the studio for an interview. He was starry-eyed, mainly because of all of his firsts, but also because he was going to appear on *Hockey Night in Canada*. When he came through the door I welcomed him to our cramped little studio that was in no way as glamorous as it appeared on air, told him his part of the show was going coast to coast, and the interview began. We chatted about how he felt, his small-town upbringing in Saskatchewan, and we replayed his goal. You could tell when the replay was on he was in seventh heaven, and then some.

When the interview ended so did the Montreal portion of the show. Instead of Redden getting up and leaving, as is usually the case with the interviewees, he just sat there, awestruck. After a moment or two I said to the producer, "Show Wade his goal again," and he did. The kid was beaming. It was a lovely moment.

∎❙❚❙

I don't know if the Danny and Dick show would work today, but it would be interesting to see the reaction if they replayed a complete game from the 1970s. The viewers wouldn't see a trace of a Telestrator, no NetCams, and sometimes two replays of a goal, but usually only one. And they certainly wouldn't get the detailed analysis of strategy that is supplied today by the former coaches and players who are in the broadcast booths. The reason for that is simple. They know a lot more about that sort of thing than I ever did.

Around the time stupefying defensive hockey was being widely criticized, and "the trap" was becoming a favourite phrase among media experts, I was talking to my buddy Bob Turner, who played defence on five Stanley Cup–winners in Montreal. He said, "You guys make me laugh with all your talk about 'the trap.' It's the same thing Toe Blake had us doing in the '50s." Any experts out there want to argue with Bob on that one?

One thing Danny and Dick had going for them was more-exciting hockey. If there were only twenty teams today it would be better, but there are thirty, and that's a killer. With their line-ups thin on offensive talent, most coaches stress defence. Doug Wilson, a former Norris Trophy–winner with the Blackhawks, said on an HNIC panel at the 2001 All-Star Game, "Coaches today coach so they won't lose." You sometimes get the feeling if every game ended 1–1, with each team getting about fifteen shots, the coaches would go home happy. In a way you can't blame them, considering the frequency with which they get fired these days, but the fans are the big losers.

When Marc Crawford was between coaching jobs and working for HNIC, I asked him if coaches ever considered the entertainment aspect of hockey, especially in light of the big bucks fans have to pay today. Marc replied, a bit sheepishly, "Not very often," by which I think he meant, "Never."

Mike Keenan once told me the attrition within the coaching ranks was due in large measure to pressure from ownership to produce and win now, not in the future. Mike ought to know. As I write this, he has just been cut loose by the Boston Bruins, his sixth NHL team.

I have been lucky in so many ways in my career, one of which was being involved one way or another with the greatest eras in the history of the Montreal Canadiens. Now people say to me, "What do you think about the Canadiens? Isn't it sad what's happening?" Yes, it's sad. The once-proud franchise is going through miserable times with a poor team. Once upon a time the Canadiens' only objective was to win the Stanley Cup. Now it's to make the playoffs again, sometime.

What's gone wrong? If I knew, I'd be working at the Molson Centre instead of at my word processor. There's a lot of talk about high draft choices who never made it, and that's happened. But in my opinion the biggest mistakes were the terrible trades made during the '90s.

For various reasons, mainly money, the Canadiens traded away their best players far too often. Chris Chelios and Eric Desjardins were their best defencemen when they were traded. Pierre Turgeon, Mark Recchi, and Vincent Damphousse were their best forwards. Patrick Roy was their best player. They're all still top NHL players, but they no longer play for the Canadiens. A team can't keep doing that and not suffer severe consequences, especially when they have nothing to show in their line-up in return. I know in this time of huge salaries most teams can't afford to keep all their high-priced talent. But the Canadiens overdid it.

■ ▮ ■

My father is well known for his career in hockey as a player and a coach. But he was involved in a couple of historic moments in hockey broadcasting long before his son got into the business.

The first hockey game broadcast on radio was played in Regina, March 14, 1923, between the Regina Capitals and the Edmonton Eskimos. The announcer was Pete Parker, and Dick Irvin, Sr., was playing for Regina.

The first hockey game televised in Canada was played at the Montreal Forum October 9, 1952, between the Canadiens and the Chicago Blackhawks. It was seen on Radio-Canada, and my dad was coaching the Canadiens. So you see, all I've been doing for the past thirty-five years is carrying on the Irvin family broadcasting tradition.

You've likely gathered by now that I am fond of historical connections. In recent years there were a couple of times when something came full circle for me. One was on the CBC show *Hockey Day in Canada*, February 24, 2001. It was all about grass-roots hockey from coast to coast. Wilma and I were in Regina visiting her family, and when HNIC found out I was going there they asked me to take part in the show.

My favourite memories of whatever hockey I played go back to my Parks League games in the '40s. Almost sixty years after braving cold prairie winters on outdoor rinks, there I was in 2001 doing the same thing as I chatted, via satellite, with Ron MacLean, who himself was on an outdoor rink in his old hometown, Red Deer. An outdoor rink in Regina and *Hockey Night in Canada*. It was like my life was passing before my eyes.

A year earlier Wilma and I had travelled west by train. When I made that trip as a kid I would look out the window at the flickering lights of farmhouses and small towns and wonder who lived there.

In the year 2000, when I was making the same trip, I found myself wondering again as I looked at the flickering lights of farmhouses and small-town Canada. That time I wondered if the people living in those houses had ever seen or heard me on *Hockey Night in Canada*. If so, did I in some small way entertain them and help them enjoy watching the wonderful game of hockey?

I hope I did.

Acknowledgements

······························

In the broadcasting business the on-air performers receive most of the attention. Over the past forty years I had my share of that, but none of it would have happened without the work of hundreds of technicians, directors, and producers who put the shows on the air. My thanks to them all.

Several gentle but persuasive hints from the publisher of McClelland & Stewart, Douglas Gibson, that it was time for another Dick Irvin book convinced me to crank up my trusty old word processor. I thank him for getting the memories flowing once again.

This is the third book I have written in collaboration with Jonathan Webb as the editor, and Peter Buck as the copy editor. As always, it was a treat to work with these two professionals.

Bob Fisher, of the Montreal Canadiens, and Craig Campbell at the Hockey Hall of Fame were very helpful supplying photographs.

As always, my family has been with me all the way. My thanks, and love, to Nancy Anne and Rob, and Doug and Doogie. This book is dedicated to Wilma, my wife, best friend, and inspiration for the past thirty-eight wonderful years.

Index

277